Be Outrageously Successful Living the Small Business Lifestyle

Sherry B. Jordan

HBC Publishing, LLC

www.sherryjordancoach.com

Ordering Information:

Quantity sales. Special discounts are available on quantity purchases by corporations, associations, and others. For details, contact Beth Bolden at the address above.

Plan It! Do It! Love It! / Sherry B. Jordan. -- 2nd ed.

CONTENTS

FOREWORD

LIFE IS WORK AND work is life. That is how it is for small business owners. The lines are blurred between work and everything else — family, friends, faith, and self. That is the way we like it. It is the life and lifestyle we have chosen. It offers everything we seek in a career and it's an opportunity to create income for today and tomorrow.

Many are confused about the difference between an "entrepreneur" and a "small business owner." These terms are mistakably used interchangeably. Nothing could be farther from the truth. To get what you want and need from the pages that follow it is important for you to know who it is intended for.

An entrepreneur is defined as "a person who organizes and manages any enterprise, especially a business, usually with considerable initiative and risk."

Entrepreneurs prefer the thrill of the race over crossing the finish line. They are always looking for the next speculative venture and thrive on the stress and chaos that goes into creating, negotiating, and sometimes hitting it big. They play to win but are not afraid to throw in the family farm as a final bet. If they lose, they move on to another game. They may or may not be emotionally involved in the outcome.

Business is defined as "an occupation, profession, or a trade; a person, partnership, or corporation, engaged in commerce, manufacturing or a service; profit-seeking enterprise or concern" and defines an owner as, "to acknowledge as one's own; recognize as having full claim, authority, power, responsibility, dominion, etc." Small depends on the industry and is defined by the U. S. Small Business Administration as "Depending on the industry, size standard eligibility is based on the average number of employees for the preceding twelve month or sales volume averaged over a three-year period."

This book is written for small business owners. For the brave collection of individuals who take full ownership and responsibility for building a profitable business that serves their needs and the needs of the people they love. It is written for those who view their business as their livelihood, their retirement, and their legacy. It is written for a group whose ideas, passions, skills, or talents inspired them to start a business and whose commitment will not let them fail. It is written for people who know the limits of their abilities and are not afraid to ask for help to keep their dreams alive.

I am one of those people. I am a small business owner. I proudly serve others who are small business owners. This book is for you — all of you small business owners — who will allow me the opportunity to participate in your small business success.

How to Use This Book

This is a guidebook for small business owners. It covers everything you need to get everything you want from your small business and the small business lifestyle. You will be guided through the development of a plan, actions and activities that will be most helpful in realizing that plan and be offered advice on how to truly enjoy being a small business owner.

You can begin reading where it suits you best. Read it front to finish or begin with the section you need most. If you do not have a plan start with Plan It! If day-to-day execution is your biggest challenge, start with Do It! If you are questioning your commitment to your small business or just not enjoying your business, go straight to Love It! Wherever you begin, be sure you read all sections. Each one has something valuable to offer.

Throughout the book you will find shaded segments that recommend actions or offer advice. You will also find challenges from me — your coach in this project.

Plan It: These recommendations guide you in creating a strategic action plan for your business. Complete the exercises. When you have finished the final one — you have a plan.

Coach's Advice: Gives you the benefit of my years of experience in business and with small business owners. These are shortcuts to help you avoid common mistakes and pitfalls.

Coach's Examples: Examples designed to help you create answers to the planning exercise questions.

Do It: Recommend actions for each section of the "Do It" portion of this book. These actions will get you the results you want.

Coach's Challenge: Challenges to push you and your business to new levels of performance. Each one asks you to do something that will have a valuable return. These are practices that seasoned business owners have learned the hard way — through missed opportunities and years of experience. They may not be easy, or convenient, but they are worth it.

Love It: As a small business owner your business and career commitments are different from those of people who work for others. You *are* the business. "Love It" gives you inspiration and suggestions for maintaining a balance between your work and your personal life. These come to you through my education, training, experience in counseling, and from clients who were willing to share their lessons and experiences for "living the life."

• • • • • • • • • • •

Plan It!

To get the maximum benefit from the book and to have a powerful plan, I recommend that you stop as you go to complete the exercises. You do not need special tools, just your own information, records, paper, and pencil. If you would like a simple guided version, check out ***Plan It! Do It! Love It! The Planning Workbook***.

Do It!

Once you have a plan you will be ready to act. It's expected that you will have some resistance to some of the actions that are recommended. No one, including small business owners, really likes to change. Most of us believe our way, whatever we have been doing, is best. I am suggesting you give these actions and the time needed to realize a return on the investment a try. They have worked for hundreds of my successful small business clients, and I believe they will work for you. Just do the action. Try not to question the reason.

Love It!

If you are like most small business owners, the primary reason for opening your own business is to be in control of your career and your life. That translates to your desire to fully enjoy the work you do and the business you own and to maximize the benefits you get from it. The Love It! section of the book is filled with advice and recommendations for maximizing joy, improving your lifestyle, balancing work with life, communicating your needs, prioritizing time, and generally loving your life and your work.

I recommend you act on as many of these suggestions as you can. Work towards change. Create the life you have always wanted, the one you expected to have when you opened your business. Be gentle with yourself. Change may come slowly.

Before You Plan

Know What You Want

Small business owners seek help from a business coach or consultant for several reasons. One of the most common is a need to understand why they are not getting the benefits they want from small business ownership. They are confused and disappointed that what they thought would be the fulfillment of a dream is falling far short of their expectations. Often, they are overwhelmed and wonder if they have made the right choice in small business ownership.

This was the case with Paul and Ann. They were passionate about pleasure boating, water skiing, and sailing. Their friends were water sports enthusiasts. They spent every leisure moment in and around the lakes and rivers within fifty miles of their home and had a dream of owning a business that would allow them to devote even more time to their passion while making a living. So, in 2018 when they learned a water sports rental and repair business was for sale, the couple jumped on the opportunity. In retrospect they realized they may have jumped too quickly without weighing the requirements, responsibilities, and demands of small business ownership. Now they wanted help to turn their situation around or find a way out.

In our first meeting they explained that, in making the leap to business ownership, they hoped for more time with each other, their family, friends, and hobbies. They also wanted to make a predictable living. What they got was a long summer season of serving clients daylight to dark, friends that wanted free service and rentals, inconsistent cash flow, unexpected expenses to promote and maintain the business, no time or money to enjoy their hobbies, no time for each other outside the business hours (which they had very few of), and fear and worry over everything in between. Paul and Ann needed a "reboot". They needed to go back to the beginning to gain a clear understanding of what motivated them to own their own business, a restatement of what they truly wanted, what was possible from business ownership, and what would be required to reach their goals. In simple terms, they needed confirmation that the business and business lifestyle aligned with their life priorities.

If you have not confirmed why you are or want to be a small business owner, what role you want your business to play in your life, and what you must contribute for it to yield the benefits and results you envision, then now is the time to do that. Right now! Read on. Reflect as you go.

Just like Paul and Ann, we begin this journey with the end in mind. You want to build a successful small business so that you can love what you do every day and enjoy your life, right? That means we must start by determining what is most important to *you.* Having your own successful small business will mean very little if in the end you find it is not in alignment with your life priorities.

Being a small business owner should allow you the opportunity to have more, not less, of what you truly want. Being the person in charge, the person who wears all the hats, and the one who takes all the risk, should allow you the opportunity to have what is most important to you. If it does not, you will quickly become frustrated, resentful, and ultimately find you are reaping no joy from the business you created.

Life Priorities

Your values should determine your life and work priorities — they are the measures you use to determine if your life is turning out the way you want it to. They are the things, people, causes, and practices that are most important to you. When the way you spend your time, energy and effort matches your values, life is usually good. You are satisfied. When the opposite is true, everything feels wrong. Often, we think that we can only live according to our life priorities when the circumstances are perfect (i.e., when you have enough money, when you are successful, when the children are grown or out of college, when you retire, etc.). The truth is you *must* live your life in alignment with your priorities *now* to feel satisfied with your life and with your business.

A simple test of priorities is to rank the following in order of importance to you. Rank them from 1 to 8 with 1 being the most important and 8 being less important.

___ Family

___ Friends

___ Hobbies

___ Faith

___ Community

___ Self or YOU

___ Work, Business, Career

___ Money

There is no "right" or "wrong." It is a personal choice. Once the choice is made, the highest ranked should be prioritized in your plans for your life and for your business.

So, what can you learn from this exercise? Look for areas to focus on in your planning process to improve your appreciation for your business and your joy of life. For example, if you ranked "family" first and you are working seven days a week, you will feel overworked or overwhelmed. You may receive feedback from your family that they feel ignored. You may feel unfulfilled in life in general. As you plan, you will want to think about how you can reclaim time to spend with your loved ones. Look for ways to outsource, delegate and set boundaries on work hours. If you ranked "community" in the top three, then think of ways to use your business to promote your community or identify volunteer programs you want to support.

Life priorities are usually fairly stable but they will change as life circumstances change. For example, when you have a young family, "family" may rank higher than "you" or "self" and as you grow older, "community" or "friends" may move up the rank. As change occurs, you may notice signs of feeling out of balance, so making this exercise a part of your planning process every year will help you identify life priorities even as they change.

COACH'S CHALLENGE

Stop now and rank the terms above in order from one through eight. These should be prioritized in order of importance to you, your value system, and your happiness, not according to what you think they should be or how you are currently spending your time.

PLAN IT!

Often "you" ranks low for small business owners. Your business is useless without you. Are you attending to your basic needs of eating, sleeping, exercise and wellness checks? If not, work these into your plan.

Your Motives

Your reasons for starting your small business are yours and yours alone. Commonly, small business owners tell me they made their decision based on a desire to control their own destiny, an interest in creating something of their own, a calling, a desire to fill a need in the community, or simply to live life at a different pace on different terms.

Whatever your reasons, it is important to be fully aware before beginning the planning process. Here are a few questions to help you evaluate your motives.

1. Why do I own a small business?

2. How long do I want to work? What role(s) do I want to play? (leader, team member, owner, absent owner)?

3. How do I want to spend the majority of my time and why?

4. What are my "restrictive thinking" or "limiting

beliefs" (i.e. what do I believe about myself, or my situation that might keep me from owning and running a successful business)?

5. What are my business strengths?

6. What are my personal strengths?

7. What do I not do as well?

8. What do I think it will take to be successful?

9. What is my mission? (See the section that follows.)

COACH'S CHALLENGE

Stop now and answer the questions above. Examine your answers. What did you learn?

Mission

As a part of your reflection on life priorities and motives, you will most certainly want to examine your "mission" for your business.

A mission describes the business purpose. It should be a statement that can travel with you through the years. A mission is what you give or contribute, who you give it to and why you give. Since being a small business owner is a lifestyle, it is important that your business purpose and your life purpose be in alignment. While going through this planning process and reflecting on your business mission, take the time to also reflect on your personal mission (or life purpose).

Just for the record, "mission" and "vision" are sometimes used interchangeably but the terms are not the same. A *vision* translates your *mission* into results and ties them to measurements. A vision is what you want to get from your mission, achievements you want to make both short and long term while you are delivering on your mission. We will address your vision in the Plan It! section of the book.

Develop Your Mission Statement

A mission statement describes your mission. Corporations, institutions and other organizations often create complicated statements that describe their mission. They sometimes inscribe this statement on posters, or plaques and use it in advertising pitches. They are often designed to attract employees, clients or a new market and is therefore more of a marketing strategy than a declaration of the true mission of the organization. This is not what is intended in this exercise. The best mission statements can be used as your answer to the question, "What do you do?"

A mission statement should be simple, easy to recite and a concise description of the purpose of your business. Here are some questions to help you get started. Be sure to state the answers to these questions in positive terms and in as much detail as possible.

- What is your business?
- Who do you serve?
- How do you serve them?
- What do you "give" them or what do they receive?
- What do you want the outcome to be?

PLAN IT!

Stop now and answer the questions above. Make a list of words or phrases that describe what you do, who you do it for and why. Now combine those words and statements into a single message. Be sure it is easy to remember and to share. Say it aloud. Practice it. Share it with your stakeholders and staff and ask for feedback. Ask them to embrace the statement.

COACH'S EXAMPLE

As a coach, my mission is to help business owners identify/clarify their "vision," craft a plan to realize that vision, and support them while they put that plan into action.

Operating Values

As a business owner you are committed to conducting your business in a way that reinforces your value system, the practices you believe are important to the success of your business, and those that will result in satisfaction for your clients. Simply put, it is the way you do the thing you do to get what you want most. In a best scenario, it will also be those things that set you apart from your competition and the reason your client or customer chooses you instead of "them."

These are operating values or virtues. Some are unspoken and expected in business practices, such as trustworthiness, honesty and integrity. Since they are expected they must be delivered, but no special attention is needed to promote them. Others are the values or standards you use to conduct your business that should be promoted. Some examples are: responsiveness, accessibility, cost effectiveness, low cost, licensed or full service, expert in [specialty] field, certified, flexible hours, etc.

What are your operating values? List your top three below. These should be values you believe will set you apart from your competition.

Operating value #1:

Operating value #2:

Operating value #3:

Operating values often change and evolve. As your business grows and matures you will no doubt change what you offer and how you promote it. Your reasons may vary. “Meeting the competition” is a common reason to adjust, or you may change your operating values to “narrow your specialty or target market,” offering less or more to those that you specifically want to do your business with.

If you breezed right through the section on operating values with no questions at all, then now is a great time to ask yourself what you could change about the way you operate your business. What would attract more of your target clients, reduce expenses, result in more profit, improve efficiency, give you a marketing advantage, or, since this is your business, give you a higher sense of success, satisfaction, or personal joy?

COACH'S CHALLENGE

Stop now and identify your operating values. Examine your answers and think about how you are using those values to build your business today. Identify any values that you would like to be known for and, when you plan, add options you will take to promote your values.

The Rest of the Story

So, what about Paul and Ann? Today Paul and Ann are living and loving their small business lifestyle. They still own their watersports rent and repair business. They relocated from the city to just minutes from their business to save travel time and to enjoy rocking on their deck overlooking the lake when they have time off. In our assessment they discovered time together and enjoying their hobbies was more important than more money in their pocket, so they took part of their profit and hired someone to manage the business one and a half days a week. On those days they spend time doing what they love most, boating and being with their friends. Realizing that they had allowed their friends to take advantage of their good nature, Paul and Ann reset their boundaries letting friends know they valued their friendship and their business, would give them great service, and offering them a "friends and family" discount. They even have "friends" special events. These efforts combined have all but stopped the requests for free rentals or special treatment. When that happens, Paul and Ann make decisions based on the circumstances. The business now offers an annual membership to their frequent users and space rental clients. This new product has made the monthly revenue projections more predictable and evened out the cash flow throughout the year. Guess what? They are now considering new passive income options including affiliate relationships, products, real estate rentals, and more. Paul and Ann have a very bright future ahead.

What about you? Are you ready to move forward? Are you clear on the motivation for owning your business, your interests for participating in that business, the values under which you will operate and the mission you intend to fulfill? If the answer is, "yes," then it is time to plan.

Plan It!

Planning Is Critical

Your business success will not happen by accident. If you want to create a business that supports you and your family and provides you with a lifestyle that brings you joy and satisfaction it will take hard work, innovation, dedication, commitment, and a little bit of luck. It will also take discipline, determination, and a willingness to ask for and accept help when needed.

You can improve your odds for success by starting with a clear and concise plan. It's that simple.

After skimming this book and deciding to read it, you may have already decided to skip the planning process thinking you may not need it. This is an example of the type of resistance I mentioned earlier. My clients Jack and Brenda learned to fight their resistance to planning, and it paid off for them. Here is their story.

Jack and Brenda own an automobile repair shop. They inherited the business from Jack's father, and Jack's grandfather before him. As a family, they have been owned the business over 60 years. In our first meeting Jack told me that the business had been "getting by" for years but had never reached its potential. At the same time, he shared they had never developed a plan or goals for success. They had always just accepted what came along as the extent of what was possible for the business.

Year after year they waited for customers to find them and ask for what they needed. When the cars didn't come, they waited and hoped — and worried.

I asked Jack and Brenda to rate their joy and satisfaction as small business owners and they both answered, "not nearly enough." They described how they worked long hours to repair cars on a schedule convenient to the owners which included Saturdays and Sundays. Brenda did the bookkeeping and held down a full-time job to supplement their income. It seemed the business owned them instead of the other way around.

Over the years the inconsistency in income had left them with debt and they occasionally struggled to pay bills. They were tired. They were also afraid that while this had been a family tradition for three generations, it may end with them. They were not sure how they were going to make it through the current calendar year and could not envision how they could ever afford to retire.

Jack and Brenda were not ready to give up. They wanted help and after years of thinking they were destined to accept whatever came their way they were willing to invest in help.

In our initial meeting we identified their goals, and I offered them hope. I had worked with hundreds of business owners just like Jack and Brenda. With great confidence I assured them that they could get what they wanted if they were willing to make a plan and stick to it. I also assured them that the right help always results in a generous return on the investment.

Three years later, Jack and Brenda have a successful auto repair business with two locations. They schedule time off and take it. Most of the administrative work is outsourced and Brenda is no longer on the payroll. They have operating reserves and savings and have started a college fund for their children. They have a team of resources including a business attorney, insurance agent, estate planning agent, financial advisor and a human resources consultant. A solid marketing plan on a careful budget now drives business to them and there is never a period when the shop is empty. Jack and Brenda have a regularly updated plan and are finally enjoying owning their business.

Occasionally, we reflect on that first meeting and how far they have come. They both admit it was a "last ditch effort." They are glad they did not give up and are grateful they are finally living the life they always hoped for. One of them usually says, "All we needed was a plan!"

All small business owners want to be successful. Some know that success is possible but they are not experiencing it. Most would agree that having a plan could be helpful and even practical and instrumental in their success. Still, planning tends to be one of the practices that often takes a back burner. It gets shoved to the "when we get around to it" list or the "when we can afford it" list or even ignored. The demands of day-to-day business tend to make planning for the future a challenge for more than 80 percent of the clients I work with.

There are a variety of reasons why small business owners do not prioritize planning besides simple resistance. The first reason is that they may not see the need. If you have a small business where you do most of the work you may think you can plan as you go or react as the need arises. Having been in business for a while you may feel you planned once (or several times) and there is no need to continue to create plans that are similar year after year. This may be a sign that you are willing to cut corners. Sometimes it works out just fine. Sometimes the outcome is similar to other situations where a lack of planning ends badly. What happens when you do not have directions to your destination? What happens when you try to put together anything without the instructions? What happens when you try to make a cake without a recipe? Sometimes things do turn out just fine. You arrive where you wanted to go, you figure out how to use all the pieces or the dessert is tasty. But more often than not you waste time trying something before going back to the map, directions or recipe to get the result you want. The point is, doing it right the first time is a good rule in almost every situation. Planning is a part of the "doing it right" formula.

You might say, "I can't make the time commitment." You may be so busy working ***in*** the business that you can't see how you can make time to work ***on*** the business. As you have seen in the previous examples, planning is not only a good use of time but it actually saves time. Facts vary on the ratio of time spent planning to time saved in execution but the majority of research tells us that planning will save you significant time in the end. Many believe that there is a better than a 1:4 ratio. That means that for every minute you spend planning you save four minutes in execution. For every hour you save four hours. For every day you save four days. Reclaiming any amount of time is important to most small business owners. This alone is a great reason to stop and plan.

Another reason for avoiding the planning process may be complexity. Many business owners say that planning is simply too difficult, they do not know where to start or they are not sure what to include.

Planning does not have to be difficult. I am going to show you how to create a plan that can work for any business, small or large. You can make the details of the plan as simple or complex as you like.

For now, let's just agree that:

Planning is critical to small business success.

Planning requires dedicated time and energy.

Planning will save you valuable time.

Planning does not have to be difficult.

Strategic Planning and Thinking

Strategic thinking is simply an organized thought process that helps you identify answers to a series of questions, building on the answers to create solutions. A collection of strategies to reach those solutions will create your plan. For example, you may have a vision to increase revenue by 30 percent in 12 months. You start by asking yourself, "What do I want?" (Answer: 30% revenue increase), then "What is my current situation?" (Answer: xx Your most recent annual revenue in dollars). Then ask, "What will it take to reach that goal?" You arrive at a multipart answer including 1) adding new products 2) increasing digital marketing 3) expanding geographic market to a new state. Finally, you determine what you will do and when you will do it to get the results you want. You have used strategic thinking to create a simple strategic plan. We will add a few other components that will make the plan a valuable tool for you to use every day.

Strategic Planning vs. Business Planning

A strategic plan is sometimes confused with a business plan. Plain and simple, a strategic plan is a type of business plan. Still, you will usually find them discussed in different circles and for different purposes. Below are a few of the differences that might be noted.

A strategic plan is most often used for managing the strategic direction of an existing business or organization. A business plan is used at inception or start-up of a new business to obtain funding or direct operations.

A strategic plan generally covers a period from one to five or more years, while a business plan normally covers a period of no more than one year.

The main objective of a strategic plan is outlining a course of action to grow a business. The main objective of a business plan is establishing the parameters of a new business including market, clients, pricing, organization structure, budget, etc.

A strategic plan is critical to the prioritizing and utilization of key resources (time, money and people) to grow revenue. A business plan is critical for securing funding.

A strategic plan is used to communicate the direction of the organization to the staff and stakeholders. A business plan is used to present a concept or idea to investors or banks.

If you are starting a new business you may want to stop and investigate your needs for a business plan. If your business has been open for even a short while, then read on. You need a strategic plan.

The Process of Planning

Planning is an on-going process. This may be the first time you have planned, but once you see the power in planning, I promise it will not be your last. Since I know you are committed to doing this right the first time here are a few things you need to know to get the most benefit from your effort. Here are answers to a few of the most frequently asked questions on strategic planning.

When should I plan?

Now! If you do not have a strategic business plan, plan now. The beginning of the calendar year or fiscal year is always a perfect time. Half year (June/July for most businesses) is also a good time. But, if it is February, or August, or October, and you do not have a plan, do not wait. Make adjustments for the time differences and start your plan now with a commitment to update it at the beginning of the next fiscal or calendar year.

How long will it take?

Planning will take the time you give it. That means you can make this as complicated as you want but it does not have to take more than a few hours. Plan when you have dedicated time without interruptions and when you are physically ready. Planning requires energy and a clear mind.

Generally, the larger and more complex your business the more time you should set aside for planning. Here are a few factors that might require more time in planning:

- Staff of five or more
- Partners
- Several layers of management
- Multiple locations
- Broad product offering
- Selling into multiple time zones
- Multiple channels of business
- Major changes expected in the planning period

Who should be involved?

Major stakeholders should always be involved in planning. Kari, who owns a digital political consulting firm, uses planning as a team-building retreat and reward for his staff. Each year he plans a getaway for the core staff members. Over a long weekend they share a house and cooking duties. They use this time to celebrate accomplishments, plan for the business ahead, and build stronger ties in their team. Kari finds, just as you will, that differing points of view are valuable to the process and that each person has something unique to contribute to the plan. It is a process that has helped them triple their business performance over the last three years.

It is also valuable to know that people are more supportive of a plan they help to create. If they are a part of the plan creation, they will be a more active participant in the execution. So, if you have others in your business that will or should contribute to the success of this plan – include them. This should be:

- Anyone who manages key projects, departments, or decisions
- Anyone who drives business through direct contact with key clients
- Anyone who has a clear understanding of your competition
- Anyone who has experience that will help you make informed decisions

What is the best type of planning session?

If you have more than one stakeholder it is recommended that you meet together one or more times to complete your plan. When I conduct planning sessions I break them into three two to four hour segments. After each session, each/all participants have assignments. The third is used to finalize the plan, assign final tasks, and set dates for further follow-up. The product from the final session is a fully completed Action Plan. But, a marathon six to 10 hour meeting is fine for an off-site planning event. Take more time if you need it to wrap up the plan. Also, be sure to have dedicated time and space for the event. Keep distractions to a minimum. This often means creating your plan away from your place of business.

How often should a plan be reviewed?

The act of planning is the most important part. Second is the act of plan review. The timing of the review is more customized. Some say weekly is best for them. Others prefer monthly and still others review their plans quarterly. Some review the plan only twice a year. What works for you and your business? The timeframe you can commit to is what is best. To help you decide, look at your Action Plan. When will 20 percent of the action have taken place? Meet just at the end of that period (i.e. if 20 percent of the action is scheduled for the first quarter then meet early second quarter to review the status of each action). If in the first review you find you do not have much to discuss you might push it out a bit for the next review meeting.

It is also important to have all the stakeholders that participated in the original process be present for the reviews. No matter what you decide, be sure that your metrics (see Setting Targets and Measuring Performance) coincide with your plan for review. If you set monthly goals review your plan monthly. If you set quarterly goals review your plan quarterly. If you would like my opinion, it is my experience that monthly is the best overall choice.

How often should a plan be updated?

Rewrite your plan as often as you like but once a year is recommended. Be sure to change or update your plan each time you have a major change in your business. Major changes can include:

- Reorganization
- Expansion
- Adding or reducing products or services
- Adding or reducing market size

COACH'S CHALLENGE

Think of your planning meeting as a high priority appointment. Be sure you have a quiet location with comfortable seating in an area that is away from all interruptions.

Be sure you and all of your participants:

Turn off computers.

Silence cell phones

Ask to be left undisturbed.

If others are participating – ask them to make all input constructive.

Focus on the future with only passing reference to the way things "have been"

TOOLS

You have everything you need in this book to create a plan. If you want a simple planning exercise workbook, check the companion to this book, ***Plan It! Do It! Love It! The Planning Workbook***.

Six Step Planning

Planning like many other processes is made easier when broken into manageable steps. It is the same concept as a recipe for your favorite dish or directions for building a treehouse. It makes the process, program, or project easier.

You will build on your plan one step at a time. Just as with a recipe or building project, planning steps should be taken in order and completed before moving to a new step. The planning project can be completed in one day or over a period of a few weeks. Work at your own pace, but I would not recommend that you stretch it out more than 30 days as the facts tend to change and other parts of your plan will need to be adjusted as a result.

The plan steps are:

1. **Design the Vision:** In this step you outline what you want to do, be, or have by a target date you select. This can be as long as you like, but is typi-

cally between 12 and 60 months.

2. **Examine and Assess:** In this step you will examine your business and assess your situation. You will identify what you have to work with to build towards your vision. You will learn your strengths, weaknesses, and opportunities. You will identify any threats or contributing factors you do not control.

3. **Set Measurements:** In this step you will select the metrics for your plan. These measurements will become your "report card" for plan progress.

4. **Select Strategy**: In this step you will select five to 10 key strategies. These are areas of focus that you feel will have the greatest impact on your business success. They are the vehicles you expect to deliver your vision.

5. **Assign Action:** In this final planning step you will identify a series of actions you will take and then assign deadlines and responsible parties to each one.

6. **Take Action:** This is the "Do It!" phase of the plan in this book.

Are you ready to get started?

Step One: Design the Vision

Think back. Do you remember the moment you decided to open your small business? Do you remember the picture that popped into your head when you first realized it was a real possibility to open, operate, and succeed by promoting your own products or services? No, really, stop and try to remember.

What did you see?

The picture that sprung into your mind's eye was very possibly the purest vision you will ever have of what is possible for you and your business. It was the vision you had for your future. It was untarnished by the mistakes, challenges and disappointments that are a real part of any small business. It might have been "dream-like." Maybe you even saw more than you now believe is possible in your lifetime. That moment, that picture, is what a "vision" is all about. The vision you have for this planning process will no doubt be different but hang on to your original vision and challenge yourself each planning period to ignore any roadblocks or thinking clouded by thoughts limited by experiences or fears.

The planning process begins with a clear statement of your vision. This is what you want to do, be, have, or have accomplished on or by a particular point in time. As your business changes and matures your vision will change with it. As mentioned above, the vision you had in mind in the beginning may be different, even very different, from the vision you will have for the next twelve months. This vision will be different from the next and so on. You will create a new vision every time you plan. You will update it as the need arises. You will adjust it as the circumstances demand.

Hopefully, your vision will evolve through a thoughtful, intentional, and strategic process. One vision might call for expansion. The next may be one of maintaining your current position and refining processes or developing systems. Your vision should be the one to serve you best at the point in time you have chosen it.

Target Date and Timing

Most often a vision is developed for a twelve-month calendar or fiscal year. That does not mean that you cannot create one for longer or shorter periods of time. Your vision is your vision. It should describe where you intend to go, what you intend to create, and how you intend to achieve all you want to achieve in the greatest amount of detail possible.

The process is simple, but it does take effort—most of which is spent getting out of your own way in order to identify what you "want" and not what you think you can "have." There is always plenty of time to bring a vision back into view. Start with the commitment to push the limits, think big, be creative, be open, and allow yourself the opportunity to have it all.

Designing Your Vision

Designing your vision can be a very stimulating and enjoyable experience. The process is brainstorming, free thinking, and even dreaming. Start with a piece of paper. Pick a date when you want to have completed the vision (most often 12 months). Then, begin to clearly state in positive terms what you will do, be, have, or have achieved as a business by the date you have chosen. Remember, your business vision translates your mission into specific terms for a specific period.

Here are a few questions you might ask yourself to begin the process:

- What is the target date for my plan?
- What do I want most from my business?
- What do I intend to create?

- What do I want to accomplish or achieve?
- Who do I want to serve?
- What do I deserve to get in return for my investment of time and money?

Remember, this is the time to be self-serving. If you do not have a stake in the business you will most likely not create the success that is possible. If you cannot determine what is in this for you then you most likely will not feel satisfied with any level of profit. Also, as you create this vision, remember to align each statement with the life priorities you uncovered earlier. Life priorities are those things that are most important to you. For example, if you value time with your family and friends you do not want to design a vision that will require you to commit to spending a large percentage of your time traveling away from home to grow your business. Similarly, if you value giving back to the community then make certain you have set aside time in your schedule and a portion of your budget to fulfill those goals.

Be Positive

When developing your vision details state them in the positive. State what you will "do," what you will "have," what you will "be," and what you will have "achieved," by the target date. Avoid creating statements about anything you are trying to avoid or do not want. Positive statements include positive action words such as develop, create, increase, design, achieve, maintain, introduce, expand, save, awarded, etc. Conversely you most often find negative words in negative statements. Examples of which might be terminate, eliminate, do not, avoid, don't, etc.

Be Realistic

As you may have already noticed there is a fine balance between wanting too much and not wanting enough when it comes to creating a vision for your business. Since stating this vision can be viewed as a promise you make to yourself you may be afraid to set your plans too aggressively for fear of disappointing yourself. The key to success is to find a balance. Challenge yourself to a bit more than you think may be easy. Know what you can do and add some percentage to that (I recommend 20 percent). I often challenge clients to set a vision just where it makes them feel a little nervous or light headed – but not queasy. You have nothing to lose but a chance to achieve great things.

This is a great time to remind all small business owners that success takes the time it takes. You can improve the outcome and shorten the timeline by planning — executing, being accountable, taking advantage of resources and more, but successful businesses do not fall from the sky. I am sure we can all identify at least one exception to this statement, one business that had explosive success on a great idea or even a silly idea (like rocks sold as pets and collectable bean bag dolls). But the majority of all businesses must follow the "farming" approach. The ground must be prepared, the seeds sown, then fertilized, watered, and finally the crop will mature and be ready for harvest. Your vision should reflect a realistic approach to timing.

As a rule most new businesses will take 18 months to three years to be profitable and longer (three to five years) to be stable and sustainable. It is typically not reasonable to think you can double your revenue year over year. If you plan to increase anything more than 30 percent you will want to have a clear understanding of the resources you will need, where they will come from, how you will pay for them, what to expect in return, and a clear estimate of sales cycles. You will also need to know who will be expected to do what. If you are counting on you and only you then you should know what "you" are capable of. A great way to approach that question is to look at what you are responsible for now and how it is impacting you, your family, your health and your life. Are you in alignment with your life priorities (there is that reminder again)? Do you have more to give or are you tapped out? Will you need resources to deliver on your plan? If so, do you know who or what those resources are and how you will engage them? Have you budgeted for the costs? All these answers fall into the questions around being "realistic" in your visioning.

That does not mean you cannot have some outstanding achievements and results and that sometimes you will gain far more than you might think possible. But it does mean that it is important to set a clear vision for a reasonable period of time, focus on your plans, believe in your possibilities, stay a steady course and be prepared to face a few disappointments. In the end, I am sure you will get exactly what you want!

Be Specific

Swiss architect Charles Édouard Jeanneret once said, "The devil is in the details." When this phrase is used it means that the failure of one or more project components can lead to the failure of the overall project or that the small things in plans that are often overlooked can cause serious challenges in the overall success.

In planning, the details are critical and begin with having a clear, concise, and unchallengeable series of statements that make up the overall vision for success. You must know exactly where you want to go, what you want to have, how much, when you want to have achieved or acquired whatever you want and often, how you plan to achieve it and what the outcome is expected to be. Be sure you fully describe each statement in your vision exercise. Give as many details as are possible and practical.

Make it Measurable

Vision details that you cannot measure make it very difficult to know if you fully achieved it. Be sure that you state your vision using details that define the date, quantity, location, number, percent, rank, or any other qualifying measurement that allows you and any other stakeholder in the plan to know and understand exactly what you plan to accomplish and when.

COACH'S EXAMPLE

2016 – 12 Month Vision:

Increase revenue by 35 percent over the year ending December 31, 2025

Increase number of active clients from 250 to 350 by October 1, 2026

Improve quality score by 10 points by end of first quarter 2022

Hire three new business development managers – Boston (May 2028), Atlanta (August 2029), Dallas (November 2029)

200 percent increase in sale of Product A following the release of Product Xa

Develop 12 new partnership relationships from the XYZ organization in our first year of membership

Schedule and take 4 weeks of vacation (March, June, August, December) this year

Lower debt by $25,000 by end of third quarter

Increase personal income by $50,000 this year
Complete the course work for and gain certification for Master xx by September 1st next year

Develop a Complete Picture

The vision for your business should encompass all aspects of your business including revenue, expense, pricing, products, client types, number of clients, staffing, systems, performance management, quality control, budgeting, marketing, sales, geography, branding, networking, public relations and more. This program is designed to stimulate your thinking for your business in the broadest most complete sense. Be sure you address each area in your vision details.

PLAN IT!

Step 1: Record your vision details. You may want to use a notebook or order ***Plan It! Do It! Love It! The Planning Workbook*** and complete Step 1: Designing the Vision.

COACH'S CHALLENGE

To get the best outcome from this exercise I challenge you to:

Set aside plenty of time.

Have a positive attitude. Forget the concepts of "impossible" or the phrase "it can't be done". Try to leave your restrictive thinking or limiting beliefs behind.

Ask for what you want. Think of this as a message you are sending to the universe. Declare it and expect it.

State your vision in positive terms. Make this vision neither an overpromise nor an under promise of what you will deliver.

Stretch your thinking. You might try stating details that make you a little nervous but not queasy. In doing that you are bound to challenge yourself.

Review for completeness (See Check your vision below)

Be sure what you have declared is in alignment with your life plans and priorities.

Check Your Vision Details

Before you wrap up your vision exercise be certain you have included the complete picture. Are all aspects of your business included? If you are not sure whether you have identified all the details here is a checklist to assist you. Check you have addressed the following:

- Revenue
- Profit
- Sales in number or dollars
- Number of clients? Active clients vs. inactive in

percentage

- Expense control: total dollars or expense
- Loans to acquire or debt to reduce
- Savings or operating reserves
- Personal income dollars or change in percentage.
- Market expansion – geography, target client increase, additional sales personnel
- Marketing changes – new campaigns, updated brand, new tactics
- Changes in the organizational structure in size or roles/responsibilities
- Training and education, certifications
- Licensing
- Investments, equipment, upgrades
- New products or services
- Price changes. Lover or raise prices
- New price packages
- Contracts or any legal needs/changes

- Partnerships to develop, expand, reduce, or replace
- Memberships or networking
- Achievements or designations to pursue or complete
- Scheduling changes, time off, vacations
- Employee benefits, rewards, performance
- Outsourcing – contractors to add, reduce, replace
- Facilities, leases, reconfigurations
- Professional services – legal, financial, etc.
- Personal goals or achievements
- Special projects or events, sponsorships
- Exit plans, retirement planning

Critical Success Factors

As you were defining your vision you may have been using some basic assumptions. They might have been as simple as an assumption that you will remain healthy all year or, for those of you that own seasonal businesses, that the summer or winter will come right on time. Your assumptions may have been more complex such as a belief that your employees are satisfied, that the level of productivity will remain the same, or that you will not experience any attrition in your current clients.

Most assumptions fall into a category of "things you do not control." It is important as you wrap up your vision exercise that you are aware of and acknowledge any assumptions you are making that are critical to the success of your vision. You may even want to record them. Make sure that anyone who participates in your planning process is also aware of the assumptions.

As you review your plan at regular intervals always review your Critical Success Factors and update them. If they change, your plan should be adjusted accordingly. For example, if you have a seasonal business that requires warm temperatures and sunshine to maximize your revenue (landscaping, exterior painting contractors, swimming pool designers, golf courses) and you make an assumption that spring weather will begin in early April you will need to make adjustments if winter lingers longer than usual and cold temperatures are still prevalent on April 20. Do not put yourself or your business in the position to have to hope, pray, and "make it up" with a longer than usual summer. That may happen but you do not want to count on it if it is not generally expected.

Here are a few common Critical Success Factors:

- Economic conditions

- Market conditions
- Staff retention
- Stable competitive factors
- Client retention
- Stable supply chain
- Weather – seasons
- Consumer confidence
- Your health or ability to contribute

Try not to spend too much time focusing on these factors, particularly if you tend to worry. Remember, most of what you will list are factors you do not control. The best defense is a good offense. Be diligent about all the factors you control and you can expect the best outcome.

Step Two: Examine and Assess

It's time to take a hard, long look at the facts. This is not always easy. As human beings we tend to overlook the truth as it relates to ourselves and anything we love. The old adage of "love is blind" extends to business for small business owners. Therefore, as you move into this second planning step it may be helpful to ask others to join you. They can offer different perspectives and viewpoints. They can help you see what you might be overlooking.

So, who do you add? You might consider adding anyone that is a key stakeholder, such as a board member, a key employee, or even your spouse (this one can be tricky). Supervisors and managers are always good choices and staff members who have contact with clients. Do not worry that you will be trapped into making changes you do not agree with. This is still your business and the final decisions are always yours. However, the act of asking others to participate will not only give you differing viewpoints that may contribute to your plan, but will also send a message to anyone consulted that you value their input.

In this planning step you will evaluate not only your business but yourself. The objective is to identify what you have, own, or employ that will help you to reach your "vision." This is an inventory of your current business systems, assets and practices. What you discover in this process is an important starting point for Step 4 (Select Strategies).

Take your time. Give this information and these questions and exercises the time and attention they deserve. Dig deep. Look at all the facts. Remember that this process is meant to help you to gain a more thorough understanding of any and all areas of your business. It should put you in touch with the performance of the past, the status of today, and the resources for the future.

If you have not done so recently, survey your employees and clients. Get to know your competitors. Examine your partnerships and practices. Evaluate your performance and the performance of all those that contribute to your success. Do a thorough examination of your records, practices, processes, and systems.

In the following pages, we will examine and assess:

- Organizational structure and design

- Overall assessment of strengths, weaknesses, opportunities and threats (SWOT analysis)
- Target client – past and current
- Your unique qualities
- Specialty – primary and secondary
- Competitors and competitive advantage
- Marketing and promotion
- Revenue, expense, and profit
- Pricing and pricing packages or bundles
- Investments and protective measures
- Staffing and staff performance
- Employee benefits
- Networking ROI (return on your investment)
- Strategic and referral partnerships
- Information management
- Client retention
- Sales and business development programs

PLAN IT!

Step 2: As you complete the exercises make notes on anything you want to change. These changes will become a part of your strategy and Action Plan. Collecting this list with pen and paper works just fine, or you may want to purchase ***Plan It! Do It! Love It! The Planning Workbook*** and complete Step 2: Examine and Assess.

COACH'S CHALLENGE

Do not rely on your memory for all the actions and ideas you will have while reading the pages that follow. Be prepared with paper and pencil the Actions pages in ***Plan It! Do It! Love It! The Planning Workbook***.

Organization Structure and Design

Poorly designed and executed organizational growth is costly for any business, particularly for small businesses where the "people costs" are among the highest percentage of fixed operating costs.

Small business owners often throw resources at a need only after the need is urgent. That means you are always in a reaction mode, scrambling to meet the demands of clients, and usually at a higher expense. Rushed hiring, which often results in making poor hiring choices, makes a less than optimal employee match leading to lower morale, increased average wages or overtime, higher turnover, and an increase in stress and strain — not on just the owner or hiring manager, but on every member of the team. Finally, this type of reactionary growth almost always impacts the quality of the work. This results in reduced customer satisfaction and expensive repercussions — mistakes, lost income and work that must be redone.

The key to managed and sustainable growth is to understand what your company structure looks like today and what you will need in a variety of scenarios for the future. It all starts with a clear definition of today's organizational structure. Once that is set, you can determine what will need to change based on the vision you have declared. Identify how and when you will add to staff, change reporting lines, delegate or realign goals. Determine the trends and signs you will look for, and be prepared to act as soon as those indicators surface.

Start by identifying the current structure. I find that drawing an organizational chart is always a powerful tool. Having a visual of reporting lines and responsibility areas is a great first step to making the changes you want.

There are plenty of examples on the internet or you may want to purchase ***Plan It! Do It! Love It!, The Planning Workbook***. There is no right or wrong organizational design as long as it works for you and your business.

The key components of a well-functioning design are:

- Clearly defined roles and responsibilities.

- Clear reporting lines and authority.
- Well balanced functions and responsibilities—no one person having too much responsibility for delivering success including you, the owner.

TOOLS

Plan It! Do It! Love It! The Planning Workbook may come in handy.

PLAN IT!

Step 2: Sketch your own chart as it looks today. Use that chart to assist you in creating the perfect organization structure for your vision. List the names and positions for all the staff members you have and indicate those you will hire TBD (to be determined) and a date you plan to hire them.

Once you have outlined your current organization you can use this same chart to build the organization in your vision. Here are a few key questions to ponder:

Will I need additional staff when I have fully reached my vision?

At what point will I need to add staff?

Will additional staff be added all at once or in stages?

If all at once: when?

If in stages: what staff will be added and when?

Is outsourcing an option for some of the staffing needs?
Can I use temporary staffing before hiring permanently?
Will additional management be needed for the changes?
Is the additional staff to be permanent or seasonal?

Predicting and filling the needs for optimal staffing and resources is a challenge for most small businesses and is especially true in the trades. It is even more pronounced in seasonal trades such as painting contractors, remodelers, landscapers, winter sports, vacation businesses, etc. They often do not know how much business a season will bring. Since overstaffing is as costly as understaffing they often play the "wait and see" game. Most of the time it is because they cannot or have not anticipated the full extent of the need until it has already happened. If you own a seasonal business or a trade business don't let poor planning impede your ability to maximize your opportunity. Plan for all eventualities and react early. You can color code your organizational chart for each situation if you desire.

Here are a few questions that are specific to your business type including:

- What are the three to five situations I might encounter in this plan period?
- What are the resource and staffing needs of each?
- What is the timing for hiring that will give me the

best pool of people to draw from and not leave me with idle staff?

- Will they be kept at reduced hours in off-season or terminated and rehired?
- If terminated: How will I keep them engaged and available for rehire?
- Can I hire staff members that are employed during the seasons that I will not need them (students, teachers, school bus drivers, complimentary seasonal workers)?
- Is there a pool of people that do not want to work full time all year (moms with children, retired, live in the area seasonally)?

PLAN IT!

Step 2: Update your budget. Changes in people always result in changes in costs — salaries, benefits, equipment, and facilities. Be sure you make a note to budget for any additional staff, promotions or recruiting needs. Update your budget with the costs of these staffing changes in the months that they occur. Add budget for benefits, equipment, and supplies. You may want to investigate outsourcing opportunities. Contact temporary agencies or locate a recruiter that specializes in small business or your industry. If you do not have a budget, be sure you record an Action to create one.

SWOT Analysis

Day in and day out small business owners are always analyzing what is going right and what is not going as well. Rarely do we prioritize building on our strengths. We tend to focus on all the things we could "fix" or improve on and dismiss those that have already been perfected or stable. During the planning process we are presented with the perfect opportunity to stop and fully analyze everything — those accomplishments that make us smile, the challenges that makes us weep, the opportunities that represent our possibilities, and the fears we have for all those things we do not control and should be prepared for.

A SWOT analysis is a simple structured planning method used to evaluate the strengths, weaknesses, opportunities, and threats involved in a business, a project, a product, a place or person.

The components of the SWOT technique for planning are:

- <u>Strengths</u>: characteristics of the business or project that give it an advantage over others and should be retained or built upon.

- <u>Weaknesses</u>: characteristics that place the business at a disadvantage relative to others and should be eliminated or replaced.

- Opportunities: characteristics the business should exploit or take advantage of.

- Threats: elements outside the control of the business that could cause trouble and should be prepared for.

To complete your own SWOT analysis start to make a list of each of the above. If you have any trouble getting started you can ask yourself a few simple questions such as:

Strengths:

- What areas of my business are going well?

- What will drive business in this plan period?

- Who or what is an asset to my business?

- What can I build on?

Weaknesses:

- Who or what drains my revenue or my energy?

- If eliminated what could make my business more profitable, efficient, popular, or enjoyable?

- What keeps me awake at night with worry?

- What areas of my business are not going well?
- What is getting in the way of my business reaching its full potential?

Opportunities:

- What did I list as strength or a weakness that could provide me with an opportunity to generate more revenue, get more clients, enjoy work more or reduce liability?
- Who can help me realize my vision?
- What resources are available to me that I am not currently utilizing?

Threats:

- What might happen during this plan period that I do not control?
- How can I prepare for it?

Once completed, these SWOT notes and statements can provide you with a wealth of information. You can and should use it to refine your vision. In these statements are hints on the strategies you create and the actions you take under each of those strategies.

PLAN IT!

Step 2: Take a piece of paper and divide it into four sections (or use four pieces of paper). Label one Strengths (S), one Weaknesses (W), one Opportunities (O) and the final one Threats (T). Identify any area, person, team, process, product, program, function, situation or other that is either a strength, weakness, opportunity or threat to your business.

TOOLS

A list on a piece of paper works just fine or you may want to purchase ***Plan It! Do It! Love It! The Planning Workbook***. In Step 2: Examine and Assess you will find several pages that will give you step by step instructions for this exercise.

COACH'S CHALLENGE

Review your SWOT statements and notes. Take another look at your vision details. Is there anything you should change because of what you uncovered in this analysis? You should have uncovered a number of actions you plan to take in the year ahead. Stop now and record them on your Action list while they are fresh in your mind.

Target Market or Client

A key element in fully developing your plan is to determine who you will serve in your plan period. This will be your target client, market, or customer — the "who, what, where and how." Choosing a specific market determines not only who you will work with, but who you will market to, where you will market, how you will market, and what you can expect in return.

Knowing who you are serving now and who you have served in the past can provide you with valuable information for making informed decisions about your future target. I suggest you review your client history in detail. Know who you have served, how, and what you gained from each client or transaction for at least the past 12 months. If you are not tracking that information I suggest you stop and perform a review that will help you gain clear understanding of who you service, how and what you gained in return.

PLAN IT!

Step 2: (A) List each client, the product or service they purchased, the price they paid, your profit, what they gained, and your level of satisfaction or enjoyment. You can create your own review form, or you may want to purchase ***Plan It! Do It! Love It! The Planning Workbook.***

The exercises in Step 2 will give you all the information you need.

PLAN IT!

Step 2: (B) If you are not currently tracking client information, add the creation of this tracking form or system to your Action Notes. You may have a system that will provide you with this information or you can track it manually with the form provided in Step 2 of ***Plan It! Do It! Love It! The Planning Workbook***.

TOOLS

A list on a piece of paper works just fine or as mentioned above or you may want to purchase ***Plan It! Do It! Love It! The Planning Workbook***.

Analyze Your Business Review

Once you have the above results, do a full review. Have you been serving the client that is most profitable, that you enjoy the most, and that wants or needs the product or service that you consider to be your specialty? If not, you may have been serving a client that is not the best fit for you and certainly not the best fit for your future business success.

Small business owners are often concerned about turning anyone away. Generally, they do not want to get specific on who they serve for fear of losing a sale. They often say "yes" when they should say "no" upon being asked to do something outside their published list of products or services. In an effort to serve everyone it is not uncommon to find that you are not serving the client you most want to work with, and therefore not making the most profit from transactions that would fulfill your vision. It is up to you, the business owner, to know who you are targeting. Speak directly to that target in all of your messages, and be willing to say "no" to anyone that does not fit into the target profile. Remember, you get what (and who) you ask for.

Choose Wisely

If you find you need to adjust your target client remember to choose wisely. Often it takes no more effort to market to those who will provide a better return on your efforts. Do your research. Here are a few bits of advice.

Make sure the client you choose wants or needs the product or service you are offering. For example, do not try to sell landscape services to apartment renters. You do not want to target newlyweds for funeral services, but you do want to target them for life insurance.

Focus on a client or market that can afford your products and services and is willing to spend money on them. As an example, focusing sales of products and services suited to persons with a level of "disposable income" such as vacation tours or spa treatments, to a market segment that is on a fixed income (elderly or college students) is not a productive strategy. You will sell the most products or services and realize the highest profit if you offer your products and services to people who not only want or need them but can afford to buy them. Also consider whether or not your target client is willing to spend money on your product or service (i.e. snow shovels in the summertime or swimsuits in the winter are difficult even if the price is right).

Be certain the clients you target are those you want to work with. One of the key reasons most small business owners take the leap into owning their own business is to have more joy in the their work life. That begins with enjoying the people that you work with whether they are staff or clients.

Primary vs. Secondary Targets

The target clients are not all equal. At any given time you might have two or more target client profiles.

There are a variety of reasons why you might choose to serve a few different target types even for limited periods of time. These include business diversification, growing a future business, testing new products or services or transitioning to new markets. Target client types might include primary targets, secondary targets, key clients and special project clients.

Your *primary target* client is the one that wants or needs the product or service you most want them to buy, is willing to pay the established price and is the client you connect best with or most want to work with. Generally it means they are the client that are the most profitable for you and your company, the easiest to serve and the most enjoyable to work with. All of your messages and marketing efforts should be directed towards this client. Think of it this way — if you can fill your calendar and your coffers with this client type, why would you work with anyone else?

Once you have determined this target expand your knowledge by understanding: where they live, work, shop; their disposable income; their buying influences or motivation; their personal characteristics; their affiliations or network; their employer; their education; and their business type. You should also include what you know about their motivation to buy and how easy or difficult they are to work with. All of this information should be shared with anyone who is assisting in your sales, marketing, or promotion efforts. They need to know who they will be attracting.

The *secondary target(s)* is also a client that wants or needs the product or service you have to offer but may not be the one that is most profitable or even the easiest to work with. These are clients that fill in the gaps. While they are not the perfect target, they might just be what pays the bills while you grow your business. They buy some of what you most want to sell. They may even be future potential targets. For now, they provide you with income while you build your specialty business with your target client. The key to serving this client is to know it is temporary and be willing to transition them out of your business when the time is right or to convert them to your target as soon as you can. The good news is that this is often easy business. Generally, they seek you out, and even if they do not want your full package, program, or product, they are loyal.

The distinguishing factor of a *key client* is that they represent a larger than normal portion of your business in sales, volume, revenue or profit. They typically are your target client who buys in a larger quantity or more frequently. You want these clients, but don't "put all your eggs in this one basket." Just a few of these can make all the difference in a successful or not so successful year or season. Similarly, the loss of one or more of these can drastically reduce your short term success.

While this client can have great value to you, they can also take advantage of their value. They may be demanding of your time, want prices that are well below your asking price, want special concessions or accommodations or demand resources. Sometimes you will find that the value they create is not worth the volume they deliver. You may even find they are less valuable overall than a few lower volume clients who pay full price and require less attention. Before granting them any special arrangements you will want to examine their net value. In your calculations, be sure you include all factors including the cost of your time, resources, concessions, etc. Know what your return is for the investment you make.

Limit your exposure and risk by not depending too heavily on this client(s) and always knowing how you will replace them should they sever the relationship.

As a rule, one client should never be responsible for more than 25 percent of your sales, revenue or profit. Avoid allowing any client to be 50 percent or more of your sales, revenue or profit. If you do not currently have any "key" clients you will want to find a few. What will they look like?

Special project clients or temporary targets are those that are typically short-term. They may be a test market or a client that you intend to only work with until you have filled your books with your desired targets.

COACH'S EXAMPLE

As a business coach and consultant my target client is a business that is already successful; sees value in having a partnership with a business coach; has a revenue of no less than $500,000 to $3,000,000 annually; are located in any state on the continental U.S.; have a staff of five to 25 people; and are in a growth or change mode. They are also energized by collaboration and follow-through on the projects they agree to; have a positive attitude; and believe they can have the success they are planning for. This client is already profitable and willing to invest in their future. My secondary target is a young growing business; in business less than five years, have less than $500,000 in revenue; and fewer than five employees. They have promise and possibilities and are willing to work hard. They have the right product for the right price in the right market. They are expected to grow into my "target" in the next five years.

Not Every Client is Right

As you no doubt discovered in the exercises on the previous pages, it is important to make certain there is value in every relationship. It may have become clear to you in this process that not every relationship has value for you and your business. These are clients you want to eliminate today or in the near future.

Consider eliminating or discouraging business with any client or market that does not serve your vision. Say "no" to any client that wants to negotiate prices below your minimum profit levels. Be aware of client types that are difficult, demanding, want a service you do not provide, do not fit into your pricing models, or have a higher cost to service.

Any client that creates negative value should not be a client you seek or keep. Eliminate them now. Do not be afraid to put boundaries on the client types you are willing to work with. Be true to your vision.

Below are some examples of client(s) you will want to eliminate and suggestions on how you might address these situations:

Not profitable: Have a standard price. If you have clients that are currently under a different price structure, change the price of products or services that you offer this client. Talk to them about how and when the change will take place. Any client that is not willing to make the change will take special handling. Be professional but firm and refer them to someone that has a lower price.

Service you will no longer offer: Be clear about the services that are profitable for you and that you are willing to offer. If you have clients that currently are using services you once offered but have eliminated, discuss with the client the change and how it impacts them. Give them a date when the service will no longer be available. Convert them to another service that is similar or serves them better.

Out of area: Set clear boundaries on your service area. If you are serving clients outside that area, inform them of the changes. If you make exceptions charge them a "trip fee" or "extra service fee." The highest cost to servicing clients outside your service area is often the time it takes to get to them and back. Time is money in almost every business. Travel time is often not recoverable and better used in other ways. Consider forming partners with other businesses that serve areas you do not intend to serve. You may find they are willing to share referrals with you for areas you serve that they do not.

Difficult client: This one is tricky. Difficult clients are often those that steal your time, your energy, and expect to receive more than they pay for. Business owners tend to avoid addressing these relationships. The fear of conflict can delay a confrontation. There is typically a price where you might be willing to work with their demands. Charge for every hour you spend, every service or product they use. Be sure you fit them into a schedule that suits you best and that they do not stand in the way of you building your business in areas that are more important to you and your long-term success.

If you have evaluated the return you get at the price you charge and still find this is not a client worth the investment, then do not delay — be direct with telling them you can no longer meet their needs.

PLAN IT!

Step 2: Outline your target client in as much detail as possible.

PLAN IT!

Step 2: (A) Identify changes you need or want to make in your target client and record the action(s) that will give you the results you want most. Vow that you will discourage any business that does not fit into one of your target types.

PLAN IT!

Step 2: (B) Refine your messages and marketing material to speak to your primary target client and only your primary target client.

COACH'S CHALLENGE

If you have determined that there are client types you are working with that need to be eliminated, and are ready to change your relationship with these clients, set a date to take that action.

Your Unique Qualities

Every small business or small business owner has qualities that are unique to them. Typically these unique qualities are the reason they believe they have an advantage in the marketplace. They are certain that the market will choose them over their competitors. They believe they have an advantage due to some fact or facts that they believe make them different in a positive way.

These unique qualities are often something a business or business owner has accomplished, developed or created. These qualities make this business or business owner a more attractive choice than others offering the same or similar products and services. Some examples of unique qualities include: education, previous work experiences, name recognition, investments, partnerships, licenses or certifications, achievements, ranking, training, talent, skill, abilities, fame, reputation, financial stability, track record, or inventions. Consumers are drawn to the product or service emotionally — they love it, need it, and want it — but they are convinced to buy based on the benefit they believe they can attain from you versus your competition. Your unique qualities help to convince them that you and your business are the best choice.

You can directly impact the consumer acceptance of your product or service by promoting your unique qualities. Use your unique qualities in your promotional materials, on your website, and in any introductions you make in networking situations or with potential clients. Be clear and specific. Always be truthful. Never make false claims.

Sometimes consumers buy products solely based on these qualities alone. Top brand athletic equipment companies use star performers for just that reason. They give the consumer a sense they can achieve more by using a product that someone who has achieved athletic greatness claims contributes to their ability. Consumers believe they will run faster, shoot farther, hit better, or win more if they choose the same product. Since we know that psychology is a contributor to success, maybe, just maybe they do indeed turn out a better performance.

While it is never a guarantee that these unique qualities will translate into business success, they are certain to have some impact on sales. Identify them and then use them to promote your business.

As you begin identifying these values remember that it is not necessary to have a large number of unique values. You should be able to identify one or more that you feel will influence the decisions of your target client to buy your product or service. This will result in an advantage over your closest competitors.

COACH'S EXAMPLE

In my practice, I promote my Masters in Psychology and 27 years' experience in corporate America. I advertise that I grew up in a family-owned businesses (father, grandfather, great grandfather, uncles and aunts) and that my husband started and owned his own business for 14 years. Some of my female clients are moved by the designation of Woman Owned Business and some of my male clients like to know that both genders are almost equally represented in their success. After years of tracking I can tell prospective clients what my success record is at any given time and often I share that I have expertise in strategic planning.

PLAN IT!

Step 2: Make a list of each unique value that you, your business, or any of your employees bring to the business. Develop statements on how you have or will use those qualities to promote an exceptional customer experience. Be particularly mindful of any you have not promoted in the past.

Specialty

Jim is a business attorney. His target is the small business owner that has a regular need for legal advice and is willing to pay a monthly retainer for a legal resource. Jim understands the demands of small business ownership and is willing to work by phone, internet, or even to travel to the client to help them manage both time and money. Jim's specialty is helping small businesses maximize their resources while keeping them "out of trouble" at a price they can afford. He uses his 15 years of big firm experience and current role as a small business owner to connect with this population and be an invaluable resource in common areas of legal concern such as contracts, disputes, starting a business or selling a business. He keeps his costs low by working from a home office with outsourced staff so he can live a lifestyle he loves and offer his services for a price that fits the budget of his target client. Jim has a well thought-out and artfully executed specialty.

Every small business should have a specialty. What is yours? Do you know? Often when I ask clients to describe their specialty, they return a blank look or answer with a long list of products or services that they offer or populations they serve. Your *specialty is typically a single product or set of products, service or group of services that you want to be known for*. It is not everything you have to offer. It is your "secret sauce," your "special recipe," your "unique design." It is that product or service that you want to sell or provide more of than anything else you offer.

Consider this, if you could fill your business or appointment books with one service or product what would it be? This might be the product or program that results in the *most profit or highest volume of sales,* but it should also be the thing you love to do most and that brings you the most satisfaction. It should be an area, product or service where you have *expert status.*

You may be one of those business owners that knew your specialty from the moment you opened your business. For example, you are committed to sustainability, want to work with brides, and love flowers, so you opened a floral design business that promotes the use of local, sustainable, plants for weddings. One of my clients did this, so her business was specialized from day one.

Unfortunately, knowing your specialty from opening day is not the most typical scenario.

Sometimes when a small business opens the specialty is somewhat clear but needs refinement. Let's say you own a restaurant that serves bar-b-que (one of my favorites). You may have a narrow focus (southern style bar-b-que) but not a true specialty. As the patronage grows you find your true specialty is pulled pork sandwiches with your special bar-b-que sauce. This dish is what you sell the most of, what you love to promote and results in the most profit. It's also better than any other bar-b-que and sauce in your city.

Often, small business owners are unclear on their specialty in the first year or maybe even the first few years. They may offer two distinctly different products or services, unable to choose between them. One of my manufacturing clients offered fish nets produced in Central America and travel trailers produced in Maine for several years before they realized they could benefit greatly from focusing on one product, one manufacturing site, one brand message and one target client.

Like my manufacturing client, many business owners can and will offer a wide range of products or services at the outset. The reasons vary, but most commonly it is because 1) they are not sure what the market needs most, so they often 2) offer their target market what they ask for in an effort to 3) generate as much revenue as possible to keep the business running, or to 4) please anyone that wants to work with them. They might also believe that 5) the more products and services they offer the larger market they can serve and the more revenue they will generate. What they don't realize is that diversification can be costly when it is not planned and executed with the right timing.

While large corporate concerns may choose to diversify and build multiple lines of business around multiple markets and product lines, ultimately, most successful small business owners conclude they can be more successful through specialization. Why? Because the more specialized the small business the easier it is for clients to remember and refer, and the more likely you are to be seen as an "expert" in the field. It is also the where you will most likely make the best return on your investment and realize the highest revenue stream.

Review Your Specialty

Your specialty should be reviewed regularly. What better time than during your planning exercise. Is it as narrow as should be? Are you still trying to sell insurance when you need to be specializing in life insurance for new dads? If you need a little help, I recommend you complete the following exercise.

PLAN IT!

Step 2: Return to the exercise you did for your target clients and add a few questions for each transaction. Do you feel the work you did for each client is the work you do best (expert)? Did you provide the product or service that you want to be known for? Does this product or service add more to your revenue or profit than any other product or service? Will this product or service set you apart from your competition?

Now review your answers. What did you learn? Are you currently offering the product or service you do the best and receiving the compensation you feel is fair and satisfying? Does the product or service you offer align with your vision for success, including work satisfaction? If you can answer "yes" to all of those questions then you are operating in your "sweet spot" and have a clear and well defined specialty. If you answered "no" to any one of the questions now is the time to make a change.

This may be a bit harder than it looks, especially if you are a new small business owner. In the beginning this can take a bit of guesswork. Still, no matter if you have been in business for six weeks, six months or six years or more, this is an exercise that will help you be even more clear on your specialty. Over time you will continue to refine your specialty until you are operating in your perfect "sweet spot."

Primary and Secondary Specialty

You can have more than one specialty—particularly early in your business. Most small businesses will have a "primary" specialty and a "secondary" specialty. For example, a painting contractor may have a primary specialty of "interior painting on historic homes" and a secondary of "special wall treatments." Or a dentist may have a primary of "cosmetic procedures" and a secondary of "veneer placement." One of these specialties will almost always become a clear specialty over time.

Remember, this is what you want to be known for and what will satisfy the Target Market "Sweet Spot" search.

Changing Specialties

Because times change—the needs of clients change, your desire to work with a particular client changes—your specialty may change. Recently, I was in the market for a new fireplace tool set. My husband and I visited a locally owned small business that specializes in selling fireplace inserts, tools and supplies. While we searched the store for the perfect pick and broom we noticed that fireplace services were far from the majority of the products and services they offered. They also sold beautiful large case clocks, furniture, designer lamps, mirrors and even lighting fixtures. We learned that most of their sales are now from large case clocks even though the business name is Johnson's Fireplace Store. This is a business that changed specialty to succeed. They still specialize in all things fireplace but they also advertise and have a following in the clock community (too bad that is not a part of their title). Had they not made adjustments in their specialty over the years they would probably not be in business today.

Do not be afraid to change your specialty but make it a practice to not make changes lightly. Changing too often will create confusion with your clients and you may lose many of the advantages that a specialty creates for you. Be deliberate about how and when you change. Do your due diligence in the market to be certain the specialty will offer you the opportunity you anticipate. Communicate effectively with your current clients. Let them know what the change will mean for them and how you plan to serve their need(s).

Eliminating Products or Services

Just because you are offering a product or service that is not your specialty does not mean it should be eliminated. Some are complimentary, such as massage might be to chiropractic services. Some are gateways to your specialty such as a hair salon that offers blow dry services to encourage clients to come back for a cut or color.

The time to eliminate products and services is when they:

- Are clearly out of alignment with your mission, vision, or values.

- Are a drain on your resources.

- Are no longer needed or accepted in the marketplace.

- Do not bring you joy and satisfaction as a business owner.

If you discover that you are offering products or services that you should eliminate, plan to do so strategically. It may not be practical to eliminate them all at once or right away. Plan for the transition. Know what you will replace that business with. Have a plan to notify clients that are using those services or products now. But do not delay indefinitely. These delays can be costly.

If you need some motivation to take those difficult steps let me warn you that your loyalty to those products and services could be standing in the way of reaching your desired level of success in your business, your long-term vision. I have never (really, *never*) had a client regret eliminating a product or service that did not meet the "sweet spot" challenge. I will not pretend that it will be easy to inform long-time loyal clients that you are eliminating a product or service that they want or need. It will not feel great to lose income from products or services you have been counting on while you replace them with those you know are better aligned with your vision. What I promise is when you are offering your true specialty to your perfect target client you will have no remorse or regret.

What services or products are you currently offering that do not support your vision? This is the time to remove them from your offering.

PLAN IT!

Step 2: (A) Clearly define your specialty in as much detail as possible.

Step 2: (B) Examine the specialty or specialties. Do you have a specialty that drives the results you want? If not, what needs to change? Do you need a more specific specialty? A secondary specialty? A new specialty? Record the details of your "primary" and "secondary" specialty. You will find an exercise for defining these specialties and recording the details in ***Plan It! Do It! Love It! The Planning Workbook***.

PLAN IT!

Step 2: (C) Refine all of your messages and marketing materials to speak to your primary target client and only your primary target client.

COACH'S CHALLENGE

If you have determined that you are offering products or services that are not in alignment with your mission, vision, values or life priorities, plan to eliminate them.

Determine when you will no longer offer those products or services. Identify those you need to notify and how. Vow that you will discourage any business that does not fit into one of your target types and do not engage in any business relationship that cannot be justified.

Evaluate the Competition

When Machiavelli wrote, "Keep your friends close and your enemies closer," I doubt he had the success of small businesses in mind. Still, the advice can be applied to one of the key components of business success, knowing your competition.

With a clear understanding of what your competitors offer and how they rate in a variety of areas including quality and service, you can identify your advantages in the marketplace and use them to attract and retain clients. You can find a path to more revenue in a market segment that is less crowded or compete better in one that is. Knowing what others offer in the same marketplace to a similar target client makes it easier for you to gain the market share you want.

The bottom line is, unless you know what your competitors offer, where they excel, what they are expert in and the opposite of each, you cannot know what sets you apart from them or what needs are not being filled. While I am not recommending this as a solo strategy, if you just focus on what the market needs but does not have from those already servicing it you will find a lower barrier to entry and escalate your opportunity to succeed.

If you have not done a competitive analysis now is the time. If you have make sure it is no more than 12 months old. Competitors come and go. Competitors change focus and direction. They enter and exit markets. Introduce and retract products. Change prices. Competitors can just as easily create opportunity for you and your business as they can create a challenge.

Do a Competitive Analysis

For as much information and opportunity as this type of analysis will provide it is one of the most valuable tasks. It is also another one of those business owner functions that tends to be pushed aside for lack of time. When correctly done the return on this analysis will yield far more than the time you will spend to complete it. Mark the time on the calendar and make it happen!

First, know who you consider your competition to be. This list should include those companies or organizations that share your target client. They offer a similar product or service, for a similar price, in all or a portion of your geographic market. They may even have a similar specialty serving similar needs or solving similar problems.

Companies will emerge in this search that can be valuable to you. These are companies that serve a different target or a different geographic market. They do not really fit the profile of a true competitor but you can learn from them and might want to keep up with what they are offering to their clients and when they are making changes.

The timing for this review is *all* the time. I recommend you be in constant review of your competition. That means that you put one or two activities a month on your calendar that help you stay in touch with what your competitors are offering. Do not wait until you notice you are losing clients to another firm to find out what they are doing and how. Stay ahead of the changes in your competitors and marketplace by keeping information on your competitors current.

If you prefer to do an analysis on a specific schedule then be sure you do it no less than once a year — twice or more will be more valuable.

Clients often tell me that they have not done a competitive review in a while because it takes too much time or they are not sure how to do it without being too obvious. Keep in mind that any business owner would be flattered to know that you consider them to be competition. That sends the message that you respect them and the work they are doing with their clients and that you are somewhat concerned that they might take business away from you.

There are a variety of ways to gather information including:

- Be a consumer. Try their products and services as a client or customer. Just make an appointment and have the experience for yourself. Be sure to take a few minutes afterwards to record your thoughts. What did they do well that your clients might appreciate? What did they not do as well that you can use as a competitive advantage.

- Hire a consumer. Hire someone or a group of people to experience the products and services of your competition and give you feedback. Be sure to gather feedback that is both positive and negative. Have them experience your competition in different days, different times of the month and for different services and price points.

- Online research. There are a variety of options with online research. Today businesses are subjected to a vast community of online shoppers and activists. For that reason you can find a large volume of information from both the competitor and from people who have experienced their products and services. Websites will tell you what a company has to offer and often what they charge. You can also find testimonials and reviews online for almost any profession or industry. Actual clients and customers log their satisfaction or dissatisfaction right on browser sites such as Google. Industry referral services such as Yelp provide consumer feedback on experiences for everything from restaurants to remodelers. Be sure you take the good with the bad. One bad review does not mean your competitor is doomed and one good review does not mean you cannot compete.

- Participate in trade organizations. Often you and your competitors will be side-by-side in trade organizations. You may share common goals on committees or projects. This shared experience gives you both a chance to get to know each other and identify your plans and focus. They cannot be expected to share any trade secrets, but it is pretty common that a little friendly competition may easily develop. Additionally, other members of the same organization will often have information they are willing to share that will benefit you both.

As the business owner, you should be constantly aware that the information is yours to collect. Be intentional about who you want to learn more about and take the steps to do that.

Analyze the Information

As you gather this information, I recommend you record it in a format that will allow you to analyze it for your purposes. The following questions should be answered or information gathered:

- Name
- Locations or geography they serve
- Time in business
- Hours of operation
- Products and services
- Specialty
- Ranking in the industry or community (if needed)
- Ratings (such as Better Business Bureau)
- Overall review scores (online)
- Pricing
- Add-on prices for extra services

Record the same information for each competitor then analyze your findings.

Competitive Advantages

Once you review your findings from the competitive survey you can identify your "competitive advantages." These competitive advantages will present you with opportunities. You may or may not choose to capitalize on these advantages but you should fully examine them and know the cost and value of each before deciding what actions you will take. Here is what to look for:

- What products do they not offer?
- What product features do they not offer?
- Where are products and services priced lower when combined in packages?
- What geography do they not cover?
- Who do they not serve?
- What hours are they not available?
- Have you been in business longer or in a location longer?
- Are you an expert in an area where they are not?
- Do you have more positive consumer feedback?
- Are your ratings or rankings higher?
- Is your price better? (The advantage could be more business or raising prices.)

The answers to these questions should be some of your advantages as they relate to each competitor.

PLAN IT!

Step 2: Identify those companies or persons in your target market who serve your target client. Complete a competitive survey in the way that serves you best. Record your findings. What is their advantage? What is your advantage? How do you use your advantage to compete with them? What, if any, cost would there be to capitalize on your advantages? What do you estimate the gain or value of the advantage to be? What actions do you need to take to capitalize on your advantages? Record them on your action plan. Repeat regularly.

COACH'S ADVICE

Never, ever attempt to build your business through negative comments or press regarding your competition.

TOOLS

If you need one, you can find a competitive survey and analysis form in ***Plan It! Do It! Love It! The Planning Workbook.***

Marketing

Sheri owns a marketing strategy firm that specializes in working with financial services professionals to launch and grow their practice. She runs her own business just like she serves her clients—with the most up to date, cutting edge, unforgettable marketing strategy and tools available. Marketing messages are clear, consistent, and constantly streaming in a variety of ways to a very broad audience. She speaks, writes, uses social media effectively, teaches online and consults for high profile clients. Sheri's business has skyrocketed to success in just a few short years because she has an advantage in the marketplace. Her advantage, she is a marketing genius.

Some small business owners have the marketing "gene" and others do not. Some know exactly how to connect the value of the product to their target clients and others struggle. Some can perform a high percentage of the marketing duties themselves while others need help every step of the way.

Marketing is a creative process. It is not surprising that it is not a strength or skill for everyone. Never fear. You can fill your marketing needs in several different ways. There are plenty of businesses that will provide these services for you. They come in all sizes and will fit into almost any budget. There are also plenty of low cost do it yourself marketing options. We will examine many of them. Before we get ahead of ourselves though, let's examine the definition of marketing.

Marketing is a noun. It is a "set of processes." These processes identify, create, deliver, and communicate the value of your product or service to your target market.

Marketing includes a process for not only attracting but retaining clients.

The type of marketing you do, or marketing assistance you engage, will almost certainly depend on your budget. If you have a budget to hire a full service marketing agency to assist in this process, get recommendations from your strategic partners or other business professionals, interview several agencies or professionals to find the one that you feel "gets" you, your business, your mission, and that you feel will give you the best return for your investment. Be sure that any contract you agree to will specify the return you expect to get and comes with their commitment to deliver.

Working with a full-service agency should result in major changes in growth and market share. These professionals know exactly how to promote you, your products and services and how to connect them to your perfect target. They offer a full range of services from research to advertising campaigns to launch events. This is the type of agency that you go to with an idea and they create campaigns to get the results you want, when you want them, from the people you want them from. Marketing services of this type are not inexpensive but, if you choose the right agency, and you have the right idea, the return on your investment will be well worth it.

Every small business owner wishes they had the budget for a full service, highly rated, marketing agency. Alas, the majority do not. If you are among the majority of small business owners you will probably be involved in all or part of the process yourself. After you become familiar with what is to be done you might consider outsourcing parts of this process to others.

Do not wait until you have that budget to begin a marketing program. Marketing is essential to any business. It is what you do to put your product or service in the hands of your target client and there are plenty of ways to do that on any budget. You will need a marketing plan from the very first day you are in business (if not before).

If you are using any of the online social media and marketing platforms such as Facebook, Twitter, TikTok, Pinterest, Instagram and more. Keep in mind that your target client tends to be supported by some and not others. Be sure you are using those that your target client will most likely use. Make changes as these platforms change. Be on the lookout for new platforms that will serve your need and the need of your clients as the internet and its players is constantly changing. Also, be aware that many of these platforms have free services and all will have services that are not free. Evaluate and update your choices as they are needed and as they fit into your budget.

Networking

For many networking conjures up sheer dread. I am one of the lucky ones. Networking has always come easily for me. Maybe it is because I had a long career in sales and sales management or maybe it is just my nature to easily connect.

Those who are terrified of the idea of networking usually have a picture of a room full of 300 people staring at them, waiting for them to drop the cocktail sauce on their clothes, trip over the carpet, or heaven forbid, to come right up to them and start a conversation.

I have good news and bad news. The good news: networking does not have to be painful. The bad news: networking is a part of marketing, and every small business owner should be networking. We will spend more time on this in the "Do It" portion of the book, but for now, know that the key is to find a balance between what you need and what you like. Then, be sure that you are getting the return you expect on your investment of time and money.

To be sure you are using your networking time wisely I recommend you evaluate your current networking commitments as a part of your Step 2 assessment. It is not difficult. Just follow the instructions:

1. Make a list of all the memberships, organizations, or networking events you currently attend.

2. How many hours per year do you devote to each?

3. What is the cost of membership on an annual basis? (Be sure to include your time. If you do not know what an hour of your time is worth calculate that before you continue. If you need a

to estimate I would recommend $500 per hour! Yes, $500!).

4. What percentage of your business comes directly or indirectly from this group (number or dollar)?

5. What is the value to your success — critical, some, none?

6. Can you improve the results by changing the way you participate? If so, how?

Do not be discouraged if you find you have been spending hours each month on a networking group or organization and learn that you are not getting any direct business from it. Consider other reasons you may be attending including:

- Does the group connect you with other business professionals that are potential partners?

- Are you learning or gathering valuable information that helps you to be a better business owner, develop new products, keep you informed on your competitors, keep you informed on regulations in your industry and/or help you prepare for changes in your market or community?

- Does this group help you to develop your leadership skills or networking skills?

If you answered "yes" to one or more of these questions you should give some value to networking with that group. It may still not be the best use of your time, and not have the right return on your investment, but you may choose to continue networking on some schedule. What you want to eliminate are those networking situations where the value is low. Those often are events that business owners use to satisfy their commitment to network by finding a group that is "comfortable" or "social" for them and nothing more.

PLAN IT!

Step 2: Follow the steps above to evaluate the value of each of your networking commitments. Decide which relationships you will keep and which you will let go. Identify your need for adding networking opportunities. Record actions on your list or Action Pages.

COACH'S CHALLENGE

In almost every small business "time is money." Be sure you are getting the return you expect on every hour you spend networking. Be willing to give up anything that does not add to your success, but be cautious. Your enjoyment has high value. Keep those arrangements that stimulate you, offer you support, prepare you for the future and/or build your community.

Marketing Evaluation Exercise

You have just completed a thorough networking evaluation. Great! The final step in your plan relating to marketing is to evaluate all of your other marketing tools and vehicles, determine what is working and what needs to change. Remember that marketing is how you promote your business. It is how you create, deliver and communicate the value of your product or service to your target client. Every marketing effort should have as much value as possible. They should be efficient and cost-effective. They should tell the story of your mission and showcase your specialty to your target client. They should be up-to-date and well-functioning.

Take time to examine all of your marketing processes and practices. Rate each area. Identify the strengths you want to build on and the opportunities to take advantage of. Any efforts that are not effective should be eliminated or reduced. If your website is out of date then give it the rating it deserves. If none of your marketing materials speak directly to your target client and your specialty is not clear then give it the rating it deserves. This is not a time to be a "light grader." It is also the time to candidly review your resources. Are you getting your money's worth? Have you engaged the best talent? Be certain you have not fallen into the trap of hiring those you feel an obligation to. For example, just because your best friend is a graphic artist does not mean they should be *your* graphic artist unless they perform on time, on budget, and give you the creativity you expect. Often, mixing business with friendship is not the right formula for getting the results you want or fostering the friendship you desire. You get what you pay for -- pay for what you want.

Remember, these tools and practices can mean the difference between you reaching your vision, or not. Ignoring them will serve no one.

Below is a list of marketing practices or tools you may use in your business today. Evaluate each. Analyze them from your client's perspective. Now, rate them one to10 with 10 being perfect.

This is not a complete list, but some of the marketing practices and processes you should evaluate are:

___ Website(s): Does it present your brand and image exactly as you would want? Are all your messages clear? Do you address buying influences? Have you posted recent reviews that will be to your benefit?

___ Social media sites including Facebook, Google Business, Instagram, YouTube, TikTok, etc.: Do you have up-to-date information? Are all those that require addresses synced and exactly as they appear with the post office? Do you have reviews and recommendations? Are you consistent in your messages and in your posting? Do you have followers? Do you tell your readers how to follow your company and how to review you?

___ SEO (search engine optimization programs): Have you had a check-up lately? How do you rank in your market area for searchability?

___ Advertising: Are you advertising where it will get you the best return? Are your messages clearly directed to your target client? Do they clearly define your specialty?

___ Online review sites – Yelp, Google, other social sites, etc.: Do you have recent reviews? Are you asking for them?

___ Events: Do you have events planned that will help you to create new clients?

___ Sponsorships: Have you budgeted to sponsor an event or cause that is important to you and your mission?

___ Public relations: Do you have a story to tell that a public relations firm could help you to promote? Do you have a public relations partner?

___ Speaking: Are you speaking to promote your business? If so, what has the return on your investment (time and money) been? Are you maximizing these opportunities to be recognized as an expert?

___ Print media: Is all of your print media up-to-date? Does it tell your story? Does it speak to your target client?

___ Broadcast media – television, radio, YouTube, etc.: If you are using these vehicles as a means to promote your business you should be getting a meaningful return on your investment. Are you?

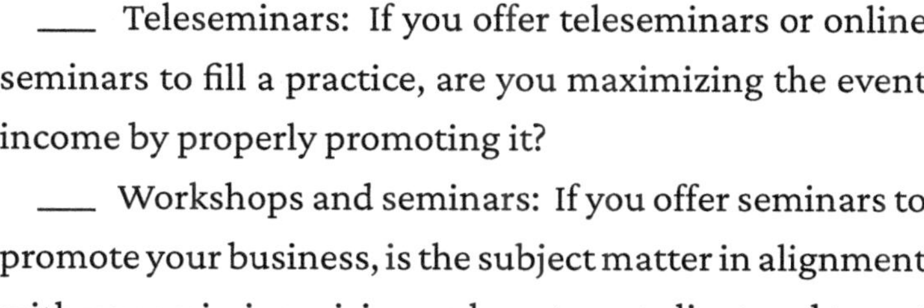

___ Teleseminars: If you offer teleseminars or online seminars to fill a practice, are you maximizing the event income by properly promoting it?

___ Workshops and seminars: If you offer seminars to promote your business, is the subject matter in alignment with your mission, vision, values, target client and target market? Do you have the right "call to action" messages to convert the participants to ongoing clients?

PLAN IT!

Step 2: Complete the exercise above. Evaluate the value and performance of each of your marketing tools and practices. Rate them. What changes need to be made? Should any be eliminated? How can you improve on those you plan to keep? Identify the need for adding new marketing programs. Record any actions you plan to take on your list or Action Pages.

COACH'S CHALLENGE

Be sure you are getting the best value for your money. I recommend that you ask for bids on any processes that renews every year. Avoid "charity" arrangements with friends or family, particularly if those parties do not take them seriously. At the very least have renewal conversations with all parties. Let them know what your plans are and what you expect from them. You will find more on this in the "Do It" section.

Money In and Money Out

Most small business owners measure their success in a variety of ways – personal satisfaction, growth, rank in the industry, employee satisfaction, contribution to a profession, an industry or the community, or the creation of a legacy – to name a few. By far, the measurement that is most often associated with performance is "money" – net profit, personal income, the rate or amount of return to investors and buying power.

While we may all agree that the "best things in life are free," money makes a difference. For the small business owner the business is their livelihood and, more often than not, a contributor to the family wealth. It carries an emotional meaning deeper than just a number on a profit line. It can be the difference in a "good" or "great" life for the owner and their family. We give money power depending on how it fits into our lives and what we think it can do for us.

How does money fit into your life? What value do you give it? Is money the way you measure your success? Do you subscribe to the "he who dies with the most toys wins" philosophy of life or the one my grandmother preached, "try like heck to take it with you."

Before we talk about how you make money and how you spend it we should talk about how you feel about it. This is valuable information and should be used in your planning process.

During a recent planning meeting with one of my clients, (we will call her Jennifer) it became clear that recent changes in Jennifer's lifestyle were putting a good deal more pressure on the "money" issues for this year's plan. Jennifer had recently had her third child. With a new baby, the expense had forced Jennifer and her husband to make tough choices about how they could and would arrange child care. After careful planning and consideration, they decided that Jennifer's husband would leave his job and be the primary childcare parent. Jennifer and her business were now the major "breadwinners" in her family. This changed the way she felt about her business and the income she produced. The desire and need to create profit and thus personal income became critical. She no longer felt she was free to "choose who she worked with" or "accept only the projects she enjoyed." She felt she had to set goals aggressively and meet or exceed her goals. After years of maintaining a "middle of the competition" price, spending when she wanted, and letting some of her collection timelines slide, Jennifer was now motivated to tighten up her financial practices. Money had a new role in her work and in her life.

Like Jennifer, it is important that you are aware of the role, importance and "emotion" of money in your business plan and in your life. Your awareness of this fact will not only determine how you spend, save, and invest, but will also contribute to a variety of decisions including your target market, the quality of equipment, goods and services, budgets and expenses for everything from marketing to personnel and your own personal income. So take a moment and give it some thought. Do you measure your success in terms of money? Is your personal income tied to basic needs for you and your family or is it just nice to have? What percentage of your 100 percent success rate do you assign to the "money factor?" Keep your findings in mind as you continue your plan.

If you gave money a high percentage weight, you will want to tighten up in every area of your business this year. A well-run ship cruises at lower costs.

If you gave money a low score, it does not mean that you should ignore good business practices and behave irresponsibility. You know the basics and, if you intend to be successful, you will not ignore the fact that too much debt is not a good thing (this means any amount that causes you to pay only interest payments or to borrow from one source to pay the other). Also know that spending too little will be costly in other ways ("cheap" will cost you valuable employees and clients and may even be dangerous if you are not keeping the essentials in good repair). Anything in the middle could be the right balance for you. Create the level of "money in" and "money out" that is the best match for you and your personality.

PLAN IT!

Step 2: Ponder the questions 1) What role does money play in my life and in my business? 2) Am I comfortable incurring a manageable debt or would I prefer to pay cash? 3) Am I willing to take risks to grow my company quickly or would I prefer to grow it safely and slow?

COACH'S ADVICE

Do not let the attitudes of others influence you in this area. Do what feels comfortable for you. Money means different things to different people. Know what it means to you and live by those principles.

The information above is our lesson in the "emotion" of money. It is important for you to understand your response to these emotions before we move to more practical business concepts like revenue, expense, and profit. That behind us, let's move on. Let's talk about how you make money, spend money, and put money in your pocket.

Keep in mind that this is cost accounting from a layman's point of view. For more complete explanations or details please consult your accountant no less than annually, whether you understand financial practices or not. Remember, your accountant is a member of your team. They can help you to determine the best accounting method for you and even help you with forecasting and budgeting. Ask for what you need. Consider accountants and Certified Public Accountants that specialize in working with small business owners. They offer a variety of services that most small business owners do not have time for and can easily outsource and afford.

Revenue

Identifying how you have been making money, how you want to make money, and ways to spend less and save more of it can be complex areas of planning. To simplify this process, I recommend asking a series of questions. The answers will inform you and help direct you to the actions you to get the income and profit results that you want.

Where does revenue come from today?

That seems a simple question that every small business owner should be capable of answering without much effort. Still, I find that many of my clients know they generate revenue from one or more products or services but do not always have a clear understanding of the percentage of revenue each represents or even if the products they think are most popular are indeed so. This information is very important in the planning process. You will need to know what is selling and what is not, who is buying and who is not. These are all answers that will contribute to decisions about market growth and expansion, investments, and how you capitalize on your target client or specialty.

Some of you may already have a system that provides you with this information. If you do – well done! If you do not, create one. Going forward you should have a reporting system (it does not have to be complex) that will make this information readily available to you. Review it regularly. Know when there is a change in your product or service mix and when there is a change in the buyer profile. This information will indicate a shift in market acceptance, competition, need, or product effectiveness.

How do I calculate product mix?

There is a very simple formula for calculating your product/service mix.

<u>Here is what you need to know</u>:

- Total gross revenue for the business overall for the period you are examining (12 months is most common)
- Total revenue by product or service (it should be the same period as gross revenue)

<u>To get the percentage</u>:

- You will calculate the percentage by product by

dividing the total gross revenue of each product by the total gross revenue of the company.

- Total gross revenue of product/Total gross business revenue = percentage of revenue by product

Do I want to increase revenue?

In simplest terms revenue is the income generated from the sale of goods or services.

For some small businesses that can be a single 'good' or 'service,' while for others it is a broader offering.

You may ask, "Why wouldn't I want more revenue?" In a small business, the generation of revenue often relies on you. You may be the one who has to work harder, longer or smarter for the total revenue to increase. My husband, having owned several businesses himself, has always referred to this as "eating what you kill." In other words, small business owners are often responsible for all of the income generated in their organization. The more they generate, the more they benefit. But, in order for revenue to increase, it also means the more family time, leisure, and personal time they have to sacrifice. If this is true, are you prepared to make those sacrifices? If you answered, "yes" then move to the next question.

Can I increase revenue?

If you are the only provider or sole generator of income, do you have more time to offer and more energy to give? If not, can you hire someone to help you? You will also want to examine the marketplace and identify what the market will bear.

Can you schedule more time on your calendar for work hours? If so, how much? Can you hire more employees or outsource portions of your work? If so, how much? The "how much" part of this means how much will your budget and your life allow? Be sure you have a budget. Know what portion of the current or additional revenue you are willing to spend to get the resources needed to increase revenue overall.

If you plan to outsource, know what the cost will be and confirm the worth. It is possible to spend a dollar to make fifty cents. Just remember what is most important to you. Is it the total revenue dollars you create or the net profit (money in your pocket)?

What is the best way to Increase revenue?

There is more than one way to increase revenue. As a matter of fact, there are so many ways that you will have to decide what is the best way or combination of ways for you.

The easiest way to increase revenue is to raise prices. Review the competitive survey you did earlier. Where are your prices in comparison with those of your competition? Is there room for an increase? Do you offer a different level of service, different volume, more convenient location, or more experience or training? If you answered "yes" to any of these questions, then you should have an opportunity to raise your prices. If you are not sure, do a price survey in your market. Be sure to survey those companies that serve your target client type.

Often you can extend your geographic market to increase revenue. In so doing you will want to be sure that you are not stretching your resources beyond your current capacity. If you are creating additional expense be certain you are accounting for that. For example, if you own a landscaping business, and decide to add another community to the area you serve, take into account the additional time it will take for you to give bids for service and for you or your work crews to travel to and from the new locations. How will you deal with the expense for travel time for both labor costs and fuel?

Simply adding more clients is a great way to add revenue. You may even have "low hanging fruit" or potential new clients that are willing to say "yes" or "buy" if you will just take the time to ask them. Who could you add to your list of active clients? Where would they come from? Are they clients you have past relationships with, or are willing to send you referrals? We will explore this further in the "Do It" section of the book. For now, all you need to know is that you do or do not have an opportunity to add clients.

Adding products or services is a great way to increase revenue and increase your opportunity to add new clients. Are there products or services that you plan to introduce? You might also consider creating packaged services as a way of increasing revenue. The objective is to bundle together services that a client may typically buy or might complement each other and discount them. You build loyalty, length of relationship and revenue with packages.

Additionally, it is recommended that you explore ways to add recurring and passive income.

Can I increase or create recurring income?

Recurring income typically comes from agreements, contracts, or retainers that you have with clients. It will smooth out the peaks and valleys in cash flow, assist in planning and forecasting capacity, and make your monthly revenue and income more predictable. Do you have this type of income today? Do you have enough? If not, can you create it? Donna, a professional development coach, has 85 percent of her clients on a six-month agreement for services. She agrees to reserve space on her calendar for them and they agree to pay her monthly which she manages through automatic credit card charges at the beginning of each month. She knows just how many hours she will work each month and how many she needs to book with new or prospective clients. She also knows how much money will be in her business bank account at the beginning of each month and uses that to manage bill paying, expenses and personal income distribution.

Can I increase or create passive income?

The easiest income is that which you gain without giving up time or energy. It's called "passive income" and almost anyone can create it. Sandra, who is a graphic designer and web developer, has a number of these relationships. In her work she has the opportunity to interact with people who need hosting sites, e-mail marketing providers, and printers. It is natural for her to refer her clients to those partners that she has created affiliate relationships with. The providers are delighted to get her referrals and realize that it reduces their sales and marketing costs. A referral from Sandra will be a client that already trusts them. They are more than willing to pay a fee for that referral. That is passive income. Some relationships are formal. You may find providers that ask for "affiliate agreements" and advertise the fee they are willing to pay for each referral. They may require that you recommend them publicly, such as on your website or by filing out a referral form. Others are less formal and are cemented with a handshake. (Something slightly more formal is recommended even if it just an email that clarifies what you agreed to.)

Examine any business you are turning away now or that you are already referring to someone else but not being paid for. Is there an opportunity to create income with an update to that arrangement?

Other passive income can come from products or services you offer to your clients from another company for a percentage of their profit.

PLAN IT!

Step 2: (A) Review your records. Identify where your revenue is coming from today. Then identify changes you can make to increase revenue. Find ways to smooth out the peaks and valleys for a more predictable cash flow.

PLAN IT!

Step 2: (B) Examine your opportunity to increase revenue through passive or recurring income. Remember, you are just setting goals and gathering information for your plan.

COACH'S CHALLENGE

Match your willingness to increase your revenue with your life priorities and budget. Spend your time and your money in such a way that it supports your priorities.

Expenses

Have you ever considered how your business and life would change if you had an endless supply of operating capital? What would it be like to never have to worry about how you would pay for new equipment, a top marketing agency, the highest rated search engine optimization firm, endless advertising, or the best talent in the business? Everything would change if you had more money than you needed to run your business. There are a few who have this luxury. The average small business owner must save, borrow, or create the capital they need to operate their business. They often find they are straining their checking account and credit lines just to fill the basic operational needs. Because they have operated without discretionary expense funds for the start-up years they often have to be reminded that there comes a time when expense management should be a selective, budgeted and objective process. If you are not there yet, spend wisely. If you are a mature business that does not have regular expense review and management process now is the time to begin. Almost every business can make better expense choices or improve their financial position with a few changes and negotiations.

Operating Expense

Most commonly, the term "operating expense" refers to an outflow of money to another person, group, or business to pay for an item or service. It is the economic costs that a business incurs to earn revenue. In most small businesses the overall goal is to maximize profits by reducing expenses without also cutting revenue.

There are some basic facts when it comes to expense management. First, it is impossible to run a business, any business, at zero expense. You must spend money to make money. The question is how much do you have to spend and how much can you expect to gain in return?

Next, you can often get the same item or service for less if you shop around or negotiate. This takes time and effort and a large percentage of business owners do not have much to spare. Still, making time to compare prices is critical to getting the most from your investment.

Finally, being well informed is the root of expense management. You must know where your money comes from and where it goes before you make changes that will improve your overall performance. This includes sound accounting practices, tracking, reporting and regular review.

Let's start by examining current expenses.

Where does the money go?

As you plan it is very important that you know where your money is going today. With that information you can determine which expenses are necessary and which are not. You can also become more aware of which expenses are not contributing to your profit margin.

Standard business practice for any small business owner is for a review of expenses regularly. Regularly for most business owners is monthly, but for you, it could be frequent. Be sure the review gives you enough time to adjust unnecessary spending or to increase spending or saving when the opportunities arise as needed.

In your review examine financial reporting documents such as your Profit and Loss Statement and the details of that statement. Additionally, look for trends and outlying expenses. You will be examining some, if not all of the following expense categories and looking for ways to maximize the satisfaction of your needs while minimizing the expense. That is fancy talk for making sure you are not paying for more than you really need or want.

Review Your Expenses

Review the following expense categories which are found in the "Expense" or "Operating Expense" section of your Profit and Loss. If you do not currently create monthly accounting reports such as Profit and Loss, add as an action in your plan:

<u>Advertising and promotion</u>: Expenses assigned to this category are for advertising and any other type of promotion that does not fit better in the marketing category. They may also be categorized separately under titles such as "sponsorships," "public relations," or "trade organizations." Let your accountant or bookkeeper help you decide. Be consistent. As you review these expenses think about what you are getting in return. Are you getting calls from print or online advertising? Are the calls converting into revenue generating clients? Can you afford to cut expenses in any of these areas or should you spend more

to get a better return? Be sure to ask for referrals and statistics anytime you make a decision to invest more in this category. Find the right resource or professional. Keep in mind that these areas often have a maximum return. If you do not see your return steadily trend up consider the value of the expense.

Automobile: Expenses listed here are related to your use of an automobile for work. As you can see below, they are often broken into subcategories. The treatment of these expenses is different for a lease versus a loan. Talk to your accountant about your expenses and let them help you maximize your position.

- Fuel: This might also be replaced with "Mileage Expense." As you review expenses in this area think about how you might save on fuel. Do you make unnecessary trips anywhere? Is your service area just the right size or too large? When the price of fuel is high or goes up this is an area that should get your attention.

- Loans: Automobile loan expenses will be displayed here. Talk to your accountant about the amount. Are you eligible to write off the total loan or some portion? Remember, if you are thinking about buying new vehicles, this area will increase. Will your budget bear the change?

Bank service charges: Service fees are recorded here. This is an area that can often be reduced by negotiating with your bank. They will almost always charge you a fee but are often willing to waive it for maintaining a certain balance or if you have multiple accounts, including personal accounts, with them. It never hurts to ask. Even if it is only $15.00 per month. That totals $180 per year. What could you do with an extra $180? Pay an employee bonus, buy a new piece of furniture or upgrade your coffee? There are endless possibilities.

Entertainment: Entertainment is a business expense category that is highly regulated. Be sure to talk to your accountant about what you can and cannot include for tax deductions in business entertainment. Then carefully examine what you are spending on business entertainment. Are you getting the return you want from those expenses?

Insurance: Insurance expenses and whether they qualify for a tax deduction often depends on your business entity type. For example, owner/stockholder insurance premiums are eligible under S-Corp type but not under Limited Liability Corporation (LLC). Both your accountant and insurance agent can help you decide on insurance types that serve you best and may even have ideas on how to use insurance to protect your business interests. The recommendation for all insurance expenses is to be sure you do not get too comfortable with an agent or company.

Keep it fresh. Shop around regularly. Be sure you get what you need at the best price.

- General liability: General liability is a cost of doing business. Your needs in this area can be assessed by you and your agent.

- Employee insurance: It is recommended that you seek the assistance of an insurance broker to be sure you are getting the most competitive programs. They can structure products and premiums that suit you and your business best. Your group does not have to be large for you to qualify for group insurance. A group can be as few as two members.

- Stockholder insurance: Life insurance, long term care insurance and "key man" insurance premiums all qualify for deduction for many business owners. With a regular check-up from your agent you can determine if you have too much or not enough to protect your assets.

Marketing: You can spend an endless amount on marketing and marketing services. Be sure you are getting the return on your investment in this area. Make sure you are spending enough to maintain your brand. In marketing you can pay $50 an hour or $500 an hour for some of the same services. Hire the best match for your budget and for the return you are receiving on the investment. Ask for referrals. Review samples of work. Start with a single project in order to get a feel for how you work together. Be clear on what you want to accomplish. Caution: do not sign long-term contracts and that you have clear escape clauses for non-performance.

Office expense: This is a broad category. It can include a variety of expenses required to support your office activities. Be consistent in what you code in this category.

Office supplies: This includes those things that are consumable in your office including paper, pens, writing tablets, coffee, cups, etc.

Payroll expenses: The number in this category represents the total amount of your payroll – both regular and overtime for the period of your reporting. It includes any salary you pay yourself but does not include owner distributions.

Payroll taxes: This number is directly related to the "payroll expenses" above. If you adjust payroll these expenses will change.

Postage and delivery: This category is self-explanatory. Are the expenses reasonable? Can you save by changing your shipping or delivery method or by negotiating a group rate? If you are manufacturing and deliver products around the country or around the world this is an area that will command attention.

Principal distribution: It is not uncommon for business owners to pay themselves a salary and then take a distribution as they can or need to. Are you taking enough or too much? Be sure you are on track for what you have budgeted this year and that you are maintaining your tax payments to avoid tax return shock.

Rent or mortgage expense: These are basic and typically a fixed cost for the facilities you occupy. It could be your store location, your office, or a portion of your home. When designating a portion of your home expense as "business" it will serve you well to discuss with your accountant as this can be a tricky area.

Telephone: The expenses in this area are a moving target. There was a time when line fees and long distance were important to control. Now, it is important to determine whether you need a land line system or if mobile phones are adequate. If you use mobile phones do you have the best plan? Finally, if you offer mobile phones to staff members, do you have the right program for them? Do you pay for all or some usage? Do they stay within their plan? My best advice in this area is to review your needs and your services regularly. Take the time to evaluate and shop for the best plan and service. The difference in monthly expense can be considerable at anywhere from $50.00 to $200.00 per month or more. Stay in touch with your provider. It is common to reduce your monthly expense just by asking.

Travel: If you have travel in your business you will report those expenses.

Expense Planning and Adjustment

It is almost certain that you will not have the same expenses in the year ahead as you did in the year behind you. Your needs change and the price of goods and services do not remain the same. The best way for you to predict what those expenses might be or should be is to ask a series of questions. Just like with revenue, the answers will guide your actions.

Consult your vision. What do you want to happen this year and how will it impact your spending? Decide if the expense is in alignment with your business and life priorities and if it will result in the outcome that you desire. You might even challenge your decisions like my client Lori.

Lori is a successful recruiter and human resources consultant. In her sixth year in business, she came to a crossroad as so many do. She had to decide if she wanted to grow her business to the next level or maintain the level of success she had created. She decided to go for it! In so doing she realized what she needed was to target a new client profile and that meant searching for and finding clients in new places. Lori had a strong network in several industries These industries had so far provided her with a steady stream of projects. She would need a bigger and potentially new client that could produce more revenue and had a more substantial budget for staffing expense and talent management. There were a number of ways to go about finding and attracting this client. She could expand her networking efforts to general managers and operations managers of larger companies which would mean joining a number of organizations; she could increase her sales time to identify prospects, calling on them and selling them her products; or she could increase her digital marketing efforts and expenses to target that group knowing that was where they most often started their search for resources. Lori chose a combination of all of these efforts but with an emphasis on passive attraction through increasing search engine optimization and digital marketing expenses. The results were just what she wanted.

What about you? What do you want? Are there multiple ways to meet the goals of your vision? What will be the cost of the solutions that suit you best?

Where can I reduce expenses?

In business every expense should be justified. Every investment should have a return.

Because the above is true, the easiest place to find unwanted and unneeded expenses is to look at the way you are currently spending. Justify every expense. Review every investment for a return benefit. Pay particular attention to a few areas that commonly hide overspending or unnecessary investment in small business.

Salaries: Often small business owners let their hearts rule their hiring and retention practices. Are you paying for personnel that are not necessary or not performing? Have you continued to raise long term employees well past their contribution? Are you so afraid of losing a key employee that you have given in to their demands for more money even though it puts them outside the range you had in your budget?

Overtime: Poor planning and lack of capacity management can lead to overtime wages. Since overtime wages are paid at 150 percent of normal wages, a saving of 50 percent is immediate if you can reduce them. Who is working overtime and why? Are they maximizing their regular work hours? Can you dissect their function and hire cheaper part-time labor to do part of a job?

Supplies and services: If your business is one that relies on supplies or the services of others you will want to pay particular attention to the price you are paying for both. Are you working with vendors that are willing to negotiate volume or loyalty? If so, have you reviewed your arrangement with them in the past 12 months? Are you over supplied in some areas and need to adjust your subscriptions or recurring orders?

Rent or lease: Depending on the market conditions in your area you may have an opportunity to improve the fixed cost for your facility or facilities. Are you paying market value today? If you are at a higher rate or if you are willing to extend your arrangement with your landlord or management agent you may find you can save. Can you reduce your office space and reduce the total lease/rent? Is it possible to move your operation to a less expensive area and remain effective?

Insurance: Just because you are a loyal customer you have no guarantee that you are getting the best insurance premium. Check rates. Survey options. You may find you can improve your costs by moving to a new company.

Marketing: All marketing expenses should be both justified and clearly show a return on the investments you are making in those areas. Are you getting what you were promised? Have the dollars you spent made the phone ring? If not, revisit the program you have with your providers. This could include print media, advertising, digital marketing, search engine optimization, direct mail or more.

Travel expense: If your business spans several counties, regions, states or even countries, you may have regular travel expenses. Are you planning your travel wisely? Do you make unnecessary trips? Are you paying for others to accompany you and if so are their travel expense justified? Are you paying extra for loyalty programs — yours or others?

Entertainment: These days, entertainment expenses do not provide the same tax advantages they once did. Are you aware of the treatment of entertainment on your tax calculation? If not, consult your accountant. Then consider whether you are overspending in this area. What do you get in return?

How do I spend wisely?

When you are a small business owner you want to spend money where it will serve you best. Since it often feels like "taking money out of your pocket" deciding to spend more, especially if the return is uncertain, can be difficult. I regret to report, there is no magic formula to make some of these decisions. There are however a few principals to apply when budgeting for increases:

- Be sure it is what you want. We all fall victim to the "sales pitch" from time to time. Be sure you are buying only that which is in alignment with your vision and goals.

- Do your homework. Get references. Research the experience of others. Make sure you can, with a high level of probability, rely on the estimates or promises you are given.

- Be cautious –ask for a trial period. No need to sign up for more than you need to. What time frame is necessary to see results? Sign up for a trial and then decide if you want to continue.

- Set clear expectations. If you are increasing staff, and staff costs, make sure you have set clear expectations with reasonable time frames. Review your situation regularly to be sure your expectations are being met.

- No long term contracts. If you must sign an agreement make sure you have escape clauses if you are not getting the results you expected.

- Be willing to cut your losses. If you find your arrangements are not working out, cut your losses and move on. If you increased staff and they are not performing as agreed dismiss them quickly or as they say, "hire slow, fire fast."

What investments should I make this year?

Making some type of investment for the future is typically a part of every small business owner's vision. This may be personal investments such as retirement planning, savings, education, professional development, insurance or wellness. It might also be investment in your staff such as training and development, teambuilding or mentoring. Investments also include real estate, facilities, equipment or systems. What investments do you want to make in yourself or your business this year?

Investments come in all sizes. I recommend you do not let a year pass without making some type of investment in your future. If your budget is strained this year think about low cost investments such as reading or team building projects.

Remember that if you do not invest in your future no one else will. You are responsible for today and tomorrow. Be sure you do not regret tomorrow what you did not make room for today.

How do I prepare for the unexpected?

Many a small business owner has had a year turned upside down because they did not prepare for the unexpected. These types of expenses are often those that we did not prepare for because we were not aware they were a possibility. Start with the expenses you know you may have (equipment that is aging, insurance premium increases, rental escalation clauses, or tax changes). Then, dig deeper. Think outside of the box. What "might" happen? How do you prepare? Do not spend too much time on what may or may not come to pass. You can only control what you can control and only prepare to the best of your ability. Everything else is wasted energy.

Is my operating reserve adequate?

The unexpected sometimes puts a strain on your business or an event threatens its existence. Stuff happens. We get sick. The market takes a nasty downturn. We lose clients without warning.

Previously you determined what expenses might pop up unexpectedly. Here you address the question, "How will I cover my normal operating costs if my ability to create revenue changes?" Are you prepared or do you just cross your fingers and hope it never happens to you and your business?

The general rule is that you are safe with six to12 months of operating reserves. Whether you have six or 12 often depends on your own need for security. Knowing how strong your need is will dictate the amount you want to target.

Keep in mind that your reserves do not all have to be in cash. A line of credit is a great way to cover a portion of the reserve amount.

Review your operating reserves and set a goal of increasing them if they are inadequate. Put that amount in your budget and treat it like a payment.

Talk to your insurance agent. Insurance is available for many circumstances that would result in your not being able to cover your operating expenses.

Is it time to change the owner's salary or distribution?

"Small business owner" is not a volunteer position. You did not start your business to work for free. Pay yourself! In the beginning it may be small. I have clients that commit to paying themselves $500.00 or even less. Still, it must be something. If you are not paying yourself on a regular basis change that! Pay yourself on a predictable date just like you would pay an employee. The beginning, middle or end of the month are popular dates for owner salary and/or distribution.

Depending on your entity type you may be paying yourself in a variety of ways. You may take a salary plus a distribution (S-Corp or LLC) or you may just pay yourself a distribution (sole proprietor). Once again, this is when you talk to your accountant about the best course of action. Let them help you to determine the right amount based on your history, tax position and predictions.

If you learn you are not paying yourself enough, consider raising your pay before you allot other expenses such as more marketing or new equipment. Would you feel more satisfied having more money to take home or to have a new computer? Now, choose.

PLAN IT!

Step 2: Review your financial records. Identify your current expenses. Then identify changes you can make to reduce costs and increase profit. Identify expenses you need to increase to grow your business, and or improve your situation. If you are not currently paying yourself, make a plan to do so. Be sure to adjust your budget to include the new expense forecasting.

COACH'S CHALLENGE

Match your willingness to reduce your expenses with your life priorities and budget.

Net Profit

For a small business, net profit refers to income or the amount of money that remains after expenses (including taxes) are subtracted (Revenue – Expenses = Income (Net Profit). As you plan and execute on your plan, attention must be paid to not only the generation of revenue but to expenses and the resulting net profit. This is the bottom line for a small business owner. It does not matter how much revenue you generate if your net profit is not enough to sustain your business and your personal income, you will most likely not be or feel successful. Now that I have your attention let's dig deeper.

It should be your goal as a small business owner to make a profit as soon as possible and then consistently thereafter. Profit will translate into personal income, or investments for your business or personal future.

With profit as a goal it is important for you to know where you are in the business development process and to set your profit goals relative to that development. Most small businesses do not generate a profit in the first months or even in the first years. This is not surprising. As a start-up most businesses do not have an established customer base for their products and services. Without customers and sales there is no profit.

Start-up businesses also have start-up costs that prevent them from making a profit. For some the cost is higher than others. Manufacturing companies, for example have to buy equipment and goods before they can begin to produce and sell products. These costs are often borrowed or paid out of pocket with a loan from the owner.

As you plan, be aware of where you are in your business development cycle and whether you should expect a profit. If it is time for you to make a profit, be sure your revenue goals are hardy and your expense goals are under control. The result should be maximum profit.

PLAN IT!

Step 2: If this is your third year or more in business you should start to see a profit. If you have not seen one, then why not? Examine your costs. Are you putting more back into the business than you intended to? Is this the best year to reinvest? Record actions you plan to take in your notes or on your Action Notes pages.

Staff Assessment—Needs and Changes

If you do not have employees or do not plan to hire employees this year you may think you can skip this section. You may feel there is plenty to do without planning for a situation you are not yet engaged in. I would encourage you to think again. While you may not have employees today, chances are you will have them as you grow. It is important to know how your business will change once you do. If you plan to add them in the next couple of years you will want to plan for them early.

Employees are indeed your best asset. The fully engaged employee cares, truly cares, about the company they work for. They are willing to invest their time, energy, talent, skills, and often their own personal time to be certain the job is done and done right. They are your business when you are not present. It is their willingness to understand the mission and vision of your company and to carry it out that can drive your success.

Some say there is a crisis in employee engagement. They would argue that employees, particularly those of a younger age, do not care about the work they do or the companies they work for. I am not arguing this point but instead would remind you that if true, then it is even more important that you select the right candidate, hire, train, develop and retain them.

Staff Assessment for Planning

Recruiting, hiring, on-boarding and retaining the right staff is a key function of a small business owner. Later we will discuss performance management in detail. For the purposes of planning, I suggest you do a quick assessment of your current staff and determine how it might impact your vision and your plans for the year ahead.

Staff Assessment					
Name	Function or Title	Salary	Rate Performance 1-10	Critical to Business 1-10	Changes/Actions Salary or Function

Continue your review with these questions and responses.

Which of these staff members are critical to the business? Your plans should include a retention plan for them.

Are promotions and/or function changes needed? If yes, you should include a plan to cover the functions they may be abandoning, including smoothly transitioning employees to new positions. Your budget should include the increased cost of any salary changes.

Do salaries need to be adjusted? If you are paying any staff member too much or too little you will want to plan for the change and adjust your budget. Reducing salaries can be tricky. Often it is easier to terminate and hire someone new at a lower cost. This is an extremely difficult choice for most small business owners. Be sure you are protecting your business by paying for what you need – no more, no less.

Do you need additional staff? This assessment was probably not necessary for you to identify if you need additional staff. The strain on your capacity and your personal time is usually the best indicator. If you need more staff, what will their function be? When will you hire them? What will it cost? Be sure to adjust your budget.

Are some staff members not fulfilling your expectations or meeting your needs? Did you rate them low in performance? These staff members may need to be replaced. The right staff is critical to small business success. It costs you time and money to protect employees that are a drain on your system. In many cases the decision to make a change is also best for the employee as they may be overwhelmed, mismatched with the position, have personal challenges that should be attended to, or are ready to make a change themselves.

This exercise is easily performed for a staff of 20 or less. It is more difficult if you have a large staff. With a larger number, you most likely have human resources professional on staff or someone who fulfills that role such as an office manager or outsource to human resources professionals. They can be engaged to help you with this staff assessment.

PLAN IT!

Step 2: Do the staff assessment above. Record any actions that you will take to upgrade staff, add to staff, improve performance, or change compensation.

COACH'S CHALLENGE

Many small business owners find they have created a culture of "family." That often makes it difficult for them to take actions that might impact their employees personally. Do the right thing for the business. That is your responsibility to be sure it is healthy and providing for yourself, your family and all of the other employees.

COACH'S ADVICE

Hire slow and fire fast. Often it is the best service you can offer a potential employee or an underperformer.

TOOLS

Staff Assessment Form can be found in ***Plan It! Do It! Love It! The Planning Workbook***.

Employee Retention

Hiring and retaining the best employees is not easy, but It is critical to maintain a low turnover rate in order to keep your costs down and to eliminate many hours of unnecessary recruiting time. One of the best ways to hire and retain the best talent is to have a comprehensive employee benefits package.

Some of these benefits are low or even no cost. Others will be more difficult for you to offer until your business can afford and support them. Begin by knowing what you want your package to look like when complete and then work towards that package steadily until you have it to offer.

Employee Benefits Checklist

Basic employee package: Every business owner with one or more employees should have these. If you do not have them today put them on your Action Plan and develop them as soon as possible.

- Handbook
- Job descriptions
- Policies and procedures

Insurance benefits: Today, insurance benefits for employers and employees are more available than ever before. Many of the restrictions of the past have been lifted. Insurance benefits are well worth exploring if you do not offer them for your employees or do not have them for yourself. Start by contacting an insurance agent or broker that specializes in employee benefits. They can help you understand your options and make the best choice for budget and return on the investment. Be sure to consider your own needs. As a business owner, disability, long term care, and life insurance can offer you and your family protection from unexpected tragedy such as an accident, extended illness, or even death. If you have key employees, you will want to examine the need to insure their life as well.

- Health insurance
- Disability insurance
- Life insurance
- Key person insurance
- Health savings account (HSA)

Retirement planning: Few employers, large or small, offer pension plans today. Most offer some form of retirement savings plans or employer contribution plans. Talk to your employee benefits agent or financial advisor about plans that might be right for you and your employees. It does not cost anything to explore and knowledge is very powerful when negotiating with potential employees.

- 401K
- Profit sharing

- Bonus plans
- IRA – SEP

Performance management program: If you do not have a performance management program, you need one—it is as simple as that. Your employees must know what is expected of them and receive feedback on how they are meeting those expectations. The creation and use of such a program is discussed in "Recruiting, Staffing, and Employee Relations." Add to your action list either the development, review, or update of your plan.

Step-by-step operating procedures: What would happen if one or more of your employees had to be away for an extended period. Is your staff cross trained or do you need to have a clear operating procedure manual to direct you or someone else in their absence? It is a benefit to your employees to have these procedures in place. It sends the message that you are prepared and they are secure. It also assists in any situation where an employee is forced to cover a position that they are not familiar with.

City, county, state and federal compliance: Rules are rules. If you are not in compliance with government rules and regulations as they relate to your employees and your industry you are at risk of penalty. Know the rules and comply to avoid costly audits and fines.

Employee survey: When is the last time you asked your employees for their feedback and opinions? If you have never done so or have not done so in the past 12 months it is time.

PLAN IT!

Step 2: Examine your employee benefits package. Be sure it is adequate to retain your best talent. If it is not, make changes that will upgrade it. Add tasks to your Action Plan for any research, development, and actions you plan to take.

COACH'S ADVICE

The value of your benefits package is based on the value your employees place on the components. Avoid making assumptions about what is most important to your employees. If you do not know, ask them. An employee survey is a great way to do that. Another great way is to discuss it with them during their annual review.

TOOLS

A sample employee survey can be found in ***Plan It! Do It! Love It! The Planning Workbook***.

Partnerships

As every small business owner can attest, wearing all the hats can be exhausting. Most small business owners have a natural ability to multi-task, because this skill is essential to success. Yet, there always seems to be more to do than we can effectively accomplish on our own.

There are two types of partnerships to consider for your plan–strategic partnerships and referral partnerships. You should have both. Both will help you to build your business but they are very different in the way you develop them and maintain them. Typically you can identify those that have been working for you by reviewing your business for the past year. Who sent you referrals? Those that send you the most referrals are the ones you might consider your natural partners. That is certainly the easiest way to develop them – naturally –but you should have an intentional plan to develop others in the months ahead.

In the simplest form, a strategic partner is someone or some entity that shares your target client but does not compete with you. They expand your network and increase your direct referrals. This is a long term relationship that is sustainable and mutually beneficial to both parties. It is usually an arrangement with no contract. Examples of strategic partnerships are an acupuncturist and a massage therapist or a cabinet maker and a remodeler. In each example these providers serve the same target client but do not overlap in services. It is natural for them to refer their client to the other provider and they will often be asked for a referral for the other service.

Examine Your Partnerships

Do you have strong partnerships today? Do you need to further develop partnerships? Do you need to build partnerships? Every small business should have between three and 10 partnerships. Read more on what to look for, how to build partnerships, and how to maintain a strong partnership later in this book. For the purpose of planning, let's examine what you have today.

Identify Strategic Partners and Rate Them

Who refers clients or business to you today that shares your target client? You might think about it like the diagram below.

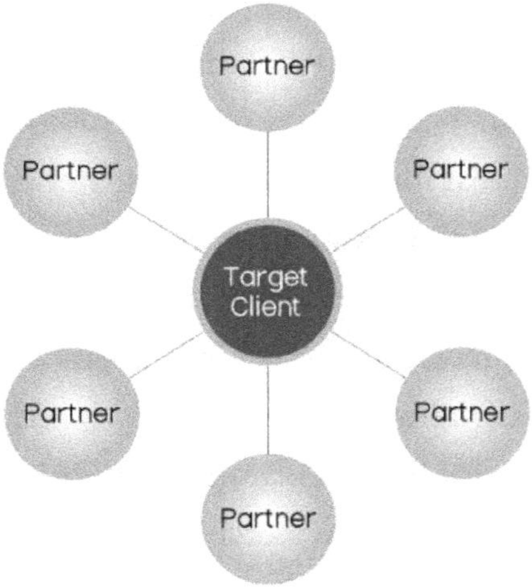

If you identify your target client and identify anyone or any business that refers clients or business to you, that also serves that client, you will have identified your strategic partners or potential strategic partners.

COACH'S EXAMPLE

As a small business coach, my strategic partners are business brokers, digital marketing agencies, outsourced human resource agencies, business attorneys and accountants – all serve small businesses.

PLAN IT!

Step 2: Make a list of the strategic partners you work with now. Rate the relationships on a scale of one to10 for communication, consistency and shared values. Any that are not rated a 10 need work. Record an action to meet with these partners and discuss your partnership or any other action that you know will improve the relationship. Now, make a list of all your potential partners either by name or business type. Record an action to locate and build relationships with those businesses. If you do not have a referral tracking mechanism add the action to develop one to your Action List. An exercise for reaching these conclusions can be found in ***Plan It! Do It! Love It! The Planning Workbook***.

COACH'S ADVICE

Not every strategic partner that you work with today or that will want to work with you in the future is the right partner. Choose wisely.

Identify and Rate Referral Partners

Referral partners are not the same as strategic partners. They are individuals or other companies or practices that refer clients to you to serve that client's need but are not necessarily a business or individual that you can regularly refer others to. An example of a referral partner is a chiropractor that may refer business to an ergonomic chair company but that company may not refer business to the chiropractor as they may target a client that buys a chair to prevent back pain. They may occasionally have a referral for the chiropractor but their relationship would not be built on an understanding that business would flow both ways. The value to the chiropractor is having a resource for their patients as a way to further support the treatment. They do not expect a referral in return.

Referral partners are often very satisfied clients that want to share their experience with others who may need or want your product or service. These are valuable referral sources as they pass the trust they have in you on to the person they refer. You will want to encourage these referrals and will learn more about how to do that in the Do It! section. For now, you just want to assess where the referrals are coming from and not coming from.

If you do not know where your referrals are coming from you will want to make every attempt to create that tracking mechanism as soon as possible. It is a critical part of your future business development.

COACH'S EXAMPLE

As a small business coach my referral partners are satisfied clients, trade organizations, and vendor sales persons that work with my target clients (i.e. a paint vendor that works with painting contractors or a pharmaceutical account manager that works with clinics).

PLAN IT!

Step 2: Make a list of the referrals you received in the last year. Who did they come from? Was it a "good" referral (your target)? Have you thanked them appropriately? What do you need to do to further develop the relationship? Record an action to meet with these people and discuss how you might make it easier for them to refer you. Now, make a list of all the people you were surprised to find were not on that list. Record an action to ask for referrals and make it easy for them to refer you. You might also want to create a referral program. If you do not have a referral tracking mechanism add the action to develop one to your Action Notes. An exercise for reaching these conclusions can be found in ***Plan It! Do It! Love It! The Planning Workbook.***

COACH'S ADVICE

Not every referral is a good referral. You do not want to encourage referrals that are not your target client. You also do not want to encourage referrals from anyone that might have a questionable reputation.

Client Retention

No matter where you are in developing your business you can easily remember what it was like to get started. How long did it take you to get that first client? If you are like most small business owners they came slowly at first and you worked just as hard to keep them as you did to get them. Strangely enough, once business starts to flow there is a tendency to pay less attention to retaining the clients you already have. Has this happened to you? You may think you know, but let's be sure. Calculate your client retention rate.

Calculating Your Client Retention Rate

Client retention can be measured in more than one way. You can either measure the number of clients (CRR) you keep or the dollars (DRR) you retain. For the purpose of this plan we will be using the number of clients you retain.

To calculate your CRR follow this simple calculation. Before you begin you will need to know:

- Total number of clients at the beginning of the

period

- Total number of clients added during the period
- Total number of clients at the end of the period

Now calculate your CRR :

Begin with the number of clients at the beginning of any period

Example: 1,000 clients at the beginning of January 1, 2014

Subtract the number of new clients added during the period

Example: 200 added between January 1, 2014 and December 31, 2014

Divide by the number at the end of the period

Example: 950 active clients at the end of December 31, 2014

Multiply by 100 to get percentage

Calculation Example:

1000 – 200 = 800

800/950 = .84

.84 x 100 = 84 percent

What did you learn? Are you retaining the percent of clients you thought you were or that you intended to? Would you like to improve your CRR?

Remember that retaining a client is a lot less costly than adding a new one. Unless you have a "one and done" (pre-paid funeral services) or "one for a long while," (new home purchase, exterior painting, internal vacuum system, irrigation system) selling your client the next product or service is often up to you. This is considered "low hanging fruit" as they most likely already know you and trust you.

Take the time now to examine who has not bought from you lately. Develop a plan to connect with them and promote doing more business with them. This could be a simple phone call or e-mail to let them know you have missed them and would like to work with them again. It could be announcing a "special offer" to "come back." At the very least this can be a client communication that updates them on what is happening in your business today (newsletter) with a general call to action.

PLAN IT!

Step 2: Review your list of past clients. Who has not bought anything from you lately? Record an action to connect with all past clients – those that have and those that have not purchased from you lately to promote the continuation of your relationship. Exercises to assist you with this project can be found in ***Plan It! Do It! Love It! The Planning Workbook***.

COACH'S CHALLENGE

If it is appropriate for your business model, make client retention a success measurement. Track how you perform in this area and set goals to aggressively retain clients and deepen relationships.

COACH'S ADVICE

Not every client that has fallen away should be encouraged to come back. Be sure you are spending the most time and effort on those that are your true target.

Sales and Business Development

Sometimes networking, marketing, and partnerships are not enough to drive the amount of business you want or need to reach your vision. If at this place in your planning you still cannot clearly see how you will reach your revenue goals then you need a sales and business development strategy.

Of the many roles small business owners play, sales and business development is often one they least enjoy. For that reason, many either avoid the activities and actions considered key to sales and business development or they prioritize the hiring of a sales person to play the role.

If sales and business development are a part of your plan for the year ahead then take the time to assess the program you currently have. Evaluate anyone selling for you, and then determine what needs to change.

Here are a few things to consider:

- Do I have a sales plan? If you do not have a plan you will want to develop one.

- Are the prospects clearly identified? If you have a sales plan then start with identifying prospects. They should fit your target client profile in your target geography.

- Are the goals clear and aligned with the vision? If you have a plan it should match your vision. Be sure your sales goals roll up to your overall business goals.

PLAN IT!

Step 2: Decide if you will have a sales and business development strategy as a part of your plan. If you will, begin by setting an action to develop a plan or updating the plan you already have. Educate yourself on the sales process. If you are ready, hire a sales person.

COACH'S ADVICE

A sales person should always fit into your plan and your budget. After a short startup period they should be a zero cost to your organization. They should more than pay for their cost in the value they bring and the new business they develop.

Investments and Protections

We all know one or two horror stories about businesses that have closed, gone the way of bankruptcy, or been forced to sell or dissolved because something unexpected happened to the owner or partners. The sad reality is most of them could have been avoided with a few protective measures.

In the last few years I have worked with clients who have faced these special challenges. One was a legal practice forced to close following the unexpected death of one of the young partners. Even these intelligent, well-trained professionals, who were regularly reminded by their own clients who were experiencing tragic circumstances, made no provision for their own unexpected tragedy. There was no "key man" insurance, no contingency or succession plan, and no operating reserves to allow for such an event. The deceased partner had contributed a high percentage of the revenue and operating funds without which the firm could not cover expenses. The spouse of the deceased, who had no interest in the firm, stopped contributing immediately leaving the other partners few options. The outcome was that they were forced to disband.

Is your future protected? Are you investing wisely? Have you had an insurance check-up? Is there a plan for your business and the families it supports if something tragic were to happen to you or a key member of your staff? You have worked too hard to build your business to put it in jeopardy by not protecting it from the unexpected and the unforeseen.

Death, legal action by employees or clients, accidents, natural disasters, illness, disability, divorce and other unforeseen events can have a dramatic impact on your ability to sustain your level of success or even your viability to operate. To avoid these circumstances you will want to take advantage of protective measures including insurance (business and personal, including life and health), defendable contracts, estate planning, and clearly defined operational processes and procedures.

Here are a few questions that can help you determine what needs to be addressed in the plan you are developing.

- Are your contracts up to date?
- Do you have a business attorney and/or an estate attorney?
- Have you had a legal checkup with them in the last 12 months?
- Do you have a business and personal insurance

agent?

- Have you had an insurance check-up with them in the last 12 months?
- Do you have professional liability or errors and omission insurance?
- Do you have a personal umbrella policy?
- Do you have a financial advisor?
- Do you have staff members that are critical to your success and if so, do you have "key man" insurance on their life/health?
- Have you executed a personal will that addresses your business?
- Do you have health benefits?
- Do you have a disability policy?
- Do you have long term care insurance?
- Do you have a disaster recovery plan?

This list is a good start but far from a fully comprehensive plan for protection. It is recommended you consult your attorney(s), accountant, financial advisor, and other professionals who support your business.

As you put these protections in place be sure to talk to your accountant about any tax advantages you may have for these expenses.

PLAN IT!

Step 2: Go to your action plan now and record any actions you need to take to protect yourself and/or your business. Start by reviewing the list of questions above. Any question you answered "no" to requires action. It is also recommended that you meet annually with your attorney, accountant, financial advisor, and insurance agent for a check-up. Put those visits down as an action to take. List an action to connect with your accountant to discuss tax implications of these expenses.

COACH'S ADVICE

Prioritize protective measures in your expenses. You cannot develop or enjoy what you have lost.

Step Three: Set Measurements

It may surprise you to learn more than seventy-five percent of my new clients report they do not and have never tracked anything in their business. Tracking and measuring is one of those activities most small business owners do not always feel is critical to their success. That could not be farther from the truth.

In his article in the Harvard Business Review in 2010, *You Are What You Measure*, Dan Ariely said it best. "Human beings adjust behavior based on the metrics they're held against. Anything you measure will impel a person to optimize his score on that metric. What you measure is what you'll get. Period." I agree with Mr. Ariely. Setting targets and tracking your performance against them is critical to the achievement of your vision. Stating it another way, you will get what you measure. It is that simple. So, what do you measure and why is it important? In a full scale business performance process there are a variety of choices to be made about what you will measure, how you will measure, when you will measure, and how these measurements will guide future measurements. Keep in mind that the purpose of tracking is to keep your attention on those indicators that are most important to your success – you want to keep it simple. The more complicated it gets the more likely you will be to stray from a commitment to regular measurement and review.

Setting Targets

Selecting targets can be simple. Think about what information will indicate to you that you are on track to meet the numbers, percentages and other goals in your vision. For example, if you want to create $100,000 in gross revenue in the planning period then you will want to track gross revenue.

I recommend you pick one or two targets from each category listed below. You should have no fewer than three and no more than 10.

- Financial
    - Revenue (gross or net or both)
    - Income
    - Profitability

    - Expense reduction
    - Savings
- Production, Products and Service
    - Dollars and numbers
    - Product mix
    - Source
    - Mix of product or service
- Customer
    - Number, type, percentage
    - Mix of clients
- Other
    - Rewards and recognition
    - Training
    - Ranking
    - Networking time
    - Pro bono services

- Education hours
- Turnover rate

Over time you will refine what you track. You will learn what measurements are the best indicators of success or trouble on the horizon, what measurements indicate that staff members are not performing as agreed, what signals markets are shifting and more.

Tracking and Measuring Performance

Tracking and measuring performance is an ongoing practice. It begins by setting up systems and reporting to produce the information you wish to monitor. The system might already be set up, such as bookkeeping. The report might be as simple as your profit and loss statement which indicates gross revenue, total operating expense, and profit – all of which you may have decided to track. It may be a less formal report. If you are tracking networking hours you may make notations on your calendar on the number of hours you spend each day in networking activities. Those notes can serve as a report. If you do not already have a system or a report you will need to create one. Automate as much of this process as possible. Any time saved is time you can use for executive thinking, planning, creating, leading your staff, and managing your business. If necessary, make an investment by hiring someone to set up a system for you or buying software that will provide you with the answers your need.

Remember, you get what you measure. Tracking is not an option. Dig in and do it right. This will be your vision report card.

PLAN IT!

Step 3: Review your vision. What have you listed as a goal that can be measured? Be sure to select the target tracking areas that you feel are most indicative of your success. Set an action to create the reports you will use to track performance and/or to set up the Targets Tracking Sheet. An exercise assisting you can be found in ***Plan It! Do It! Love It! The Planning Workbook***. Record the action to update and review your Target Tracking reports regularly (monthly is recommended).

COACH'S CHALLENGE

Take another look at the targets you have set. Are you being reasonable? Have you been aggressive enough? If it is true that you "get what you measure" then I challenge you to set your goals appropriately and as aggressive as you feel is reasonable.

STEP FOUR: SELECT STRATEGY

We learn about "strategy" very early in our life. It is how we get what we want when we want it without expending more time, energy, or other currency than we have to. If you have children you know what I mean about learning early. I still picture my boys huddled behind the garage with their water balloons planning an attack on the pet dog. Even before the age of 10 they knew that, in situations such as these, every move counted. They would have only one chance to reach their target or one chance to catch him off guard. Taking the right action at the right moment could mean the difference in that poor pet's escape and their delight. They used strategy to get exactly what they wanted with as few moves as possible whether that was play time, teenage adventures, or college budget negotiations. Those boys were and still are strategic thinkers.

How about you? Do you naturally identify and develop strategies and think through every move that will help you to reach your target? If not, don't worry. Learning to think strategically, creating strategy and developing your tactics can be learned through practice.

Strategy is a plan of action designed to achieve an overall goal. Strategy is broken into categories and comprised of tactics (in this book they are referred to as "actions"). Together they are the primary means and methods you will use to move from your current status or situation to the vision you developed. It is your "system" for delivering on your vision.

Overall, most plans have between six and 12 key strategy categories. The actions in each strategy make up a plan for achieving a particular goal which you have listed as a part of your vision. For example, if your vision includes your intention to "increase revenue by 30 percent," you will have a strategy category entitled "Revenue" and a goal listed to "increase revenue by 30 percent." You will then list all the tactics (e.g. actions) that will help you achieve that goal. The actions might include "raising prices by 10 percent," or "adding (list the resource) as an affiliate to create passive income." Think of strategies as a way of sorting and organizing tactics you plan to take to get you from your current situation to the vision you have designed. You can set it up like a recipe with one step building on the next or just list all of the actions in a random fashion with a goal to complete them all by the end of the plan period.

One final note, if you are confused about the difference between "strategy", "tactics" and "actions" don't be. Think of "strategy" as the attack plan and "tactics or actions" as the move you take to get to the target and win the battle.

Typical Strategy Categories for Small Business

After planning with hundreds of small business owners I have concluded that most have very similar key strategy categories (from this point referred to as just "strategies") plus one or two that are specific to their industry or a special project they have undertaken. If this is your first strategic plan you may want to adopt these standard choices as your strategy. As your planning process becomes more customized to your business you will have more customized strategies.

Sample Action Plan forms can be found in ***Plan It! Do It! Love It! The Planning Workbook***, or you can create your own form from the sample on the following page.

Action Plan					
Strategy: Marketing and Sales					
Goals: Change the marketing approach to reach a broader range of target client in the (insert) community. Expand customer boundaries to include (insert) and (insert). Increase sales calling by 20%					
Project or Action	**Start** (Qtr, Mo, Day)	**Deadline**	**Owner**	**Complete** √	**Comments**
Action, Task, or Project					

Income, Financial, Revenue, Expense

This strategy is the one that includes everything relating to money. Here you record any actions you plan to take that result in more or less revenue, income, expense, savings, investments, or profit. Typical actions would include price increases or decreases, changes in salaries or personal income, or change in the rate of savings. This area also includes expense reduction, debt consolidation or settlement, securing loans needed to run the the business, or capital expenditures such as new equipment. In this area you will also record any actions related to reserves for operations or savings for future expenses. Actions relevant to your income or expense management such as a change in your accountant or bookkeeper is found here as well. A typical action might be to “pay off credit card xxx” or “increase (insert product) price percent.”

Networking and Partnerships

Finding and forming partnerships is a very effective way to extend your reach and grow and develop your business. This will almost always be a key strategy. Only those that no longer want to grow or are winding down their business will not have some action in this category. Actions should relate to identifying individuals or groups of similar or like-minded business people, connecting with them to expand your business community or referral network, and creating business opportunities together.

Included in this strategy should be the actions of evaluating current networking practices and identifying new networking opportunities.

All partnerships should be reviewed no less than annually. In this strategy it is recommended you develop actions to review strategic and referral partnerships, set meetings to discuss opportunities and improve relationships. If you do not have partnerships or do not have effective partnerships, record actions that will help you identify the right partners and build relationships with them. If you are not sure how to choose a partner or build relationships check out the index entries on Partnerships. You can also talk to your business coach or consultant about your needs and desires and they can help you to plan for these powerful arrangements.

Typical actions would be to "meet with [insert name] to discuss partnership" or "evaluate the percentage of business referred by [insert name]."

Products, Services and Packages

It is important you constantly review and refine your full offering of products and services. For that reason you will always have a "Products, Services, Packages" strategy. The actions should be those surrounding the examination of your current offerings and any additions, updates, upgrades, expansion, or refinement you plan as a result of the examination. Typical actions might be to "review current [type] packages" or "examine the satisfaction rate on [product]." They might also be to "eliminate [service] for [market]" or to "create a new package to introduce [product(s)]."

Client Management and Retention

Business owners work hard to identify, engage and satisfy customers and clients. The most difficult and most expensive part of this work is the first sale. Every sale after that one takes less effort, energy and expense. For this reason alone every business – small or otherwise – should have a vibrant "Client Management and Retention" strategy. Actions found in this strategy will include how you manage client information, how you track buying habits and client satisfaction, and a communication plan that keeps you and your business in regular contact with those who have experience working with you or buying from you. It should also include "good will" programs such as how you reward or acknowledge a loyal client or customer. Typical actions might be to "upgrade the CRM (client relationship management) system" or "develop a client survey."

Marketing and Sales

Marketing and selling are parts of an equation that equals production and profitability. They are often confused and sometimes considered to be the same, but the definitions and the functions are quite different. In the simplest sense – "marketing" is a noun and "sales" is a verb. Marketing is a "process" of promoting your products or services to your potential marketplace. The key concepts in marketing are: advertising, branding and identity, distribution, promotions, social (media or marketing), service, market research, public relations and sales. Typical marketing actions might be to "refresh the website" or "develop a marketing campaign to attract [insert population]."

Sales is one of the key concepts of marketing and is the act of selling your products or services for a profit. All businesses need both a marketing and a sales (or selling) strategy. Actions in this strategy will include those associated with any of the marketing concepts or with selling your products or services such as, "plan and execute a door-to-door spring promotion" or "set retail sales goals for each employee."

If you have a sales staff you are encouraged to split this strategy into two strategies—marketing and sales.

Recruiting, Staffing, Employee Relations, Performance Management

This strategy will be slightly different depending on the size and make-up of your staff. If you work alone and your plans do not indicate a change in this status for the plan period, you will not need this strategy. If you have employees, they need consistent attention and dedicated support. Actions in this strategy should be centered on managing employee performance, rewarding results, career development, succession planning and an ongoing recruiting strategy. If you do not have a performance management program make it your first action item. Typical actions might be to "schedule performance review with [name or all employees]" or to "review and update the sales bonus program."

If your plan calls for adding employees you are encouraged to hire slowly and methodically. Your actions should be centered on developing a recruiting process, developing job descriptions, new job posting on [job board], first, second, third and final round interviews, employee offers, onboarding with expectations, goal setting, performance reviews and evaluations. Typical actions might be to "write the job description for [new position]" or to "post for the [position] on [job board]."

Operational Efficiencies, Processes, Procedures, Systems

In small business, time and resources are often not plentiful. This means it is more important in small business than in any other organizational type to have the right systems, efficient processes, and clear procedures. This strategy might include developing a procedure for [almost anything], delegating [anything], software purchases, training and anything else that will help you to organize, reduce time in any process and engage all the resources you have available. Typical actions might be to "create a system for travel time tracking" or "create a check list for [any process]". Other actions might be to "track time on all projects" or "research new software for [X]."

Facilities, Equipment

Where do you work? What equipment do you use to do your job, produce your products, or support your staff or clients? Will there be any need for change in these areas during the plan period? Actions listed in this strategy will include finding and securing new or additional work location(s), satellite locations, storage facilities, maintenance as required, any changes in your lease or mortgage, reorganizing work areas, expansions, upgrading your work areas, changes needed in surrounding areas such as parking lots, street or easements, access ways, etc. It will also include the purchase, replacement, or maintenance for equipment, furnishings, and decorating. Typical actions might be to "replace computers for [names or positions]" or "identify new location for the [location] office."

Training, Education

Training and education are key contributors of long-term success. If you plan to be in business for more than one year you need a strategy for training and education. If you have staff you can benefit from identifying and scheduling not only your education needs as an owner but the training and education needs of your staff members. Decide in advance how much you are willing to contribute to the training budget. How will it be split between you and your staff? Will you contribute 100 percent or ask for the staff member(s) to make a contribution. Typical actions might be to "schedule sales training for [name]" or "find a workshop on effective communication for the next staff meeting."

Executive Development and Leadership

This strategy is one focused solely on the leaders of the business. If you work alone it may be just you as the business owner and executive. If you have staff it should be you and your leaders and managers. Just as you evaluated your employees for their needs in training and development, do the same for yourself as the owner and any members of your leadership team. Your needs for training and development can be a part of the "Training and Development" strategy if you have a small staff or no other employees in a leadership position. Actions in this strategy might include identifying skills that need improvement (yours or others), or to improve performance today or in the future. Included in these actions might also be those for succession planning. Here you might also identify your leadership team for the future and their needs for development. You want them to be ready to step in when the time is right.

Typical actions might be listed as "develop a succession plan" or "schedule a leadership development assessment for [name]."

Legal and Compliance

Every small business has some level of legal and compliance responsibility. This could include reviewing your contracts and auditing for state or federal regulatory compliance. It could also include employer responsibilities such as posting notices or filing applications. If there are only a few you might consider adding these actions to the "Operational Efficiency" strategy. If there are more, create a separate strategy and give it the attention it deserves. Be sure to consult your business attorney and human resources expert to identify all of the actions appropriate for your planning period.

Typical actions might be "contact [name] business attorney for annual review" or "update [type] contracts."

<u>Special Project(s)</u>

If your vision includes the completion of a special project or projects, you will want to create a separate strategy to outline the actions and timing for each.

Sample Strategies with Goal Detail

Here are a few sample strategies and the goal they plan to achieve. Any of the combined strategies can be separated if that simplifies planning for you. Your Action Plan will be fluid for the full period of your plan. If you start with more than five action items for any one goal then you may want to create a separate strategy for that goal.

Strategy: Income, Financial, Revenue, Expense

Goal(s): To increase revenue from $150,000 to $225,000. Increase profit margin from 17 percent to 22 percent. Realize a personal income increase from $55,000 to $70,000.

Strategy: Networking, Strategic Partnerships, Referral Partnerships

Goal(s): Increase networking hours to 15 per month. Identify and develop relationships with three new strategic partners and two new referral partners.

Strategy: Products, Services, Packages

Goal(s): Increase the (insert) product sales from 20 percent to 50 percent. Develop bundled services packages for the [insert] services.

Strategy: Client Management and Client Retention

Goal(s): Develop and implement a client retention program. Set up a client communication calendar.

Strategy: Marketing and Sales

Goal(s): Change the marketing approach to reach a broader range of target clients in the [insert] community. Expand customer boundaries to include [insert] and [insert]. Increase sales calling by 20 percent.

Strategy: Personnel, Staffing, Performance Management

Goal(s): Develop policies and procedures for staff management including handbooks, manuals, goal setting, tracking, performance management and accountability. Develop a staff expansion plan.

Strategy: Operational Efficiencies, Processes, Procedures, Systems

Goal(s): Set up system for [insert]. Increase productivity by 15 percent. Streamline the [insert] process.

Strategy: Facilities and Equipment

Goal(s): Inventory equipment and replace any that does not meet the quality standards. Negotiate expansion lease. Relocate [date].

Strategy: Legal and Compliance

Goal(s): Update all contracts with a new confidentiality policy.

Strategy: Special Project (Spring Tradeshow)

Goal(s): Generate 25 new client leads.

PLAN IT!

Step 4: Identify the strategies you will use to get you from where you are now to your vision. Combine those that seem to logically fit together. See the samples above as they are the most used by small business owners I work with. List your strategies and the goal you plan to reach in each.

COACH'S ADVICE

Do not wait to plan. If you have not been working on your plan as you read you can complete this chapter and then return to the beginning exercises or stop now, go back to the first exercise and complete the first four steps.

TOOLS

Sample Action Plan forms can be found in ***Plan It! Do It! Love It! The Planning Workbook*** or you can create your own form from the sample in this chapter.

Step Five: Assign Action

Mark comes to my annual group planning event every year. Every year he works diligently throughout the day to focus on creating a plan that will guide him to the vision he has designed for the next twelve months. Every year he declares his intention to complete his plan and follow through with the action. Every year he falls short of his vision. It's just his nature he says, "I just can't seem to do what I know will get me where I want to go."

Twice a year I offer a group planning day for small business owners. It is a great way for them to plan together. They feed off each other's energy and ideas while they focus on their own business and vision. We work through Steps One through Four during the event and each participant then commits to completing Action Plan within one week and reporting their outcome to the group. This system works great for 95 percent of all participants. The other five percent, like Mark, never seem to follow through. All the effort is not lost. Just working through the process helps every business owner to organize their thinking. But, failure to complete the planning process with an Action Plan (tasks, tactics, actions, deadlines, and assignments) often means they do not realize the full benefit of the process. In other words, it is nice to know where you are going but if you do not follow the directions you could end up anywhere.

The most difficult part of the planning process is the first three steps. From here it is a matter of sorting, prioritizing, and when appropriate, involving others. So, resist any temptation you have to stop and just "take it as it comes." Finish your plan.

Choose a Format

There are plenty of formats for your planning document. You can use project planning software, an excel spreadsheet, or a simple notebook or paper. Whatever you choose it should be readily available and easy for you to use. If the plan is being used by more than one person it might be best to choose something that can be shared online from multiple locations.

A sample of an Action Plan can be found below or in ***Plan It! Do It! Love It! The Planning Workbook***.

Action Plan					
Strategy: Marketing and Sales					
Goals: Change the marketing approach to reach a broader range of target client in the (insert) community. Expand customer boundaries to include (insert) and (insert). Increase sales calling by 20%					
Project or Action	Start (Qtr, Mo, Day)	Deadline	Owner	Complete √	Comments
Action, Task, or Project					

Create a Custom Document

You can certainly create your own customized plan documents. There are plenty of options. For the most up to date options browse for "planning documents" and review the large selection available.

No matter what you decide, I recommend you include these action plan components:

- Clearly state the "Strategy Title"
- Define the "Goal(s)" of the strategy
- List each action, task, or project that will contribute to the success of the strategy
- Record the quarter, month you plan to begin the action, task, or project

- Set a deadline for completion
- List person responsible for the action, task, or project (it may just be you!)
- Provide a section for comments that you will use during review or as a way of communicating with others that share your plan

Develop Action in Detail

Some business owners think and plan in what I call "chunks." They might list a big project; record the start date, deadline and owner without detailing the steps of that project. If that works for you then do it that way. If you need more detail then break it down into smaller deliverables. For example, if you are planning to have your contracts reviewed, one owner may say:

Action Plan					
Strategy: Legal					
Goals: Protect the business while being fully compliant with all city, state, and federal rules and regulations.					
Project or Action	Start (Qtr, Mo, Day)	Deadline	Owner	Complete √	Comments
Example 1: Contract Review	May 2016	June 2016	Self		Review all client contracts
Example 2: Contact Attorney	5-1-16	6-1-16	Self		
Meet with Attorney	6-1-16	6-15-61	Self		Review all client contracts
Distribute Updated Contracts	7-1-16	7-30-16	Admin		New and update any that are expiring in 90 days

You know if you are a detailed or "big picture" thinker. Use what works best for the way you think and process information. Be certain to consult other members of your planning team. They too will have a preferred way of processing information. It will have to work for everyone for it to be effective.

Share Responsibilities

This is an opportunity for you to do what you do best and delegate the rest. It is also an opportunity for you to engage your stakeholders in the plan and get their support and buy-in to deliver on the actions, tasks, and projects that will result in success. Sharing the load also makes reaching your goals less of a strain on you.

Choose the person or persons most likely to complete the action with the best performance. Delegate the action to them and then back away. Allow them to complete the action and report their progress in regularly scheduled planning update meetings. This is a great way to develop your staff and future leaders. Give them a chance to show you what they can do.

Set Start Dates and Deadlines

Often during the planning process business owners identify the actions and responsible parties but have trouble putting start dates and deadlines on their plans. Maybe this is because they are used to just doing what comes next and do not like to be committed to specific deadlines. More probably, they are not sure how to prioritize their time, capacity, and calculate the value of the completion of the action. If, however, they do not assign dates and deadlines, those actions, tasks, or projects tend to never start, let alone never complete.

Set a reasonable start date and deadline for each action. In the planning process, owners often want all action completed now. There is a tendency to front-load the actions into the first three months of the planning period and then to have to adjust missed dates for actions that could not be worked into the schedule.

Start by prioritizing the actions that will have the most value to your plan and spread lower contributors over time. Do your best to follow through with your plans. This is your plan. If you miss the date or deadline, identify why and make changes and updates. Find a new date and set a new deadline. Keeping the plan in "action" is what the plan is all about.

Your regular review and updates will be important to keeping these dates and deadlines current. Thus begins the "Do It" part of your small business life and lifestyle.

PLAN IT!

Step 5: Create the Action Plan document. Use a format and style that are comfortable for you and others involved in your plan. Record Strategy Title, Goal(s), each action, target Start date, completion Deadline, responsible Owner, and any Comments.

COACH'S ADVICE

Fill in all of the blanks. Set dates and deadlines. Prioritize. Be reasonable. Fight the urge to set all start and deadline dates in the first one to three months of the plan.

TOOLS

Sample Action Plan forms can be found in ***Plan It! Do It! Love It! The Planning Workbook*** or you can create your own form from the in this chapter.

Do It!

Step Six: Do It!

Plan your work and work your plan." The origins of this statement are unknown but it has been quoted as inspiration by many from Vince Lombardi to Margaret Thatcher. Translation: having a plan is of little use if you take no action. You know what you want and what it will take to get it. Now, do it! You have a plan — "work the plan."

This section guides you through the action of building, growing and maintaining your small business. You can think of it as the sixth step in planning: taking action to deliver your vision. Using your plan as a roadmap, you will move from your current situation, one milestone at a time, to the place you want to be: your vision.

Along the way I will give you advice based on my experience and the experiences of my small business clients. Avoid the mistakes, pitfalls, and missed opportunities of hundreds of successful business owners. Adopt new practices. Create new systems. Change your behavior.

Watch your business thrive. It all starts with your commitment to be accountable to this plan that you created in the previous section of the book.

Accountability

Once the plan has been created it is easy to think you have completed the project. This is just the beginning. The good news is that having committed your goals in writing with a planning exercise makes you 40 percent more likely to achieve your vision. But why stop there when you can increase your odds? Some research suggests:

- If you tell someone else, you are 60 percent more likely to achieve your goals.

- If you make a regular investment of review and accountability your odds go up to 95 percent more likely to achieve your goals.

If you are like me, you want what you want. Let the first act of "doing" be to identify when and how you will stay on track with your plan. Start by engaging your stakeholders for the full length of your planning period. Ask everyone to do the same. Consistency is as important as accountability.

Plan Review

Reviewing your plan regularly is powerful reinforcement. Decide how often you will review your plan and put it on the calendar. Think of this date and time as an appointment with your best client: you and your stakeholders. Resist delaying the review when something else comes along.

I would advise a monthly review. If your plan is designed to move more slowly, with dates and deadlines more than three months apart, then you may find that quarterly works best for you. Never let more than six months go by without reviewing and updating your plan. For most people that is half of the plan period. If you let any project go unattended for more than six months it is likely not going to produce the results you want in the plan period.

If possible, have your plan review in person with all of the stakeholders involved. If you are in business alone review it with your coach or an accountability partner. As mentioned earlier, avoid the temptation to delay these meetings or cut them short due to some current issue or interruption. Reviewing the plan is just as important as creating it, maybe more. Make it a priority. Make sure anyone you choose as an accountability partner will do the same.

Accountability Partner(s)

Reviewing your plan with someone or a group of people outside your business is even more powerful. Each person that is included will have some sense of ownership for the plan and can offer new ideas, perspective, and input.

If you do not have people or peers that you can rely on as accountability partner(s), look around for someone who would be a good partner for you. There are plenty of other small business owners that could benefit from the same support. Choose wisely. Not just anyone will do.

Find the right partner. Look for someone you trust that has a similar sized business as yours. You might consider asking one of your strategic partners. That is a great way to share ideas and help each other move your plans along. Share your commitment to this plan with them and ask for their commitment. You might even choose to sign a contract to emphasize importance.

Set a schedule and keep it. I recommend that you put dates on the calendar for the year or plan period. At the very least, plan the next meeting while you are wrapping up the current meeting.

Decide in advance what you will review together and how you will present the information. It is not good enough to just "send it over" and let them look at it. You want to take the time to collect the information, analyze it, conclude your findings and then share them with your accountability group or partner(s). As mentioned earlier, meeting in person is always best so that you can be sure you have the full attention of each person.

Set a policy of confidentiality. Some of the information you share with each other will most likely be confidential or proprietary. You will have chosen a partner that you can trust, but you should also be clear with all the parties that the policy of confidentiality applies to any information shared in your accountability meetings.

Determine in advance how you would like to be held accountable for your outcome. What would you like your accountability partner to do or say if you meet your goals? More importantly, what do you need if you do not meet them? This is typically the way you prefer to be motivated. Do you like a "carrot" or a "stick?" Be sure you share that with your partner. If you are playing the same role for them, be sure they share how they like to be motivated as well.

Make a change if you are not getting your needs met. Partners that serve you best are those that take this process as seriously as you do. It is my hope that the partner(s) you choose will be exactly what you need, but, do not allow a weak accountability partner to bring you down. If the partner you choose shows signs that they are not committed, make a change quickly. Signs can be:

- canceling or rescheduling more than one time
- not being prepared
- allowing interruptions
- cutting meetings short
- not paying attention

- not giving good feedback
- not holding you accountable in the way that you agreed
- or any breach in confidentiality.

DO IT!

Find an accountability partner(s). Set up a calendar for a meeting to review outcomes. Prioritize these meetings.

COACH'S CHALLENGE

Get started right away. Work your plan. Take action! Use the information in the following chapters to reach your goals. This section of the book will follow an outline that coincides with the typical strategies for most small business owners.

COACH'S ADVICE

Choose an accountability partner right away. If you have staff you may decide to be partners for each other. If you do not, then find someone that you trust to share your plan with and to hold you accountable.

TOOLS

Download an accountability contract online. There are plenty to choose from.

Income, Financial, Revenue, Expense, Savings

Many of you may be at a place in your business where you feel you live "hand to mouth." This phrase comes from sixteenth century Britain when record numbers of people had precious little food to eat due to famine. When they were lucky enough to be offered food they would literally put it straight into their mouth mostly to ensure no one else could get to it first.

Often small business owners go through a period, most common in the building years, when they feel there is little or no money to manage, let alone enjoy. They struggle to pay their bills. They put themselves and their needs lowest on the list and never seem to have anything left over for anything other than the basics. If you are here, it's time to move on. This book is about living a life you love as a small business owner. This includes having enough money to cover your needs *and* your wants. Have faith. It will get better. Just keep working your plan and find the support you on need in a partner, strategic partner, a key employee, a coach, or an organization that sticks with you through every challenge. (Often having someone outside your home and family is best as you want to be sure you are present to enjoy life when in personal situations.)

Every small business owner needs money management practices. If you do not have them, it is time to create them. The best way to make sure you have enough money for all you need and want is to know where it comes from and where it goes. This all starts with a budget.

If you have advanced beyond the suggestions that follow you can find assistance in learning more complex practices such as forecasting, calculating return on investments, risk management calculations and more from your accounting partner.

Create a Budget

These days there is a budget for everything from the calories you consume to the plans you have for retirement. It can be overwhelming even to think about attempting such a process for your business. Many clients tell me they do not have a budget and may never have had a budget. Often they will remark that, "I have it all in my head," or "I know how much money I can spend before I need to stop," or "I pay my bills and put the rest in my personal account."

You may think that because you are a small business you do not need a budget. You could not be farther from the truth. You take more control, reduce expenses, and begin to save the minute you begin to plan and record the actions.

A budget is necessary for you to manage the financial aspects of your business. It does not matter if you are just starting out and know where every dollar is coming from or if you have long since considered yourself successful and are making plans to invest in future growth. You need to be well informed about all of the financial aspects of your business.

Contrary to what you might believe, budgeting is not all about restricting what you spend or focusing on debt that needs to be reduced. It is about how much revenue you are generating, where it is being spent, and then how to make adjustments to improve your cash flow. This often translates to putting more money in your pocket every month.

So, if you have a budget — well done! Review it regularly and keep the practice alive. If you do not have a budget, create one. You can find plenty of them on the internet for free or visit www.planitdoitloveit.com for a sample and template.

A budget does not have to be complicated. The budgeting process does not have to be daunting. Just decide to do it and follow the directions below. Here is everything you need to help you create and maintain a small business budget.

Block out the time to develop the budget. It can be a part of this planning process or you can make it an action item.

Approach with a positive attitude. The excuse many clients give is they do not want to know how deeply in debt they are or how little revenue they are generating or that they have obligations that seem to stretch on forever. The budget process is all a part of being a well-informed business owner and is never as bad as you think it might be. Most business owners report they are relieved when it is over.

Use the facts. Make sure you are using real numbers. Calculate annual costs and use averages.

Anticipate change. Investigate any increases you are anticipating and use the higher costs. Include any changes you are planning in employee expenses either in additional staff, salary increases or changes in benefits. Include any increase in rent or taxes and any changes in assessments. Are your costs going up? Are insurance premiums rising? Is the rent adjusting? Conversely, can you eliminate a loan payment or equipment contract that will be satisfied? Can you negotiate lower service costs?

Involve others. Include others in your budgeting process. It is difficult to remember every line item. Ask them to contribute any expense changes they anticipate or purchases or investments they recommend.

Have realistic expectations and set realistic goals for change. When you recognize what needs to change, set achievable goals. One of the biggest budget killers is unrealistic expectations. This is a covenant you are setting with yourself and your business. Make sure you will not disappoint yourself.

Set a schedule to review your budget regularly and keep it up to date. If you keep your budget current, updating it will be a breeze in the years to come. Some like to review their budget monthly along with their profit and loss and other financials. Others review their budget less frequently. I recommend you review your budget no less than quarterly and update it no less than annually.

The intention of every small business owner is to make a profit. That may seem like an unnecessary statement but it is worth emphasizing. This means your goal is to always have more "coming in" than "going out" and a positive number on the "net income" line of your profit and loss statement. If you do not, then you will want to identify what might be keeping you from achieving this position. Your best resource is a small business accountant who can help you strategize.

Spend Wisely

Now that you have a budget — use it! Your budget should include all areas of anticipated spending. This will give you guidance on when and how to allocate and spend your hard-earned revenue. Do not get ahead of your plans. It is easy to do. Today there is credit available to anyone with a clean credit rating. It is usually more than you want and almost certainly more than you can safely manage. Resist the urge to "buy it now" and "pay for it later" or "pay on time."

Some use of credit is expected to manage your cash flow but it should never be excessive. Notice I have not given you guidelines for what is safe for you. Talk to your accountant and/or your financial advisor if you have any concerns in this area. Keep it manageable. If you spend more than you make the money has to come from somewhere to keep your business operating. Somewhere is usually from your income first or even your personal savings and then from others who are close to you. This is a slippery slope and can be difficult to recover from if you slide too far down the hill.

Save for Security

One of the most common challenges of small business owners is the need for financial security. Your operating expense creates an ongoing "overhead" which must be covered on a regular basis. Most small business owners worry about what will happen if their flow of cash is interrupted, if they get sick and cannot work, if there is a snow storm and the store is closed for seven days, or if customers do not come and the coffers are empty. The best way to address this concern is to have funds available for emergencies. We call this "reserves." Some call this cash reserves, others operating reserves, or even emergency reserves. The meaning in the case of small business is the same. It is money set aside to safeguard your financial stability. If you do not need the cash, it slowly earns interest. If you need it, it is there and ready to get you through a crisis.

How much is enough? This is open to debate. At an absolute minimum, the reserves should cover your daily living expenses (since those come from your business) plus your daily business expenses for three months. Six months would be wiser, and some planners recommend a full year. Set aside the amount that creates a feeling of safety for you.

Often, I am asked if a line of credit can be used for this purpose. Of course it is good to have and in the case of an emergency can be used, but a line of credit becomes debt. Debt must be paid. If you choose to use a line of credit be sure it is only a part of your bigger "reserves" plan.

Invest in Your Future

If you are just getting started you may find it hard to believe there will be enough money one day to invest in your future. You will be successful and there will be enough to invest. So, plan on it. Do not wait until you feel the time is right. Plan today. Start by finding a financial advisor that is a good match for you and your needs. Financial advisors have target markets and specialties just like you do, so find one that works with your personal profile and who has a specialty in the areas which interest you most. Together with this professional decide how you will invest in your future.

Brad, who owns a remodeling company, tells me he will work until he cannot get up in the morning. Many small business owners feel just like Brad. They love what they do and they plan to do it for as long as they are able. Still, the day may come when you have a change of heart or when your health is not cooperating. You want to be ready for that day. Not afraid, just ready. I promise you it will make your working days more enjoyable to know that you have options.

DO IT!

(A) Record the actions to create or update your budget. Or, stop now and create a budget for your business. Be sure to include all expenses, real and anticipated, and include a savings and investment plan.

DO IT!

(B) Record the actions to meet with your financial advisor and talk about your plans. If you do not have a financial advisor, record the action to find one that is a good match for you and your plans.

COACH'S CHALLENGE

Having a budget for your business is a great first step. I challenge you to stick to your budget. I also challenge you to also have a budget for your life. If you do not have a personal or family budget create one now. It will help you to see what your needs are and how that might put demands on your business success.

COACH'S ADVICE

Going deeply in debt early is one of the biggest mistakes small business owners make. Be sure you get outside advice before you spend outside your means. Look at all the consequences of your plans.

TOOLS

Free budgets for small business are easy to find online. Review a few of them and select the one that meets your needs best.

Revenue Generation

"Money makes the world go round." While this is far from true it often feels this way. Money creates more worry than almost anything else in life. Where will it come from? Do we have enough? What if it stops? Because worry stems from fear and fear drives action it stands to reason that revenue generation is a dominant focus in small business ownership. Few small business owners can say they are never concerned about revenue generation. Those who make that claim typically consider their business to be more of a "hobby" than a "lifestyle."

Just like every other component of your plan, revenue generation starts with a strategy. Once the strategy is in place then you can create everything you will need to support it. Here is what you will need to know to create a strategy:

How much revenue do I want to generate? This should have been decided as a part of your vision process. If not, stop now and decide on an amount.

How much will come from each product, service or channel? If you offer several products and/or services decide how much revenue will come from each. You may have already done this as a part of your vision exercise. If not, this is a key component of managing revenue generation and should be a part of tracking and reporting. Determine how much revenue you expect to get from each product, service, or channel of production either in total dollars or in percentage.

Do I have everything I need to generate the revenue projected? If you have not reached this level of revenue generation in the past, examine your resources including staff, facilities, equipment, and capacity to be sure they are adequate to produce the revenue you project.

How much will be too much? It may be hard to believe but you can generate too much revenue, produce too many products, and agree to too many projects. If you are producing beyond your capacity it will impact not only the delivery to your current clients but put your future success in jeopardy.

How will we know we are on track? This should have been part of your Target Tracking exercise. Monitor the targets and metrics you have chosen. They will give you the information you need to manage capacity.

Now, align your entire organization to deliver on your revenue generation strategy. Keep in mind it is the responsibility of the entire organization, working together, to execute this strategy. Every staff member should be aware of your revenue generation goals and know what their part is in delivering on the strategy.

ADVICE FROM YOUR PEERS

"As a small business owner your vision can sometimes outpace your ability to deliver. Just because you can calculate the amount of business that is possible for you and your organization does not mean you are ready to deliver on that projection. It takes only one bad experience for many clients to try the competition. They expect you to deliver what you promise and are typically not forgiving if you do not. Be sure you are not always in reaction mode. Make sure you have the staff before you promise the service. The sales numbers are meaningless if there is no profit. One great job is meaningless unless that client would refer you or come back for their next job" Nancy Long, Boss Lady, Sisu Painting, Inc.

DO IT!

Review your revenue goal. Is it appropriate? Have you set it high enough? Is it manageable? Did you take all resources needs into consideration. If you have not communicated your vision to your staff do so now. Make sure they know what their role is in delivering on the vision and in particular on delivering on the revenue generation goal.

COACH'S CHALLENGE

Make it a regular practice to communicate updates on your vision to all of your stakeholders including your staff. Engage them in reaching the goals that are set. Celebrate with them when you reach milestones.

Price and Pricing

Business owners beware. Setting and keeping the price of your goods and services is harder than it might seem. You may think all you need to do is charge as much as you can, and people will buy if they can afford it. There is far more to price and pricing than such a simple approach.

Price is a key component of any revenue generation strategy. The price you charge is typically based on the cost of the goods, plus the cost of production or the value of the service and a profit margin. It is impacted by what the market will bear or the tolerance for the price you charge in your target market. You might think you always want to have the best price possible. This is not always true. The one exception is if you have a "most affordable" or "lowest cost" marketing strategy.

What you want is the price which will get you the results you expect. Price can be used to:

- Increase or decrease sales.
- Increase or decrease market share.
- Control capacity
- Change product mix.
- Increase market awareness.
- Introduce new product lines or services.
- Eliminate product lines or services.
- Capture market segments, etc.

The important thing to remember about price setting is that it has a direct impact on revenue and therefore on profit. Adjustments in price, even temporary adjustments, must be planned, monitored, and budgeted.

Price Setting

So, how do you set price? First, you have to know your market well. Know what others charge for the same or similar products and services. Next, you must know what your target client is willing to pay and what they can afford. Never, I repeat, never, undervalue your products or services without a clear plan on why you would do so and how you remain profitable or recapture profit later. You may think this is a silly comment. Who would undervalue their products or services? It is a fact that a majority of my clients in start-up or early phases will undervalue their products, and services, fearing their inexperience has some deflationary impact on their offering. Wrongly, they believe the only way they can attract a client is to "give it away." They often undercut their competitors by 30, 40, 50, even 75 percent without realizing the price they put on the product or service is often the value the client will perceive.

People must feel they are making valuable investments when they purchase from you. They will justify the outcome based on the experience they have. Make sure the experience matches the price and charge what your market will bear. If you need one more reason, I will quote one of my clients, Samantha, who regularly reminds her staff members, "Don't try to manage anyone's checkbook but your own. Every client has the right to say 'no' if the price is outside their budget."

Increasing Price

We reduce prices from time to time, but this is the exception in small business. Most often when we consider price, we are hoping to justify an increase. Remember, it is the fastest way to increase revenue.

If you are planning for a price increase or if you just want to make sure the price you are charging is a best match for your target client and market, the place to begin is with an examination of your current pricing and the sales associated with it over some period of time. I recommend the past 12 months. List your products and the current prices for each. Calculate the number and dollar volume you sold, produced or generated in the past 12 months.

Pricing, Revenue, Profit Exercise

Product Or Service	Unit (#, Hour)	Price Per Unit in $	Cost to Produce Per Unit	Profit in $ per Unit	# Produced in past 12 Months	Total Profit ($) by Product/Service in Past 12 Months	Percent of Total Company Revenue

Now examine your findings. Answer these questions:

- Are you fully aware of what price similar products or services are offered for in your marketplace to your target client?

- Is every product profitable?
- Where does the most profit come from?
- Does the profit come from the products aligned with your specialty? If not, are you willing to change your specialty?
- Is there room for an increase in price in any area? If so, will it still attract the target market you have chosen? If not, are you willing to change your target market?
- How much will a price increase change your total revenue? Profit?

DO IT!

If you are uncertain of any answers to the questions above stop now and do your research (see Competitive Review in Part 4: Examine and Assess). You must know who is offering what and for how much in order to know how you will compete against them.

COACH'S CHALLENGE

If you do not have reports that are designed to give you this information, you can review them regularly I would recommend that you develop them and review the information on no less than a half-yearly basis.

TOOLS

Price and pricing exercises can be found in ***Plan It! Do It! Love It! The Planning Workbook***.

Recurring Revenue

When I first started working with John he had not had a vacation in over five years. He worked nights and weekends and most holidays as a tennis coach. He loved tennis but it was not the reason he failed to step away and renew. He was afraid that if he did not take every opportunity he had to meet with clients the money would stop. He was the sole provider for his family and they had a tight budget. As you might guess, there were many facets of this issue to work through over time, but the first of these was to set up a flow of recurring revenue so the money would come even when John was not on the court.

For your business to be able to operate without you, you need revenue that flows when you are not selling. One way to do this is to create recurring revenues. These are goods or services you have "pre-sold." They are due on a particular day or in a range of days (the first through the 15th of the month for example) and might be charged in advance or in arrears. You can count on this revenue to arrive on a pre-determined date whether the goods or services are being delivered then.

In John's case this turned out to be an annual membership of his tennis services. For you it might also be a retainer for services not yet performed, as with legal services or human resource services. Or monthly services such as might be charged by a landscaping provider or digital marketing provider. No matter what you have to offer you can almost always break it into portions you can charge for over a period of time.

As with most arrangements between a small business and a client, there are a few cautions to making recurring revenue a successful practice.

Always have an agreement. It does not have to be a contract but you should have something in writing which specifically states what the client is paying for, when it is due, and what happens if it is not paid or not paid on time. Be sure both parties acknowledge with a signature, initials, or via a reply to an e-mail.

Charge a late fee. Pick a grace period for the fee to be paid, put it in the agreement, and if it is not paid on time, charge it. You can decide if you want to waive it for that random missed payment but you will want to follow-through with the charge — letting them know you have done so.

Have a start and end date. There should always be a date when the agreement starts and a date when it ends.

You may choose to continue an agreement based on the original terms but you'll want to have an end date. Use the end date to review how the agreement works. It is also the perfect time to raise prices if you find you did not bid on the project properly or it is requiring a higher cost of goods or service time to perform.

Include consideration for unavoidable situations. For example, if you are a landscape contractor and you live in Texas you will have days when there is so much rain that it is impossible to mow a lawn. Identify how many days this might happen a year to a single customer and include that in calculating the overall price. Be sure to advertise that the fee includes an estimated number of days when services cannot be performed so that you are not constantly calculating missed days and reducing fees.

If you have a client who does not comply with the terms of any part of your agreement — chronically late with payment, chronically late in arrival, does not perform as agreed, or any other noncompliance — it is an indication they do not value the arrangement, or it is possible they believe the arrangement is more flexible than it is. Start by reminding them of your agreement and clarifying that it is not flexible. If they continue to operate out of compliance, I recommend you terminate the arrangement.

DO IT!

If you do not currently have recurring income programs take the time to examine the possibility of adding them. They will not work for every small business but do not decide it is not possible without examining it fully. Check your competition. Do any of them offer recurring programs? If so, how could you do the same? Make it better?

COACH'S CHALLENGE

Be sure you price recurring program appropriately. Never discount them too deeply. The right amount is a portion of what you save from generating new clients each month and/or in collecting from clients each month.

Passive Income

Who isn't looking for "easy money?" Everyone wants it. Some find it. They find it in passive income.

In the most general sense, the word "passive" means "without effort." Who would not want to make money without trying? It is not quite that simple, but it is a great source of income with low effort or not as much effort as traditional revenue generation. The most difficult part of passive income is the set-up. Planning and creating streams of income can take months or years.

First, let's define passive income. Passive income is revenue or earnings you derive from partnerships, products or other enterprises you collect with a type of income acquired automatically with minimal labor to earn. Some examples might be real estate partnerships or rentals you do not manage, products you have created that are sold online, or even book sales.

My client Karen has done a terrific job of creating passive income in her business. She is a chiropractic physician and wellness expert. The bulk of her income comes from creating wellness program plans for large corporations to offer as benefit to their employees.

Karen has produced a series of "how to" videos and online support tools to guide employees through the wellness changes they want to make in their lives. She offers a membership style program in which the employee or employer pays a flat monthly fee to have access to the tools and information. This program represents 30 percent of her overall income but does not demand more than 2 percent of her time in materials, updates and maintenance.

It is not critical for you to have a passive income, but you should consider any options you have either now or in the future. If you want to earn more, work less, and have time to enjoy your small business lifestyle you should build sources of income which do not require your day-to-day involvement. Either that, or create a variety of income streams which do not need your full and constant attention. Whether you are just starting your business, or you have had it for a while, I recommend you think about how you can shift some of your revenue generation to passive income.

If you are interested in creating a stream of passive income there is plenty of guidance online or in books written by small business owners who have successfully created millions in passive income. Do your homework. Decide what works for you and the business model you have already developed. Include your desire to add passive income in your plans.

DO IT!

Take the time to investigate all of your income sources. Are you generating revenue from all products and services? Are you maximizing the income you can generate from each? Do you know what you are generating from where? If not, be sure you set up reporting systems that will provide you with that information, readily, constantly. Think about your future. If you do not currently have a passive income decide how you might add it and when. Remember that multiple streams of income are important to create security.

COACH'S CHALLENGE

Set your price and keep it. Remember that your business is not a third world bazaar where you are expected to haggle over the price. Your price is your price. Once you are clear on what you can and will charge set a policy to not negotiate. If you decide to offer something for "free" or "pro bono" recognize it as that. Remember that the price you charge is often the value that your clients will put on the product or service. Let it have the value it is worth.

Networking, Strategic Partnerships, Referral Partners

This strategy is aimed at developing new business with the help of others. You, the business owner, may be directly involved or not. This is an opportunity for you to maximize your greatest resource: time. Think about how you are spending your time while you are developing and mastering networking and partnerships.

Networking

It is time to get out there and promote what you have to offer!

For the small business owner, networking is a great way to build relationships to promote business through referrals or partnerships. It is also a great complement to other marketing practices.

Get out there and show them how proud you are of the products or services you offer! Yes, that is what networking is all about showing the world you believe in what you offer. While networking is a key component of business and promotion. It can also be one of the most difficult practices for the small business owner. Limited time and lack of skill often make this one of the most challenging responsibilities in business success. The key is to choose only those activities that are the best fit for you and your business and stick with those that result in the right return on your investment.

Still, master this skill and you will reap great benefits. Networking and building relationships that drive referrals and revenue is a cost effective way to grow your business and should be considered part of your marketing strategy. The type of networking you do, with whom you do it, and how you do it should be consistent with your marketing goals. Attend events that will put you in contact with people who might be potential strategic partners, customers, or provide you resources for growth and education. All the while keeping in mind that your time is valuable, and it is important that you get a return on your investment of time and money in the short and long term.

Some people consider themselves to be natural networkers. They love crowds. They do not miss an event. While they may mingle regularly, it does not necessarily mean they are effective. This group sometimes confuses social activity for a valuable marketing action. Networking has to be done with purpose and intention. You should always know what you want from participation. Set goals for each event. How many people will you meet? Is there a person from a particular company you need to connect with? Be clear on what you will do when the event is over as follow up is essential to maximizing your networking efforts.

There is another trap for the "natural" and that is overuse of networking. Every networking commitment and event must produce results. There must be value for you to invest your time and money. If you are someone who thinks you might fall into this category, evaluate your regular networking activity using the process below and then cut any membership, affiliation, or event that does not yield the right return.

While I have known a number of "naturals," some who were effective and others who needed to adjust their commitments, the majority of small business owners I work with avoid networking all together because they find it so uncomfortable. Most of them imagine a room filled with 300 strangers sipping cocktails and trying to sell them something. Effective networking is not that. As a matter of fact, networking comes in many sizes and styles. The large event is one of them but there are also smaller gatherings of like professionals and peer group meetings (paid and unpaid), professional organizations, one-on-one coffee meet-ups and more. Find what works for you and do it consistently. Commit the time to get to know others that frequent these events. The more people you know the more comfortable you will be.

DO IT!

Review your calendar for the past months. Did you participate in networking events or activities? What was the return on the investment of time and money? Now, make choices on how you will spend your valuable time based on your findings.

DO IT!

Decide how many hours of networking it takes to create one new client. Put networking on your calendar as an appointment. Keep your appointments.

COACH'S CHALLENGE

Never attend an event without your business cards. Always practice your introduction ("elevator pitch") before you attend and make it specific to that event. Set a goal(s) for every event you attend. Meet at least one new person that can benefit you or your clients. Follow-up and follow-through.

Develop Partnerships

Every small business owner needs partnerships. They save time, energy, and effort in finding, vetting, and adding new clients. They will provide the resources necessary to conduct your business in a more efficient and cost-effective manner. Finding and forming strategic partnerships is the single best way to extend your reach, attain your goals faster, and realize your vision. Dedicating a portion of your time to developing partnerships with the right persons or organizations is time well spent.

There are two types of partnerships — *strategic and referral.* You should have both. Both will help you to build your business, but they are different in the way you develop them and maintain them. I recommend that you have between three and 10 total partnerships. You can decide how many of each will work best for you. The magic number is the one that will send you the amount of business you can manage without pushing you over capacity.

Referral partners are individuals or other companies or practices who refer clients to you to serve that client's need but are not necessarily a business or individual that you can regularly refer others to. Referral partners can also be satisfied clients that want to share their experience with others who may need your product or service.

Strategic Partners

As you learned in the "Plan It" section of this book, a strategic partnership or strategic alliance is a long-term relationship with another business owner who shares your target client and target market and with whom you can partner for mutual benefit. The relationship should have sustainable benefits that make sense for both parties. This is a relationship that will immediately expand the network of potential clients for each partner and therefore, should reduce your marketing costs as well as reduce the time spent networking and promoting yourself or your business. Often partners will work together to set goals and share projects which will benefit them both. Strategic partners make great accountability partners.

The full benefit from this type of partnership begins with the selection of the partner. This process takes time and devotion from both parties. Not just anyone will do. Start slowly. Test each other. Be sure you have the right partner before you start to promote them. You might think of this process as similar to finding a mate for life. Start with "attraction," followed by "dating," then "go steady," before you "get engaged" and then "marry for life." Choose wisely to realize the greatest value now and in the future.

Who makes a good strategic partner?

Effective strategic partnerships are not based on personal chemistry or common interests — though these are important factors to consider and often make the relationship more enjoyable.

There are, however, two critically important factors which are absolutely essential in an effective strategic partnership: both parties must serve the same or a complimentary target client; and they must have the same business ethics and values. A well matched partner may offer a complimentary product or service to your target client or they may offer the same product to a different client or different geography. For example, if you are a financial services consultant with a specialty of working with young families, you might look for insurance agents or agencies who serve the same client, or you might also look for other financial services consultants who serve "ready to retire" clients. Both can refer business to you and you can refer business to them. Another example is a remodeler in the construction industry who specializes in kitchen and bathroom remodels in the metropolitan area. They might find partners in electricians, plumbers, interior designers or cabinet makers who serve the same market. Or, they might look for remodelers who cover markets outside their service area.

Best matched partners are most often of similar size, serve the same or complimentary geography, have equal education and training backgrounds, are members of the same professional organizations, have similar business strategies, are in similar growth patterns, and have a similar customer service strategy or guarantee. They are also dedicated to the service delivery and quality of work.

As you begin your search you might ask these questions:

- What service or product does your business provide?

- Who is your target client?
- Who else provides a service or product to the same client that does not compete with me?

You might also return to Step Two of Plan It!, *Examine Your Partnerships* on page 124 and review the diagram. Create a diagram like this for your business.

Where do you find strategic partners?

Very often, you will meet your potential strategic partners through satisfied clients. These clients may have recommended you to each other or you may have worked together for that client. In either case this client will endorse your work quality, creditability, service delivery and reliability.

Vendors are another great resource. Vendors serve a wide range of clients. They are helpful in finding another small business that serves a similar market but does not want to serve yours. For example, you own a massage therapy practice which specializes in on-site sports massage. You might work with your laundry service to find another massage therapy professional who specializes in home visits or in maternity care.

Another way to connect with potential strategic partners is to attend networking events or trade organization events where they are likely to participate. If you are a Certified Public Accountant you might find bookkeeping professionals, payroll specialists or financial planners at one of your professional events.

Finally, do what their potential clients do and search for them online. Look for those that have high ratings and reviews. These review sites are not just for potential clients. Reviews and testimonials online are a great way for you to screen and vet potential strategic partners. By seeing what their clients have had to say about them you can decide if they are a good match for you as a partner. Review their social media community sites (Facebook, Google+, LinkedIn, etc.) to learn more about their "personality." What news do they think is important? Who do they endorse? How large is their community (followers, likes, etc.)?

As a rule, the more you trust the referral source, the shorter your period of vetting the partner will be.

Synergy Breeds Success

Selecting strategic partners is a process of matching more than just a target client. It is imperative that you also have a match in values, beliefs, ethics, personality, quality standards, and customer services standards to name a few.

You may already know business owners with whom you share a connection or likely referral network. In other words, you share some of the same kinds of clients who provide an obvious and mutual benefit for working together. But even more important than those obvious connections is the question of synergy. Sharing the same client is one thing, but do you share the same ethical values and commitment to best practices? Do you share the same standard of conduct? Do you share common goals? How do you match in personality? Until you can answer all of these questions keep your working relationship with a potential partner casual and cautious.

The Magic Number

What is the right number of strategic partners? How many is too many? Simply put, there is no perfect number and, as long as they are managed properly you cannot have too many. Earlier I mentioned that you should have between three and ten total partnerships — strategic and referral — and that the number should depend on your needs, the partner's ability to refer business to you and capacity. If you must have a number to strive for, I would suggest you work towards five. Find five partners and develop them into partnerships that are active and healthy and that contribute a meaningful percentage of revenue to your business each year (the percentage is up to you). Emphasis is on "active and healthy."

Active and Healthy Partnerships

For a strategic partnership to be effective long term, each partner should have a solid understanding of the other's goals and objectives and be willing and able to wholeheartedly support them. The best and most effective strategic partnerships merge the personal credibility of each partner with the goals of each company and the resources to make things happen. Both parties in this partnership should be committed to the success and best interest of the other party in every referral. They should make it their practice to find ways to introduce their partners and promote them at every opportunity. These are healthy partnerships.

You can have a healthy relationship with a partner but if you never realize any gains in revenue or profit from the relationship it is not "active."

"Active" relationships are those that have a regular flow of referrals. The nature of your business will dictate the number. A regular flow may be as many as a few a week to one per quarter. Set goals together on how many referrals each can expect to get from the other. Track them. If you do not see the number that was promised, discuss it. Avoid relationships that send referrals to you sporadically and randomly and then demand that you rearrange your workflow, schedule, or capacity model to accommodate them.

Know what is expected of you

As small business owners, most of us are intensely passionate about our businesses. We have a vision of where we want to go, and we do not want to compromise our values to get there. Therefore, we must approach the process of selecting a strategic partner with cautious optimism. Not everyone will be the right fit. In fact, the majority of people whom you meet will not become a strategic partner. Sometimes this is because they want you to compromise on your product, your service, or your price to serve their client. Before you commit to being a partner know what they expect of you in all aspects of serving the referral they send you. Any partner that does not respect your mission, vision or values is not a good choice.

Partner actions will reflect on you

When you refer a client to a strategic partner it is important to realize your client interprets this as a recommendation. They expect to get the same level of service you offer and provide for them. Since this is true it is important to be clear with any referrals you may give before you have had enough experience with the partnership to be certain they will "deliver." You are in danger of damaging the relationship you have with your client and your partner if you take this trial period too lightly. That happened to my client Anne.

Anne is an organizational development consultant. She specializes in working in the construction industry and had a long-term relationship with a client who specialized in demolition for commercial projects. When this client asked for a recommendation for a business attorney, Anne gave them the name of someone she had known only a few months. The relationship she had been developing with the attorney was going well. They had synergy in their businesses and liked each other. They had done a couple of small projects together and those had been successful. Both knew the fee structures of the other and, while they never quoted a price, Anne felt comfortable giving a price range to her client for the work and project they planned to do with the attorney. The attorney was expanding her business and was looking for larger projects. The project Anne's client was shopping for was perfect. Anne shared the contact information with her client who, transferring the trust he had with Anne, immediately hired the attorney and made assumptions about the cost.

The contract was signed with a clause that allowed for additional charges outside the scope of estimated hours. The client, again trusting that Anne would only recommend someone that was as expert in their field as she was in hers, was pleased with the estimate and proceeded with the work. At the halfway point in the project invoices started to arrive at Anne's client's office for "charges outside scope of contract." Final costs were more than double the original contract estimate and far exceeded the estimate Anne had shared with her client. Anne's client blamed Anne for recommending a business attorney that did not have enough experience in the project size to properly estimate costs. Relationships between all parties were permanently damaged. What went wrong? How could that have been avoided?

That first mistake was recommending someone without knowing whether she was capable of the scope of work. The second was not telling the client that her relationship with the attorney was new and while she had delivered just as promised on other projects she was not sure what to expect in this situation. Anne could have suggested more research or work samples. Lastly, never, ever quote price for anyone else even if they are a partner. Sharing a range or giving out published, dated, price sheets can be acceptable but to be safe remind your client this is the latest information you have and they will want to confirm it before engaging in an arrangement.

You do have to start somewhere. Partnership relationships are formed one referral and one project at a time. Begin with caution and follow-up with anyone you refer for feedback on their experience.

Start, Familiarize, Commit, Plan, Measure

As in any successful personal or professional partnership, the need for mutual commitment toward continued improvement never ends. Once you find the right partner, the real work has just begun. Here are a few steps to keep in mind as you enter into a strategic partnership relationship.

1. Take time to get to know each other well before you decide to recommend each other.

2. Work together for a while before you decide to

endorse each other's work.

3. Formalize your commitment to each other. Be clear on your expectations of the other and be sure they are clear on yours. Share your goals for working together.

4. Be in regular communication. Offer feedback and share ideas.

5. Plan together. Once you are certain of your desire to have a long term relationship and you are comfortable with endorsing each other's work, then begin to plan together. Annual planning is a minimum.

6. Measure results and adjust.

7. If the relationship is not what you expected it to be — terminate it immediately. There are plenty of potential partners out there. Use your time and resources wisely and protect your reputation.

Remember, these are long and committed relationships. Do not enter them lightly. Once they are developed, be sure you evaluate them regularly and work together to grow and improve.

DO IT!

Identify one to five new potential strategic partners. Assess the value they could bring to your business and that you could bring to theirs. Contact them. Set up an appointment to discuss a potential partnership. Record a date to review your relationships (your next planning period is a great choice).

COACH'S ADVICE

Caution, caution, caution. Be sure you do not tie your reputation to the wrong partner. Take time to do research, get referrals, check for online reviews, confirm licenses, and introduce partners to your clients with a disclaimer until you are certain they are the right partner for you.

Referrals and Referral Partners

If strategic partnerships are the single best way to extend your reach then referral partners are the single best way to quickly build loyalty with new clients. For this reason, they are among the most valuable resources for your business. They deliver — at no cost to you — clients who already trust you. They cut your sales cycle dramatically and reduce your overall marketing costs. A referral partner does not expect anything in return. They are just sharing a resource with someone they have a relationship with.

In most cases, referral partners have had a positive experience with your products or services and they trust you and your team. Generally, clients obtained in this manner will be more profitable and more loyal. They will buy sooner and stay longer.

Often referral partners are satisfied clients who simply want to help a friend or family member by sharing the experience they have had. You might ask a friend for a recommendation on a hairdresser, massage therapist, a dentist or a doctor. As a potential client, you trust them because your friend has had a good relationship. Similarly, business owners may want to help a colleague or a client by sharing your service or products if they fill a need or gap they cannot fill for their client or your product or service is a compliment to the product or service they offer. An example would be a couple's counselor who might recommend a colleague that specializes in grief or loss therapy when their client's parent dies. The motivation for the referrals from a personal source or business source may differ, but the result is the same. Referral partners drive business to you and are advocates for you and your business.

Create Tracking Systems

Often business owners have referral partners and are not aware they do. This could be you if you are not tracking where your business is coming from. If you do not currently have a referral tracking system it is recommended you develop one. It does not have to be elaborate but should provide information which will assist you in identifying the origins of your business and in tracking how and when you acknowledge the referral. Plenty of tracking software is available for a wide range of prices. For some, a simple spreadsheet or list will do. Use the one which is right for you and your organization. The tracking systems should be simple to use and kept current. It should be reviewed regularly, no less than quarterly, and the results should be used in a follow-up system.

Every new client should be asked how they learned about you. This information should be cataloged, sorted, reviewed and utilized in identifying how the new client found their way to you.

Once you identify those sources a pattern will start to emerge. You will find business comes from a variety of sources, some random and others from very specific individuals or other sources who repeatedly refer you to friends, family, business associates, clients and others. Those who send you multiple referrals should be considered potential referral partners.

Some business owners are in favor of a tracking system but inconsistent in asking clients how they found them. This feels intrusive to some business owners. Often they do not like being asked these questions and transfer their feelings on to their clients. If gathering information from your client is a challenge for you then you might want to take advice from Jill.

ADVICE FROM YOUR PEERS

Jill is an internal medicine physician that owns her own clinic. She was spending hundreds of dollars per month on magazine advertising to attract new patients. In her own words, "We discussed tracking referrals in a regular staff meeting but then I never asked for reports or reviewed statistics until my coach asked for a report. I was shocked to learn that I had not gotten even one new patient as a result of the magazine advertising. I was also shocked to learn that sixty-five percent of my new patients were coming from client referrals and thirty-three percent were coming from one client who also was a personal fitness trainer. Imagine my embarrassment that I had never acknowledged those referrals and my relief that I could cut thousands of dollars in advertising expense by canceling the magazine ad campaign."

Who makes a good referral partner?

The first rule for developing referral partnerships is to consistently deliver what you promise with the right level of customer attention and service. Delivering the right experience or product is imperative to developing loyal clients, building partnerships and to the overall success of your company. W. Edwards Eming put it best in saying, "Profit in business comes from repeat customers; customers that boast about your product and service, and that bring friends with them."

Some referral partnerships develop on their own. These are typically satisfied clients who have had the right experience with you, your products, your services, or your team and just want to pass it along to others. If they are individuals, they are typically "connectors" that have a reputation as being someone who always "knows someone" for almost any need. These partners might also be business acquaintances or members of your professional network who know you and your offering(s) well and trust that referring you to their clients will help them to build their own relationships and/or their business.

The Magic Number

Just like with strategic partners there is no magic number. Typically, referral partners are sending fewer regular referrals than strategic partners and therefore will not strain your capacity. You should base your referral partner target number on the number of relationships you can effectively manage. How many relationships can you acknowledge, foster and develop? How much time will it take for each? If your referrals are coming from satisfied clients a simple thank you note is often good enough. If they originate with another business owner it may take more time and attention to keep the relationships healthy and continue the flow of referrals. A regular meeting with business referral partners is common in which you will thank them for the referrals, ask for any feedback they are receiving, and explore ways to deepen the relationship.

Where do you find referral partners?

If you are searching for new referral partners, which I hope you are, there are a few common places to find them including:

<u>Identify competitors with a full practice or business</u>. Some of your competitors may not be taking on new clients either temporarily or permanently. Find a few you can build relationships with and agree you will help each other by referring business when either of you reaches capacity. The best way to identify these sources is in professional organizations you both belong to (another good reason to be a member of a professional organization). Caution, this situation often results in a discussion around compensation or referral fees. Be sure you know your industry, and state and federal requirements if you decide to pursue or pay compensation for referrals.

<u>Identify professionals or businesses who prescribe or recommend your products or services to their clients</u>. This may seem like a strategic partner candidate and in some cases it may be, but most often this is a referral partner. For example, you may own a bakery which specializes in gluten-free products. A referral partner may be a nutritionist or a naturopathic doctor or other medical

professional that prescribes a diet change which includes eliminating gluten from a client's diet. It is not likely you will have a customer looking to you to refer them to the dietary prescriber because they think they may have a gluten allergy. By the time they reach you they have already had a diagnosis. It is more likely the prescribing professional will be offering resources for a patient/client for which they are recommending the dietary change. The same might be true if you provide energy efficient products. Find designers, contractors or energy companies that will refer you and your business to their clients.

Join a referral group of members who are also looking for new referral partners and are willing to make a commitment to get to know you and your services and share them with their network. They will ask you to do the same. There are a number of these groups in every major city in many countries. Search online for the options in your area and then visit the group. In most cases these groups allow you to visit several times before you have to commit to membership. Take your time and make sure the group is a good fit for your business and your personality before you join. Remember, the group members are not always potential clients. In many cases they are new businesses with limited budgets. It is their network you are interested in. Who do they know? Who do they work with? Who could they refer you to?

Identify businesses that serve your client in other states, particularly if they are in close proximity. I live in Portland, Oregon. Vancouver, Washington is just over the river. I have clients that get referrals or give referrals across state lines if they are not licensed in those states — therapists, attorneys, contractors and many more must have a state license to operate. In this particular example these may also be potential strategic partners if you refer business reciprocally, but serving as a resource for their client is often all that is needed. To develop these you can start by networking across state lines or you can meet these resources at conferences.

Identify clients who have sent you regular high quality referrals. Acknowledge how important they are to you and reward them for their referrals.

Appropriate Thanks

Identifying your current or potential partners is just the first step. To have the best results from these relationships you must get involved with them. At the very least you should acknowledge the referral, and thank the referring party. Not just once, but every time. If there is a large flow of business a thank you at regular intervals is appropriate. This acknowledgement does not have to be a grand gesture. Sometimes the simplest acknowledgements are the most impactful. I recommend to my clients they do the unexpected. If your client expects an email, send a handwritten note. If they expect a phone call, send a bouquet of flowers or basket of fruit. Whatever you choose, make sure it is something they value. Not everyone wants a dining gift card or game tickets. (More information on this subject is in the later section on Client Retention and Management).

DO IT!

Identify one to five new potential referral partners. Define the value they could bring to your business and how having you as a resource might benefit them. Contact them. Set up an appointment to discuss a potential partnership. Record a date to review your relationships (next planning period is a great choice).

COACH'S ADVICE

Be sure you are not violating any rules, ethics, or regulations that govern your occupation or license.

Products, Services, and Packages

Deciding on the products or services you will offer in your business may be the easiest part of business ownership. Why? Because most small business owners start their business with talent, knowledge, experience, passion, skill, ability, or a design to create something they believe other people will pay for. Those are your products or services. Still, no matter what you started with or how you are performing in your market today, it is important that you make it a practice to constantly review, update, add, or eliminate products and services as they serve your business goals best. Times and needs change. So should what you have to offer.

Research and Development

You may think that "R&D" is only for big business. Not so. You too should engage in a regular practice of researching your market, your competition, and your clients' needs—then developing new products, services or enhancements to your current offering to keep them fresh and up-to-date.

As Heraclitus said, "The only thing that is constant is change." Because this is a fact of life, it means that whatever works today may not work tomorrow. To maintain steady business growth and security it is important you stay ahead of the "change curve".

A regular practice of market and competitive research and analysis will give you most of the information you need to serve your target clients well into the future.

1. Survey your clients

Recently I worked with Bob and Carol on the expansion of their landscaping business. They knew they had a very limited offering of services which included mowing and trimming. They were baffled about what services they should add and what should be added first. They were considering everything from landscape design to gutter cleaning. The more they talked about it the more confused they became. They brought the problem to one of our sessions and we discussed how they might proceed.

First, they needed to know what their current clients wanted. They decided a simple survey could help them to gather that information. They decided to contact each client personally to ask a series of questions which would help them understand the products and services the client valued most and those that they would purchase if they were available. The survey was short and simple. They used the contact as an opportunity to tell each customer how much they appreciated their business.

Bob and Carol got great feedback. They discovered that 85 percent of their clients rated the relationship an eight or better on a scale of one to ten. The majority were happy with the services they offered and the way they offered them. They learned that 100 percent of their clients were very pleased they had taken the time to get their opinion. Several offered a few ideas for new services they would be willing to pay for.

As a bonus, Bob and Carol asked for and got seven new "excellent" online reviews.

Bob and Carol marked their calendar to do another survey the same time the following next year. They believe, and I agree, that making a client survey an annual event is both a part of research and development and also a good client retention and marketing strategy.

This type of annual survey is great if you have clients with regular, reoccurring services. If not, you may want to survey your clients when they purchase your products or services. Develop a few questions which can be asked at the time of purchase to gain valuable information about why they do business with you and what it would take for them to do more business with you.

COACH'S EXAMPLE

Questions Bob and Carol asked their clients:
What products or services are most important to you?
What services to you want that we do not offer?
If we added the services you want would you be willing to add them to your plan?
On a scale of 1-10 how well are we serving your needs?
What could we do to get a 10 rating?
What do you value most about our relationship?

2. Research Your Competitors

Bob and Carol also needed to know what members of their target client group wanted but went elsewhere for because Bob and Carol didn't offer them. These were clients they felt they were not currently attracting, or they had lost to their competitors. They could identify a few reasons why they thought they didn't have these clients (i.e. loyal relationships to someone else, not having been introduced yet, lured away with a low start price, etc.), but they expected that one of the main reasons people might not be engaging their services was a gap in the service offering. Knowing they could not be all things to all people they decided to do some research on how their competitors were servicing some of these clients. Then, they could determine what additional services they might offer, and what they could expect in return for those additions.

The research started with their friendly competitors. Bob and Carol, like most small business owners, know others that are in their field. Over time they have agreed that there is enough business to go around and they share information to make business easier for all of them. The intent was certainly not to take clients from these businesses but to understand how they served a similar client and to get some new ideas of their own.

Gathering information from true competitors was a bit more difficult. Bob and Carol used a variety of approaches to gather the information they needed including:

- Calling with direct questions
- Acting as a potential new client
- Reviewing websites and online review information

They could have continued their research by hiring consultants, survey companies, secret shoppers, etc., but both Bob and Carol felt like the value of the information was not a good return for the cost of those types of services.

3. Contact Previous Clients

Like many other small business owners, Bob and Carol wanted to know why they had lost a few clients they really enjoyed working with. They knew they should have asked more questions when the clients left their service but also felt like they might be more willing to share now that a little time had passed.

They made a list, conducted the calls, and were surprised at how open past clients were about sharing their reason for making a change. The reasons ranged from change in their budget to the need for services that Bob and Carol did not offer. The information on services was particularly helpful and was included in their evaluation on product expansion.

Adding Products or Services

Once Bob and Carol had all the information they needed from their research they evaluated:

- Which products or services did the market want most?

- Which products or services would be the easiest to add?

- Which products or services should result in the most additional revenue?
- What costs would be associated with adding each product or service?

Bob and Carol handled their research and development process perfectly for their business. You might want to follow their lead on some of the same practices or use new or different ways to gather information. No matter how you approach it, you will want to follow a similar pattern of:

- Evaluating what your current clients need and want.
- Identifying what others are offering to your target market that you are not.
- Identifying why clients stop working with you.
- Determining which products or services you want to add to attract your target client and increase your revenue.

DO IT!

Prepare and conduct surveys with your clients if you have not done so in the past 12 months. Do a competitive review if you did not complete one as a part of your planning.

COACH'S ADVICE

Business size does not matter. Research and development is a must. Make sure you have a regular practice of gathering information that will help you to retain clients, sustain your business and prepare for the future.

Bundled Packages

You may have decided to add products or services or just keep what you have for now. No matter what you decide, the next step in following through with a product or service package strategy is to determine what might be bundled together to improve efficiency, sales and revenue.

To be most effective, bundled products or services should be designed to benefit both the client and the business owner. No matter what products or services you are offering the advantages typically follow a similar pattern:

The client gets:

- A discount for buying a number of products or services at one time.
- Reduced processing time (payment, ordering, etc.).

- May get a feeling of status if the packages are designed in levels (example: Silver, Gold, Platinum).

- Enjoy the same things they would have purchased separately at a reduced expense.

The owner gets:

- Assurance of a longer relationship with a client.

- Consistency in income and cash flow (such as a retainer package spread over a period of time, e.g. monthly for one year).

- Reduced processing costs.

- Valuable information they use to manage inventory or capacity.

If you do not already offer packages of bundled products or services, you will certainly want consider adding them.

Creating bundled packages is simple. Just follow these steps:

1. Make a list of products or services that your clients typically buy together or over a short period of time.

2. Calculate the total value of the package as if you

were charging them for the individual product or service.

3. Discount it by some percentage (10-25 percent is usually enough to motivate a buyer).

There are rules for success in offering these packages. Failing to follow them can actually reduce your revenue or your profit. Be sure you follow them when selling a package.

Rules for Bundled Packages

Package price is due in total, up front. You will be asked if they can pay a portion. The answer has to be "no" or you have defeated the purpose.

Be clear on the refund policy. In most cases there is no refund.

Any refunds are calculated on a percentage basis. The penalty should be no less than the discount. From time to time something will go wrong and you will refund on a package. Just be sure to calculate the percentage discount if refunded.

Price for profit. Be sure you have not discounted so much that you no longer have a profit in the sales. Zero profit x [any amount] is still zero.

DO IT!

Examine all packages. Ask the same questions you asked regarding individual products or services and make changes that align the packages you offer with your specialty and target market or client.

Client Retention

As with friendships, we have clients for a reason, clients for a season and clients for a lifetime. They all have value, but the most consistent value comes from long term loyal or repeat clients. These are clients you "retain" through one project or service and they return for more. They might want more of the same or something different. Monica owns a restaurant. She tells me her clients may come for dinner once, then lunch, then dinner and cocktails. Often they will bring others with them, refer, or even buy gift certificates to give away.

Retained clients are valuable for a variety of reasons including reducing the cost of attaining new clients and the likelihood they will refer you to others.

Retention

The length of time you target for client retention depends on your business, your products and services. It depends on the characteristics of your target client and on the "life" of what you offer. Monica hopes her clients will be loyal customers for as long as she owns the restaurant which she plans to be at least twenty years. A pediatric practice goal might be to have patients stay throughout childhood and into adolescence. In contrast, a weight loss center may have a goal to retain a client throughout their weight loss and up to one year following for maintenance. Every business has different target retention periods. What is yours?

So, what is the right client retention rate (CRR) target? You may think it should be 100 percent, which means you never lose a single client or customer. Reaching that number is both impractical and improbable and would not allow you to choose the clients you may want to eliminate for whatever reason. A strong target is between 85-90 percent.

This number will vary from business to business. The best number is the one which fits your business and your industry. Do your homework. What is the industry standard? What CRR do your competitors have? Finding this information is not always easy. The need for this kind of intelligence is a great reason to be a member of a professional group. They often collect and share this type of information with their membership. You may also find that peer groups are helpful in identifying targets for CRR.

By tracking your CRR you will get an indication of not only how loyal your clients are, but other valuable information such as whether you are delivering on the promises of your product or service quality; the performance of your employees in offering good customer service; and the value of your product or service in the marketplace. More importantly, having a record of these numbers over time will help you to identify when you are not serving the needs of your clients and marketplace. You can then find ways to improve.

Client Retention Strategy

Yes, you should have a strategy for retaining clients. With rising new client acquisition costs it is more important than ever that small businesses actively and intentionally retain clients.

Studies from the U.S. Small Business Administration and the U.S. Chamber of Commerce have found acquiring new customers is more costly than we may have once thought. They report it can cost as much as five to seven times more than retaining an existing client. This is a staggering number. Combined with the fact that customer profitability tends to increase over time, this should be more than enough motivation and incentive to have a well-defined strategy for keeping each and every client that is profitable and meets your target profile

The client retention strategy starts with just giving your client what they expect: the right customer service.

Customer Service

If you notice your customer retention rate is not what you would expect, the first area to examine is customer service. Are you delivering on your promises? Do your clients feel their expectations are being met? Do you show your appreciation for their patronage? If you do not know the answers to these questions, or if you have not surveyed your clients lately, then you may have a customer service issue which is impacting your ability to retain clients.

Research tells us 13-15 percent of clients leave because they are unhappy with a product or service and over 65 percent of all clients who leave do so because they are unhappy with the service they received.

Luckily, customer service statistics can be improved. Here are a few simple tactics that every small business can use to do just that:

- Hire the right people.
- Make customer service a part of your training program.
- Set customer service goals in your performance management process.
- Set clear expectations with clients.
- Set targets for customer satisfaction.
- Reward acts of customer service excellence.

Hiring the right people for your team is critical for so many reasons. The primary one we are interested in here is hiring people who can and will deliver great customer service. Be sure you include customer service questions in the interview process. Consider giving the top candidates a personality test to help you to identify the best match for communicating with—and serving your target client. If you are not sure what those characteristics are, work with a professional counselor or consultant who can interpret the results for you. Consider hiring a human resources professional or recruiter to help you. Look for one that specializes in working with small businesses as they tend to be right for your budget and understand your particular needs.

Once you hire the right staff members *make customer service a part of their training program* during the on-boarding process and continue that training as a part of your ongoing commitment to education. No matter how long someone has been on your staff they can always benefit from a refresher on subjects such as customer service. You can also use training time to solicit feedback from team members on ways you can serve your clients better.

It has been said that you must "inspect" what you "expect" from employees. The best way to do this is to set customer service goals as a part of your performance management program for employees. Then review and give feedback on performance. Some may say this is too structured or too time-consuming a process, but if you do not treat the customer service goals of your company like they are important, no one else will. Anytime you find a staff member is not meeting the goals repeatedly you must take action. Think of it as business "sabotage" and then decide how you will handle it. This may sound like harsh treatment, but allowing any one person to impact your client retention on an ongoing basis is dangerous to the health and long term success of your business.

Tom Peters says, "The formula for success: under promise and over deliver." This is a great start to setting clear customer expectations, but it is not all you should consider. Let clients know what they can expect and when they can expect it. Be sure they understand what it will cost and when and why those costs might change. Finally, be very clear with your clients about what their part of the arrangement is and the consequences should they not keep their agreements or promises.

Set targets for customer satisfaction. Make sure everyone in your organization who contributes to customer service understands the expectations of the customer and does their part to deliver. Once you do this you will need to measure customer satisfaction. Learn how you will do this and follow through. Customer service rating tools are numerous. Make sure you choose one that is simple to use and make it a required part of any transaction. (Example: If you are using a rating card you might have a goal to average a "Good" rating from clients.)

Always reward the behavior you want most. In this case, reward customer service excellence. Recognize employees who give the best customer service. Recognize individuals who are mentioned in reviews or feedback from clients. A monetary reward is not necessary. Everyone likes public recognition (some say even more than money). There are some simple and easy ways to publicly acknowledge a customer service job well done — staff meetings, group emails, celebrations, or reward certificates presented in public are a few ideas.

As you add these practices to your business keep in mind that customer service has both an external and internal component, we have clients we serve and clients we work with — other staff members. Both must be well served for the business to be healthy and happy.

ADVICE FROM YOUR PEERS

"As a pleaser, I wanted to take care of my clients. I tended to promise to deliver on an unrealistic timeline. I then had to follow-up with a note saying the project was delayed only to learn they were not in a big hurry to begin with but were now disappointed that I had set a delivery date and then missed it. I learned to ask for their expectations before I promised something they did not even need and to feed in extra time for mistakes and unforeseen issues. I now have a much more effective process with much lower stress and rarely miss deadlines." Lori Rush, President, Rush Mentoring Services, LLC.

DO IT!

What is your customer satisfaction rate? If you do not know, discover that right away with customer satisfaction surveys. If you do know, add any actions needed to improve or retain your current rating to your to your action plan.

COACH'S CHALLENGE

I challenge you to evaluate every staff member and to rate them on customer service delivery to both the external and the internal customer. Anyone that does not meet your standards must be counseled. If the below standard behavior persists take action.

Client Management System

We have already established that keeping clients is as important, if not more important, as getting new clients. It reduces your cost of client acquisition and the longer they stay, the more valuable these clients become. The longer they stay the more they spend, the more they refer you, and the more valuable feedback they offer you. With this fact in mind, it may surprise you to learn it is very common for small business owners not to have any type of system to manage their client information. They often do not know where their business comes from, including who their clients are, how they found them, what they want and do not want, how to contact them and more.

Others have a system, but they do not use it.

To retain your clients you have to have a fully functional client management system. It should be aimed at meeting the needs of your customers through regular communication and at driving more revenue by keeping your customers engaged and interested in working with you and your business.

Know what you plan to do with your system. Know what it can do. Do not over buy for your needs. Check for "free" resources first — some of the systems you are already using may be capable of meeting the need. Sometimes something as simple as a spreadsheet will do. Be sure it is a system that is simple and efficient.

Once you have a system set up, use it!

Uses for Your Client Management System

Here are some of the uses for a small business client management system:

- Store client information for easy access

- Record referral information — understand how they find you; measure marketing effectiveness; manage partnerships

- Manage prospective client information — increase sales!

- Communicate with clients or subscribers — communicate quickly and easily with all or portions of your client population

- Provide information on client behavior — including amount and number of purchases; type of purchase; timing on purchases; buying influences

- Helps you make decisions on products and services to keep and develop

- Helps you to identify clients who no longer buy from you; retain current clients; address issues that caused them to leave; update and refresh your records

- Protects information from departing employees.

Client Communication

Clients are much like family and friends when it comes to communication. If you do not communicate, they will not know you care. Communication with past, present, and future clients is imperative in generating new clients and retaining those already working with you. Failing to do so will result in losses. Sometimes they just "go away" because they forgot about you, did not remember how to get in touch, or assumed you did not care enough to be in contact. Other times the competition will steal them away if lack of communication causes them to question your interest in meeting their needs. In any case, you do not want to take a chance you will lose a hard-earned client just because you do not stay in touch. By the time you realize it has happened it will probably be too late.

Being consistent is very important. An occasional email, direct mail piece, or a blog share is not communication. It is a random act of information.

Tips on Communication

Here are a few tips on how, when and what to communicate:

- Have a plan and follow through.
- Be consistent and make it a priority.
- Do not overdo it — make sure you are sending enough, but not too much, information
- Do not make assumptions on what they want to know — ask questions and generate communication that responds to the answers you receive
- "Speak" to your "target" client — the language and information you use should be directed at the client you want most
- Focus on your "specialty" when you are promot-

ing products — do not "sell" anything you do not most want people to buy

- Make it simple and easy for them to obtain and retain the information you are providing — keep it short; no complicated packaging

- Tell them you appreciate them — again and again

- Ask for their business — again and again!

- Tell them who to contact anytime they have a question or a problem — again and again (you get the point)

One last tip, tell your target client how to stop receiving your information if they do not want it. You do not want to become a nuisance. Most people are overloaded with information today. I spend a few minutes each morning "unsubscribing" or deleting information I did not order, do not want to receive, or am no longer interested in. I am not alone. Consumers become very disenchanted when the information they are receiving does not meet their needs. There is a fine line between just the right amount and more than is helpful. Respond quickly if you see a pattern of higher than usual unsubscribe messages.

Appreciation or Loyalty Programs

Client appreciation programs or loyalty programs are valuable, but not easy to administer for every business model. They may or may not work for you and your business, but you should consider them to be certain you are not missing an opportunity.

Building on the 80/20 rule, client loyalty programs are designed to take advantage of that small percentage of your clients that represent most of your business. The objective is to reward their loyalty by offering them something they value. This usually comes in the form of a discount card, a "punch" card, loyalty number/code/scan giving you a free item when certain amount is purchased, or a status level (silver, gold, platinum) that offers you additional or discounted services (airlines are great at this — love that fast lane!).

If one of these programs is a good fit for you and your business then you might ask, "Why give something away?" There are a number of reasons starting with a loyalty program encourages repeat business. When people have options to choose from, sometimes the mere knowledge they may earn a reward from a particular retailer is enough to influence their choice.

If properly managed and utilized this type of program provides valuable information about your clients and their buying habits. You can collect information from the members of your loyalty program to learn more about who buys from you and why, where they live, and depending on the questions, who else they buy from, what they value, etc.

A loyalty program can serve as low-cost advertising. If customers see your name on a membership card whenever they open their wallet or on an email when they check their inbox, you are taking advantage of low-cost advertising.

If you decide to add a loyalty program then here are suggestions on how to make it work best for you and your business.

Loyalty Program Setup and Operation

Have an opt-in option. If you want high participation in your program, let people opt-in. On your website or at your cash register, give customers the opportunity to join your loyalty program. Let them agree to receive regular or occasional special offers from your business.

Keep track of email addresses with your client management system. Add them immediately after they agree to join.

Keep it elite. If you want to limit participation to those customers who spend the most, you could consider offering invitations to a select few.

Issue membership cards or numbers. Create a real or virtual membership card that customers can use to track their purchases and earn discounts. Membership cards can be a major influence on buying behavior but customers need to know where they are in the earning process.

Communicate regularly. Set up a schedule and communicate regularly with loyalty program members so they feel like they are part of an elite group and are reminded to participate. These emails (or texts) can be filled with useful content, descriptions of new products and special offers.

Reward Structure

The rewards for your loyalty program can be structured in dozens of ways. The program should be one that is easy to track and simple to sustain for a long period of time. Here are a few options for you to consider:

Buy x, get one free. This is the method used by coffee companies, fast food establishments, bakeries, etc. and gives the member a free item once they have paid for a predetermined number.

Discounts. This option is a good choice for a service-based business. It offers a discount on future orders to customers who spend above a certain amount. For example, award a 10 percent-off coupon for every $100 the customer spends on a single order or day.

Memberships or clubs. Most supermarkets offer a club-style rewards program, which tracks their purchases and permits certain advertised deals only to those who are a member. This method may work well for businesses that are keen on targeted advertising.

Pay upfront discount. Small business owners can offer their regular customers an incentive to pay ahead. This can also help with cash flow management.

DO IT!

If a loyalty program will work for you, decide how you will structure and manage it. Set dates for a launch and design a marketing campaign that will attract the clients you want to participate in the program.

COACH'S ADVICE

A loyalty program is easy to implement and difficult to terminate. Be sure you are prepared to support a program for a long period of time. If you are not sure, you might try offering a short term "special" to test the results.

Marketing

After years of working with hundreds of small business owners, I have concluded most small business owners secretly hope to eliminate marketing and have their target client magically find them.

Why is there so much resistance? Well, the reasons range from marketing is expensive to creating the right message is daunting.

Many claim they are not creative enough to develop marketing messages or confident enough to deliver them.

An overwhelming percentage say they simply do not have time for either. The bottom line is, marketing is critical to business success. The sooner you accept that it is an integral part of building a business the sooner you will see the results you want and have the opportunity to enjoy the benefits.

You do have choices in the way you execute this strategy. You can do it yourself or you can pay others to do it for you. Whatever you decide, do not wait for your ship to come in—swim out to it. Tell your story. Give the world what it wants—a compelling reason to buy—whether that be you, your products or your services.

Low Cost or No Cost Marketing

If you are a small business owner just getting started you may ask "What is most important?" and "What will fit into my budget?" There are always a few marketing practices even the most meager of budgets can, and should afford. Here are some suggestions:

Business cards: While the business card may seem like an "old school" marketing tool it is still valuable and cheap. Get them early and share them generously. Set goals for passing them out. Make notes on them making them more psychologically more difficult for the receiver to throw away. Use them as a "leave behind" (with notes of course) on any potential client you drop in on.

There are plenty of low-cost printing options on the internet. Many provide templates that can serve you well in the early days. Never go anywhere without them.

Website: Most people today (some say 90 percent up from just 65 percent only a few years ago) start their search for everything on the internet. If this is true, then a website is a must. Not only can it drive new business your way but it gives you credibility. A website does not have to be a bank breaking investment. If you are even a bit creative you can do it yourself with free or low-cost tools such as Wix, Weebly, Fat Cow or the many more that pop up daily. You can also find a number of very talented web designers/developers in every price range. Do your research. Look at their portfolio. Have clear agreements to protect yourself and be sure it will serve your needs without additional expense.

Online review sites: Most online review sites are free. Which ones are popular in your market? The internet provides all business owners with an equal and unique opportunity to learn from the experiences of their competitors' past clients without ever having met them. Consumers have always had a powerful influence on the decision of others to select a particular business or provider, but a singular voice now touches millions. All they have to do to share their story is to find the business on the internet at one of the many sites that allow reviews, recommendations or customer comments and they can help you get your next client or steer them away. Generally available to everyone are those found on Google, Facebook, Yelp and LinkedIn but there are new general review sites each year. Others are more specific to a trade such as Psychology Today which provides information and listings for mental health professionals or Houzz.com which showcases the products and services of those who build, remodel, design, provide services for homeowners, or those that aspire to be homeowners. Still others are available only to those who are members such as Angie (formerly Angie's List). No matter where the comments are listed you can count on the fact that they are powerful. Recent research shows as many as 87 percent view an online testimonial or review to be as credible as a referral from a friend. Do not miss this opportunity!

<u>Social media</u>: Build a community online. Be sure you have a Facebook professional page (free) and a Google+ page (free) for your business and, if you are in professional services, consider LinkedIn. You might also want a Twitter account or an Instagram, Tumblr or YouTube account. Some of these are free at a basic level and offer additional services and options at low costs that may serve your business well. Once established, keep them active. Post several times per week. Talk to an expert about what makes your page(s) "relevant." Resist the temptation to believe those who say having a social media presence is meaningless (they are out there). We know for a fact po-

tential clients check you out even if they do not "follow" or post comments. They learn about your business brand and personality thorough these platforms.

Speaking and presenting: Look for opportunities to speak, either about your products and services or on a subject important to your target client. Anytime you are the person on stage you have the status of "expert." When you are an expert people want to do business with you. Local service organizations are always looking for someone to fill their programs. Occasionally you will even be offered a fee. But be willing to do it for no charge if the room is at least half full of potential clients and you are allowed to market your services to them, including a follow-up email or onsite marketing materials, or both. Always make follow-up a priority.

Referral groups: These were mentioned previously as a way for you to build referral partners. Early in my business I was a member of a referral group and found them to be valuable then — and now. I am still in touch with many of the members of that group and often refer my start-up clients to them.

Many small business owners can benefit from joining a referral group. This group typically meets once a week and is comprised of 20-50 representatives from many business types. Most of them are owners. Each group allows only one member from each occupation so you have little or no competition. The objective is for all members to support each other in growing their business. There is a price for membership. To know if it is right for you, identify what a new client is worth and decide how many you might realize from being a member of this type of group. Be patient. It typically takes six to nine months to realize any real gain.

Strategic partnerships: A few of these can increase your business immediately. As mentioned earlier, these are partnerships with other businesses that share your target client but do not compete with you. In general you serve the same client and often at the same time. Be careful who you choose. Remember, your client assumes you are recommending them and guaranteeing the service they expect to receive. Try a few test projects and be sure that is what is happening. If the project goes well, proceed with caution until you know you can trust each other.

I have implied the marketing tactics above are at little or no cost to you. Before I close I want to remind you there is always some cost. You and your time are the cost. What is an hour of your time worth? Before you decide you cannot afford to outsource be certain this is the best use of your time as a small business owner. If you find outsourcing is best for you, hire the resources for a reasonable wage, temporarily or on contract. Find someone who has experience but fits into your budget. If you are not sure about any of this, invest in a meeting with a business consultant that specializes in start-ups and ask for advice.

ADVICE FROM YOUR PEERS

"The magic of marketing is content, contact and consistency. Sadly, many business leaders get wrapped up in the content and miss two-thirds of the equation. Your content doesn't have to be a 12 page white paper. A singular, 350 word newsletter each month is fine. Just get started. Marketing is like a muscle: you must use it to build it."
Sheri Fitts, Founder, Sheri Fitts & Co.

DO IT!

Examine the suggestions above. All small business owners, start-ups or well established, can benefit from making some or all of these a part of their marketing strategy. Add any that you feel will contribute to reaching your vision.

COACH'S CHALLENGE

Add at least one of the suggestions to your marketing strategy for your plan period. Set goals and track the results.

For Fee Marketing — Priorities and Resources

As mentioned earlier, engaging a full service marketing agency is a luxury most small businesses cannot afford. That does not, however, mean you should try to do it all yourself. Remember, you should always do what you do best. This commitment will bring you more joy and will generate the most success in your business. Delegate or outsource the rest.

Marketing should be a high priority for outsourcing. A good indication you are ready to outsource is when business has reached 70- 80 percent capacity. Typically, at this point you can afford the services and you will need them for your business to grow.

Marketing should also be a high priority for outsourcing if you cannot or will not give it the attention it needs. Marketing is necessary and if you find you do not have the time, knowledge, or desire to be fully engaged in marketing practices then fill the void by hiring others to do it for you. You can start small and stay in your budget.

If you are still struggling with the decision on when to hire, decide what it will take to fit these professional services into your budget. The calculation is simple. Calculate what a client or sale is worth to you and your business in profit. How many of them do you need to cover the cost of a marketing professional? How many new clients or sales can you create if you reclaim the time you typically spend on marketing? Now decide if you are ready.

Once you have made the decision to outsource there are a variety of service providers in every market who support small business. You will find plenty of contract or freelance options in almost every community. Here are a few for you to consider and the benefit for you and your business:

Search engine optimization (SEO): If I only had a few extra dollars in my budget every month I would spend it here. Having the right formula helps potential clients find you on the internet. It is "attraction" type marketing and today it is necessary. All you have to do is set it up and let it work for you, but it is much more difficult than it may seem, and the rules are always changing. Maintaining your optimized position (highest ranking on the search engine or internet page) can be a full-time job. Find a company with experience in your industry and market area; that can give you credible references who will share positive results; who has made investments in cutting edge software which guides their decisions; that fits into your budget without a lot of "add ons;" and that presents you with a clear plan for how they will increase your traffic. Have them begin with an audit of your system. This can give you a good indication as to how you might work together. Most companies offer the audit as a stand-alone service and some even offer it complimentary. If you do not know where to start, start on the internet. Any SEO company worth their fee should be easy to find.

Website and website maintenance: Most small business owners today are well aware they must have a website to look professional and be taken seriously. They know consumers search for information online and they form opinions about whether or not you are credible and can meet their needs before they even make contact. All of this is based on the impression they get from your web presence — the most crucial piece of which is your business website. Investing in a website is just the beginning. Formats go in and out of style. Content gets stale. Pictures look dated. Remember you have one shot at making a good first impression and that impression has to be kept up-to-date. Most small business owners do not have the time or the expertise to keep their website current. Consider hiring someone to do this for you. Often your web designer/developer will offer a longer term maintenance price at a reduced fee. Be clear on what they will be doing for that fee and sign on for only what you need. Avoid hiring anyone with no experience or a friend or relative that likes to "putter" with web development and design as a hobby. As with most things, you get what you pay for. In today's market a web site for small business can cost between $750-$10,000 depending on the designer's experience and more complicated needs such as e-commerce sales. The average cost is around $3,000. A maintenance package should be between $100 and $1500 per month depending on how much ongoing work is required. The average for a small business is $150 to $250 per month. Ask for bids and gain a clear understanding of what value you get for the cost.

Social media: We can debate all day about whether writing is an art, a skill, or a craft, but no matter what you believe, telling your story is a powerful marketing tool. Today your business personality and community can and should be created online with blogs and social media posts. If your business can benefit from communicating with your community, consider outsourcing this part of the marketing process to someone who writes for a living. Create a calendar of writing assignments with them that is consistent with the messaging plan you will be using in all other campaigns. Make sure they focus on your target market and use key concepts and terms which are important to your target client. My campaign focuses on those things important to small business owners such as revenue, profit, hiring employees, motivating employees, designing marketing campaigns, etc. What will you focus on?

Graphic design: Today there are some very low cost providers for graphic design services. While this may be the point where you start, do not stay there long. Resist the temptation to download free or low cost templates. They are available for general use and will not send your unique brand message to your target client. Instead, I recommend you find a freelance resource that fits your budget. Work with them to create graphics for your business card, website, print material, stationery, signs, etc. that are uniquely yours. Be sure to use the information you uncovered in your brand exercise when you are creating logos, color schemes and other elements. Ask to see samples of their work to make sure their creations appeal to you and, if you already have images in mind, that they have created similar images for others.

ADVICE FROM YOUR PEERS

Cameron owns a handy man business. He is a one man business who works in high-end neighborhoods in Seattle. He says, "Outsourcing marketing is the best decision I ever made. I knew from the very beginning that I did not, and maybe even could not, perform those functions. I do not have a creative bone in my body and am not techno savvy. So, I found a freelance marketing company on Craig's List. They were just getting started and were willing to do my marketing for a very reasonable fee. I calculated what an hour of my time was worth and realized I could afford them for eight hours a month and still make a profit if in those eight hours I signed up just one new client. More advice, working with someone that had just started their own business meant they did not have good systems in place. They were still finding what worked. I am sure I spend more hours than should be necessary managing that relationship. If I had it to do over, I would find someone more established that could take more of the burden more quickly."

DO IT!

Identify what you can outsource. Investigate prices. Get recommendations Review your budget and make sure that you can justify the expense.

COACH'S CHALLENGE

Outsourcing may give you a sense that you are losing control. Fight through that. Test some of the outsourcing options that have been recommended for marketing. Control the trial period, but be sure you have given it enough time to work. While you are testing, use the time you reclaim to grow your business, put systems in place, or enjoy the time as leisure.

COACH'S ADVICE

When you outsource, be sure you have clear agreements on what work will be done, when, how, and what the charges will be. Do not sign long-term contracts until you know how you will work together or be certain there is an escape clause. Hire someone you can have a professional relationship with (i.e. avoid friends, relatives, and charity cases).

Buying Influences

To be effective at marketing, we must understand what makes your client "buy." Buying is an emotional response that we justify by identifying a benefit that it has for us.

Think about your last purchase. What was it? Why did you buy it? If you are like most consumers it was because you wanted it. But, to be sure you were making a wise decision; you probably justified it by identifying the benefit that it had for you. You might have decided that it was a wise investment — it "saved" you money. Or, you may have determined that it would help you to "make more money." At the very least you might have admitted you deserved it because it made you "feel better." No matter what you purchased you will have worked through that short purchase justification process. That is the same process every client or customer goes through when choosing to buy anything from you and your business. Knowing that, you will want to determine why your clients buy. What motivates them?

As stated earlier, buying is an emotional response. People buy because they want the product or service and they justify this decision with one of several benefits defined broadly as influences. Here is an example. You drive by the car lot on your way home and see a bright red convertible on the lot. It's the car of your dreams. You can just feel yourself behind the wheel. You had not planned to buy a new car and it would be the most extravagant purchase you ever made. You hesitate. Then you think, a closer look won't hurt. You turn in and look it over. You feel the leather and grip the wheel. The salesperson comes over and offers you the keys for a test drive. A little test drive — why not? It drives like a dream and you know everyone is looking at you with envy. You feel younger, more successful and you begin to think about how you could own this car. You simply must have it! You run down all the reasons why buying this new car will be good for you. It's a popular model so you know it holds its value and will be a good trade in (make money). It is the spring sale and they are offering special financing (save money). The dealership is very close to your house and it will be very easy to bring it in for maintenance (save time). They have offered to take your car on trade and let you drive the new one away today (safe effort or make it easy). The crash rating is very high, and you would feel safe even driving with your children (feel better, security and confidence).

You make an emotional decision and are influenced to say "yes" by several factors. Your clients will do the same thing with your product or service. Marketing should offer them clear motivations that match these influences and stimulate their buying choice. Make it easy for your client to say "yes." Understand what influences their buying decisions and give it to them in all of your marketing materials and messages. Start by knowing the most common influences.

Common Buying Influences

Influence #1: I will save money. This factor is the one most often promoted. "If you buy my product or service, it will save you money." The inference is that you are selling your product or service at a better price than someone else or that owning the product or using the service will save the buyer money. Saving money can be achieved in a variety of ways. Is your product less expensive than others on the market? Is it more cost effective to purchase (i.e. online or in more locations)? Make sure your target client knows exactly how you will save them money.

Influence #2: I will save time. Limited time is one of the most common complaints of people today. The faster we go the more behind we get. Almost everyone is looking for ways to reclaim time or find a shortcut to the same results. Show your target client how you, your product or your service will save them time.

Influence #3: This will make [insert something important to you] easier. Who is not looking for convenience today if for no other reason than it is expected to save them time? It is a sure bet that most of your clients could benefit from anything that will make something that is important to them (process, procedure, task, experience) easier.

Influence #4: This will make me feel [safe, secure, confident, better]. Home alarm companies promote safety. Insurance companies promote security. Undergarment companies and dental brightening agents claim to give more confidence. Personal services and travel companies promise to make you feel better. What about your product or service? What does it have to offer your target client?

Influence #5: It will help me make money. Almost everyone wants to make more money or have more money. If your product will help your target client improve their buying power or increase their earning power be certain that you tell them how.

Once you understand how you or your product or service will influence your target client's buying behavior you will want to make sure you spell it out for them in clear, concise messages in all marketing materials, advertising messages, promotional vehicles, and even introductions and greetings. Give them examples. Testimonials from satisfied clients are powerful.

Their Influences are Not Your Influences

Be sure you do not transfer your own situation, thoughts or buying influences onto your target client and then make choices on how you will market based on how you would react.

It is a simple fact that we sometimes cannot get out of our own way when it comes to marketing and/or selling our products or services. The sum total of all we have become shows up in every part of our small business. One of the most common challenges we create for ourselves is transferring who we are and how we think onto the decisions that our clients will be making about doing business with us.

Recently I was working with the owners of a well-known hair salon that serves clients from luxury communities and accomplished professionals including a number of celebrities. The discussion was around staff stylists and their resistance to promote the sale of hair products.

Not surprisingly this salon sells hair products that are considered the top in the industry. The price of a hairspray may exceed $50.00. The cost for a single product may exceed 50 percent of what the staff stylist will be paid as their percentage for performing a service for that client.

Logically the stylists know their client can afford it, but they often hesitate to offer the products because it is not something the stylist's own budget would allow. Since their income is far less than that of their client and their budget is more limited, they think differently and resist encouraging the client to buy the product even though the client could benefit from its use. This stylist is transferring their own concern about money on to their client and it is costing the stylist commission and the salon owner's revenue on the product sales.

This example plays out several times a month in my office and it seems to be most common with new business owners who are worried about revenue and profit, worried about paying their bills, and believe that everyone has the same life challenges that they do. Remember, your job as a business owner is to make your product available to potential clients at the price you have determined it is worth, and their job is to manage their own budget.

DO IT!

Identify the influencing behavior of your target client then make it easy for them to justify by pointing out the benefits. Example: "Let me save you time and money by..." Review all marketing material (advertisements, brochures, messages, etc.) and marketing vehicles (websites, digital marketing sites, review sites, etc.). Be sure the benefits are clearly defined for your potential clients.

COACH'S CHALLENGE

Review your attitude and your messages. Make sure you are not transferring your influences or feelings to your clients. Do your job. Offer your products and services to potential clients at a fair price. Let them manage their own buying and budget.

Sales

A number of the small business owners I work with have a sales background. Many had the opportunity to be a part of a sales team and worked for organizations that provided formal sales training. This experience gives them an advantage in small business ownership. They know how to promote themselves and their products and services. It comes naturally to them to set goals, network, build strategic relationships and manage their client information. If you have a sales background, great! You can apply those skills to selling your own product or service. If you do not have sales background, do not be dismayed. Sales, and the act of selling, can be learned and there is ample information out there to help you. Some of the best sales people I know religiously followed the process they learned to reach the top of their leader boards. You can do it too.

Make it your business to read, watch, and learn from the many books, videos, and workshops that teach sales techniques and offer tips from experts in the field. If you shop online, look for reviews on the available resources and buy those that have the highest overall reviews. They should teach you sales basics such as:

- Prospecting: The search for potential buyers

- Sales calling: Different types of sales contacts including cold calls, appointments, and telesales

- Closing the sale: Getting a positive "buy" response

- Selling styles: Understanding the various selling styles, including knowing which one suits your situation best and how to use them. They include relationship sales, consultative, collaborative, etc.

- Value creation and value propositions: Relaying the value your product or service will have for a buyer

- Negotiation: Ability to hold a discussion aimed at getting an agreement which suits both parties

- Overcoming objections: Knowing the common objections and ability to overcome them

If you have a sales team you will need a different set of skills and abilities including:

- Goal setting: Setting goals with, and for, your sales team; which contribute to your vision; which are specific, attainable, reasonable, and measurable; with timeframes and review processes

- Motivating: Motivation implies encouraging and urging employees to perform to the best of their capabilities to achieve the desired goals of the organization. Even if they are self-directed, sales professionals will achieve more if they are properly motivated.

- Coaching: Getting the best performance from team members through coaching techniques and supporting them to achieve goals. Give them clear feedback.

- Communicating: Communication is the key to sharing your vision and relaying what role each person has in that vision.

- Influencing: This is the power to affect a person, thing, or course of events and in the case of sales it is your power to guide them to the results you want.

- Rewarding and Recognizing: A very important component for any sales practice. It is most effective when finding out what has value to sales persons and giving them ways to achieve it (time, money, awards, etc.).

Many of these will be discussed in more detail in the Executive Development and Leadership Skills on page

268. All of these skills have been well covered by hundreds of books and videos. Do your homework. The side effect is increased sales, revenue and profit.

Capacity Planning

Just because you can sell does not mean you should always do so. Overselling and exceeding your capacity can get you into big trouble. Over promising or making commitments to deliver on a deadline you cannot meet will result in a loss of trust. It may also lead to poor quality if you rush to complete a project or squeeze in just one more appointment. Your hard-earned business can evaporate if you do not deliver as promised. Dissatisfied clients are like elephants, they have long memories and carry a lot of weight. They will move on but not before they have made a big impression and possibly destruction on everything they pass.

From time to time we will all get ourselves in a jam. Maybe you lose an employee or your equipment breaks down. The next thing you know you are behind schedule with your current business and all future business is being pushed back. Now what do you do? There are some simple tactics to protect your business reputation.

Remember that managing to capacity is a part of managing by the numbers or metrics. As small business owners we have a tendency to say "yes" to everything that comes our way until it is too late and we are in over our heads. Know your capacity and do not take on more than you can manage.

If you find yourself in an overcapacity situation, face it as quickly and as directly as possible. Do not try to hide or catch up if your deadlines are at risk. Communicate the changes with your clients. Tell them what to expect and when.

No small business owner enjoys complaints, but they can be considered "gifts" that help you manage your business. Some say for every one complaint you get you have ten more who did not bother to contact you. Do not ignore any complaints you receive. Address the complaint with empathy and a willingness to find a solution to satisfy both parties. This includes reviews you get online. Post a thoughtful reply and offer to connect live to address the issue.

ADVICE FROM YOUR PEERS

"Devise ways to turn down clients before you actually need to. It feels counter intuitive when starting out, but a time will come when your gut tells you that you need to turn down or walk away from a client. You need to be able to trust your gut and walk away, but it's hard if you don't know what to say." Tara D., Founder, Jenkins Davisson, LLC

DO IT!

(A) Identify what skills you need to sell your products and services and start to develop them. If you manage sales people identify what sales management skills you need to develop.

DO IT!

(B) If you do not know what your capacity is, find out. If you have products this may be a production or shipping capacity. If you offer services this may be a performance capacity. Your business coach or consultant should be able to help you determine capacity.

Recruiting, Staffing, Employee Relations

All successful small business owners reach that crossroad in their business when they have to decide if they want to grow by adding staff, and whether those new hires will be permanent or temporary, full-time or part-time, regular employees or contractors. Growing in this way is exciting. It also adds a layer of complexity the majority of small business owners feel they are ill-equipped to handle. Recruiting is an art. Managing staff is a skill. Both are often underdeveloped when you are ready to hire your first addition. Rejoice if you are in a position to decide whether you need staff — you are among the successful. But, before you hire, learn the basics. Be prepared. Ask for help if you need it. Taking the "learn as I go" approach to recruiting, hiring, onboarding, and managing staff can be costly.

Recruiting

The need to add staff often comes as a surprise. You wake up one day and realize you are out of time and out of energy. You are working every minute of every day that is physically possible and you cannot beg, borrow, purchase, or steal another minute.

You may have taken on more work than you can process or are already behind in delivering on your commitments when it becomes clear you need help. You are now in a position of not having enough resources to keep up with the work you have, nor the time to hire the staff you need. You find yourself in a hurry to find resources.

Rushing to hire can be the beginning of a failed hiring process. It takes time to locate, evaluate, and secure the right addition to your team. Do not rush this process. It will cost you time and money. Unless you are extremely lucky, you will have to endure several rounds of turnover before you slow down to do it right.

Avoid Pitfalls

1. <u>Rushing to fill the need</u>: No matter how much you want the right resource to come quickly it will take the time it takes. Hiring the wrong resource fast will just mean you have to do without the right resources longer.

Mack and Karen own a small manufacturing firm that is on the rise. They needed a new operations manager. They knew having this person on board would offer them an opportunity to grow even faster. Less than a week after posting the open position, they hired the best of the candidates that applied even though she did not have the skills or experience they needed. Two weeks later, they were frustrated. The new hire had to be terminated and the process restarted resulting in additional fees, lost time, and energy. They were lucky. Sometimes it is not so easy to unravel what you have put in place and start again.

2. Waiting too long: Hire when you first see the need, not when it has become critical.

Richard owns an accounting firm. Every year he waits until tax season has already begun to hire the help he knows he will need. He rushes to plug the holes. Every year he is frustrated when the best resources have already been hired and he has to make do with "B" or "C" tax preparer talent — none of whom become permanent team members.

3. Hiring the "possibility:" See the candidate for what they are and only what they are. Do not hire on potential unless you have the time to develop it.

Mark is an optimist. He sees potential everywhere, including people. When he began building his marketing agency he hired creative people he believed he could develop into project managers. He soon learned that just because they wanted to learn project management did not mean they could do the job. His team blossomed as soon as he hired experienced, creative project managers.

4. Hiring for comfort instead of contribution: Dan, like so many other small business owners, started his consulting business on his own expertise. Quickly he needed to add staff. In the beginning he relied heavily on candidates he "liked' and he felt he "connected" with. Disagreements were high from the start and turnover was common. When we analyzed the situation, we realized Dan was hiring himself — over and over. He was hiring his comfort level but not hiring the right skill sets or experiences to fill the gaps. Once he looked for complementary skills his team flourished and client contracts increased.

5. Looking for an "A" player in a "B" pile: Mike always wants the best sales person, but his compensation plan is not competitive. His hope is that he will find a "diamond in the rough," a real "A" player who is only asking for a "B" wage. This is a lose-lose strategy. Even if you are lucky enough to hire someone with more potential than their experience reflects, they will not be happy with an under-market salary for long. In the end, you still have turn over if you cannot retain the right talent.

There are many resources on the subject of hiring and retaining the right employees. The examples above are just a few of those I see recur with my small business clients. As you prepare to hire a team here are a few tips.

Tips for Hiring the Right Match

- Take your time!
- Be clear about what you need.
- Look for the right skills, abilities and experience
- Interview candidates more than once (I recommend a minimum of three interviews — phone, in-person, follow-up in person)
- Get multiple points of view — ask others to interview candidates
- Give them a project to test their skills or an on-the-job interview.
- Make sure they are the right personality fit (consider a personality test)
- Check their references.
- Do a background check.
- Search their "online presence" — Social media sites, professional resources (LinkedIn), name search

ADVICE FROM YOUR PEERS

John and Margo are both CPAs and own an accounting firm which employs ten people. Their business has doubled over the last three years and in that time they hired an office manager that, while very talented, repeatedly gets complaints from clients and staff about her attitude. She does not return phone calls, speaks abruptly, and will argue if challenged on any subject. Even more disconcerting is her consistent lack of follow-through on deadlines and deliverables. Two years of gentle talk and prodding followed. Finally, after an incident that resulted in the loss of their longest client, John and Margo terminated the employee. John now says, "All I could see is that she was brilliant in her technical work. I was aware of a few incidents but felt the good outweighed the bad. I wish I had paid more attention. After her departure we learned that we had lost dozens of clients and that the turnover we had been concerned about was primarily as a result of her management style."

Onboarding

Hiring is just the first step to building a high performance team. Once you've hired new talent, you must then onboard them in such a way that they know what is expected, settle in quickly, perform at their highest level of capability, and become a long term asset for you and your business. Onboarding refers to the way new employees acquire the necessary knowledge, skills, and behaviors to become effective contributors to your business team.

Early in my career I landed a job selling mortgage insurance. I was amazed I was chosen because I had only a minimum of experience in the industry. I was a long shot in a field of otherwise experienced candidates. I have often pondered the question of me as their choice especially considering their onboarding practices.

Knowing little or nothing about sales and not much more about mortgage insurance, I was counting on a lot of instruction and guidance. I was surprised when on my first day of work I was handed the keys to my new company car, a manual of guidelines, a list of current clients, and instructions to "go sell mortgage insurance." I am pleased to report I did figure it out and in a few short years proved myself worthy of the position. However, I have often wondered how much more productive I could have been and how much faster I would have had success if I had been given the right support from the start.

Think of onboarding as your opportunity to get more from your new hires more quickly. The more they know about what you expect of them and how to deliver on those expectations the larger their contribution will be to your business success.

Tips for Onboarding

Remember that this process is just as important as the hiring process. Give it the time and attention it deserves.

1. Give them a tour. Take the time to show them the landscape. Show them where they will work, rest, take breaks, have their lunch, etc.

2. Introduce them to the staff and clients. Some introductions might be done on their first days. Other introductions may take time. To be formally introduced sends the right message to everyone involved. The message is: this person is my choice and I want you to accept them and trust them. If they are working from a remote location be sure they meet all the staff members they will work with, including those who might be in a headquarters or other supporting location.

3. Set clear expectations. Give each new employee a complete job description. List for them exactly what you expect them to do. Tell them when you expect them to have mastered tasks and functions they may not be familiar with. I recommend expectations with timelines. Outline what is expected in 30, 60, 90, 180 and 360 days.

4. Give them resources. As a part of setting expectations be clear on where they go for information, feedback, and training. Always let them know you are open to questions and feedback and who they can go to if you are not available.

5. Give them an employee handbook. This should be a compilation of all the policies and procedures you have adopted for your workplace. These are a great reference source on the first day of hire and months and years into the future. If you do not have an employee handbook, create one or have one created for you. It should include policies on vacation, sick time, dress code, tardiness, breaks, equipment usage, social media practices and more.

6. Ask the employee to share their goals. By doing so you will have a better understanding as to how you can keep them satisfied and retain them as an employee. You are not responsible for meeting all of their career goals, but you may choose to contribute to their success in a way that binds them more closely to you. One of the best ways to do this is to consider paying for all or some portion of training or education. Tell them how they qualify and what you expect from them in return — such as years of service or repayment of tuition if they leave within a predetermined number of years following the contribution.

7. Let them know how they will be measured. Give them an overview of how you conduct your performance management process. If you do not have one develop one. Let them know when they will be reviewed.

8. Set dates for review and stick to them. It is suggested you review progress at the end of the first 90 days and then no less than annually thereafter. For a more compre-

hensive program you should consider reviewing progress quarterly or every six months.

9. Get them on board and up to speed as soon as possible. You will be glad you did and they will be too.

ADVICE FROM YOUR PEERS

"Hire when you first have the notion that you will need the help. It takes time and you do not want to feel rushed. Hold several interview meetings and do not settle for any candidate that does not meet your minimum requirements. Never hire thinking you can "change" them or "grow" them into the employee you want. The right person is out there. Find them and then onboard them with a slow and deliberate process. It takes six months to get them from hired to fully functioning. Anything else is a miracle." Dennis J., Owner, Jordan Mortgage Company

Performance Management

You may think you are too small to have a performance management process. No business is too small. If you have just one employee, you need a performance management process for staff. If you have only yourself, take the time to review your own performance.

Performance management is a systematic process used by employers of all sizes and types to review and measure the effectiveness of individuals in reaching the goals and expectations that have been set for them or by them, and how they contribute to the overall mission of the organization. This process may or may not be formal. It may be verbal or written. It might happen several times a year or just once. It should be what works best for your needs.

For small business owners I recommend something simple but powerful. You want your employees to know that you take this process seriously but do not want it to be too intimidating. The outcome should benefit both the employee and the owner and it should be used as a tool to develop your employees into the most productive, satisfied and loyal employees possible. You can also use performance management as a way to begin the succession planning process. Build a staff for the future one person and one year at a time.

In this process you will evaluate key areas of performance. These will be slightly different for each person. Most employees are measured on technical skills, communication, judgement, relationship building, productivity, customer service, citizenship (respect, compliance with rules, commitment to the mission) and personal development. Depending on the position measure them in areas which are specific to their position. If they manage others add measurements for developing others, management, leadership, etc.

Typical Performance Management Review Process

While it is true you can have a verbal review process, and often owners will do this for new employees in early stages or as a "check-in" type review monthly or quarterly, the most effective reviews are in person and in writing.

1. The employee is given an opportunity to review themselves. Many skip this step, but I always find it to be a great way to start the process. It allows them to think about what they expect and allows you to see where your assessment differs.

2. The employer/owner gives the employee a written review report. Create a standard format (or find one online) and use it consistently.

3. A discussion is held regarding the details of the review. This should be scheduled and uninterrupted.

4. The employee has an opportunity to respond to the review. Give them time to respond, but not too much time. Put a deadline on the response date.

5. Set goals for the new period. This can be done together in your meeting, or you can set goals for them on the review and have them add their personal goals in their review.

You should be prepared for differences of opinion. No person can see themselves as others do. During the review process you may find your employees have quite a different view of how they perform than you do. This is a great opportunity to work toward a common understanding that will benefit you both.

Tips for Effective Performance Management

1. Keep it simple. You will have to live with the program you develop. Develop a simple format and stick with it. There are plenty of templates online to get you started or ask your human resources professional.

2. Have a calendar for reviewing performance and keep the commitment. You can choose to review employees at a regular interval all at the same time (many large organizations do this every December) or on their work anniversary. Using the work anniversary allows you to spread out the process if you have multiple employees to give each of them the time and attention they deserve. Using a single target date allows you to compare employees to each other as well as to their goals. No matter what you decide, set the dates and keep them. Nothing says, "We don't really care," more than missing your performance management commitments.

3. Be honest. Avoid being too tough or too easy in your review process. Neither will serve you well. I like to start by telling the employee what they are about to hear is "my viewpoint of their performance in the most direct manner possible." Then I proceed to use the "sandwich method." I tell them what they did well first, then those things they did not do as well, and finally I let them know

how they contributed positively to the overall mission of the organization and how I plan to reward them.

4. Give examples. For all levels of performance, give the specific examples you used for measuring the performance. Be clear about what they did well and not as well. I recommend you put notes in an employee's file throughout the performance period so you can remember the specifics.

5. Be fair. It is possible that employees well-liked by their reviewer will generally get better marks and a more positive delivery than those that are not. Our emotions have a vote in almost everything we do in life. Be careful to leave yours out of this process.

6. Ask employees to set personal goals. Part of this process should be to allow the employee to set some of their own career goals and, if appropriate, ask for your help in meeting them. The act of asking them to set goals for themselves says you care about what they want from their life and career and are prepared to listen and, if appropriate, support their goals.

7. Avoid tying raises to every review. Often employees expect to get a raise at review time. This may be the time you tell them what their salary increase will be, but I recommend you separate review from salary or compensation change. In small business, employee performance cannot always be rewarded at the level you would like, or they may expect. Your budget must be able to support

the increase. Separating the review and compensation change dates will change the level of expectation they have for getting a "good" raise if they get a "good" review and vice versa. I do reviews on anniversary dates and announce raises (or bonuses) at year end. I let them know I am tying it to their overall performance, and how they can contribute and share in the benefit.

Let me emphasize one more time: performance management is critical to the outcome you can expect from your staff. Make time for it.

Reward Results

Employees should be rewarded for the contributions they make to your success. A salary increase is one form of reward but not the only one.

Rewarding results is an extension of the "token system" used in modifying behavior. When one of your employees does what you want them to do, reward them. If they respond to rewards, which the majority of all people do, they will repeat the behavior that will get them the same or better results so that they can be rewarded again.

Often we think of money (bonus, salary increase, or other monetary compensation) as the only way to reward someone. This is certainly a common reward method but it is not the only one. What is important is to reward the employee in a way they consider valuable. This may or may not be money. Some research indicates that a public "thank you" in the form of an announcement, certificate or recognition statement is more powerful than some sums of money. If you do not know what motivates your employees, find out and then develop the rewards.

Here is some information you may find valuable from Gallup. Notice that money does not appear on the list of what the employees polled considered "core" to their satisfaction.

The Gallup Organization has surveyed numerous industries, organizations and individuals over a period of more than 20 years. Through their survey results they have identified 12 "core elements" or needs of employees that link them to their organization through satisfaction. In short, these elements are what employees "want" and "what motivates" them to maintain their employment with a particular organization.

The 12 Gallup "Core Elements"

1. I know what is expected of me at work.

2. I have the materials and equipment I need to do my work properly.

3. At work, I have the opportunity to do what I do best every day.

4. In the last days I have received recognition or praise for doing good work.

5. My supervisor, or someone at work, seems to care

about me as a person.

6. There is someone at work who encourages my development.

7. At work, my opinion seems to count.

8. The mission/purpose of my company makes me feel my job is important.

9. My coworkers are committed to doing quality work.

10. I have a best friend at work.

11. In the last 6 months, someone at work has talked to me about my progress.

12. This last year, I have had opportunities to learn and grow.

SOURCE: Adapted from First Break All the Rules, p. 28, by M. Buckingham & C. Coffman, 199, New York: Simon & Schuster.

Tips for Rewarding Results

- Match the reward with what the employee feels is valuable

- Reward as soon as possible after the results are complete.

- Reward in public — make it special.
- Combine rewards with a "thank you" for your contribution statement.

Note: If you are rewarding sales results with compensation you need only reward publicly when expectations have been exceeded.

Avoid Rewarding Negative Results

Recently my client Carolyn, an insurance agent, asked for help to sort through a situation with one of her employees. It was performance review time and this employee was expecting a raise. Carolyn had inherited the employee from her predecessor when she retired. The employee, whose attitude grew worse every year only to be matched by her unwillingness to do what was expected of her, was expecting a raise this year just as she had expected and received one every year for the past 15 years. Carolyn, who had gone along with the raise since she took over the agency, had decided it was time to do something other than reward poor performance. The trouble was, this employee was the last connection to some of the older clients and she was afraid that if she did not give her a raise she would quit and not go quietly. To complicate the issue, the older clients were leaving in record numbers and this seasoned employee did not seem to be doing her part to retain them.

As Carolyn was explaining the situation to me she realized she was being held hostage and she did not like the way it felt. She was ready to do whatever necessary to turn the situation around. In translation, she did not plan to reward poor performance with a raise just because she was afraid she might have to replace a few clients.

Reward the results you want and you will get the results you reward. No employee has a right to a pay increase or bonus unless you have promised it to them in a contract. If they are not contributing to your business success in a positive way your best vehicle for sending that message is to give them a less than an average increase or no increase at all. If they did not earn a bonus, do not pay it.

Avoid other types of rewards for the wrong results including public recognition (positive or negative), promotion (to move them out of the way), or special projects (never reward "negative" with "special").

Tips for Managing Poor Performances

- Be direct.
- Address the issue as soon as it is recognized.
- Be sure you deliver your message in person and in private.
- Give them examples of the behavior that created the situation.

- Tell them how they can improve.
- Help them to set goals to return to a positive contribution.
- Set dates and deadlines for improvement.
- Monitor the situation.

If the situation does not improve you will have to decide how long you want to carry a liability. If you do not believe the situation will improve then terminate the employee in accordance with any policies you have set or employment regulations that apply. If you are unsure what is required, seek counsel from your business attorney.

ADVICE FROM YOUR PEERS

Nate is a dentist. He bought his practice from a mentor who had served his small community for over 30 years. As a part of the purchase he agreed to retain the employment of the office manager who had been with the practice for 15 years. In the beginning she was a valuable asset, but as time went on and Nate changed software and practice systems the office manager became a roadblock to progress. He followed all the advice for performance management, but the situation did not improve. Twelve months after we first discussed terminating her Nate gave her notice. Nate's advice to you: "Do not wait just because you dread the conversation or to avoid conflict. An employee like my office manager can steal time, profit and progress. I gave her far too much power for too long."

Employee Survey

In the Gallup results in the previous section, one of the 12 core elements of employee satisfaction related to being asked for an opinion. Asking for feedback, even if you do not make changes as a result, is a powerful tool for building employee loyalty. If you have not surveyed your employees in the last 12 months, create an action item to do so. If employees are your best asset, you need to know the status of their employee satisfaction. Hiring and training is expensive. Your best strategy for retaining them is to meet their needs as much as is practical and possible. Do you know what is important to them? What would make them more willing to be committed to you and your organization? It is recommended you survey employees annually.

In a recent meeting with my client, Adam, we discussed his frustration with his annual survey. Adam says, "It seems that asking their opinion opens the door for them to complain about everything instead of engaging in helping the team." Adam is right. You will have a number of employees who feel that, if you are asking, this is their opportunity to get everything off their chest;

ask for everything they want; tell you what they like and do not like about how your run the company; complain about everything from not enough parking to vending machines that do not meet their dietary needs; etc. You get the picture.

This outpouring of criticism and complaint may seem petty and distracting to you, but they now feel heard. Feeling heard leads to feeling valued. There is always more good than bad that comes from this process. Take a chance. See what happens.

One way to manage the tone of the feedback is to ask your employees to be constructive in their comments and to remind them you will not be making changes based on every request.

No matter what feedback you receive, view it as an opportunity to learn more about your working conditions, your staff, the perception others have of you and your leadership style. Do not take it personally. Learn from it. If the majority asks for change, consider it.

Typical Survey Questions

- Do you feel appreciated?
- Do you have what you need to do your job efficiently?
- Do you know what is expected of you?
- Do you feel you get the right amount of feedback?

- Are you doing what you do best every day?
- Do you feel you are recognized for the contributions you make?
- How can we help you meet your career goals?
- Do you have suggestions for improving working conditions, processes, or systems?
- If you could change three things about our company or your position what would they be?

ADVICE FROM YOUR PEERS

"One of the core issues about employee surveys is in regards to managing expectations and in creating new expectations where there were none before. I certainly have observed more communication about what we can do to make 2 Brothers better after doing employee surveys. And, when those conversations happen between employees who have the capacity to see the business as a whole they are highly productive. When they happen between employees who do not have the experience or desire to see that the business is a combination of competing priorities, they tend to create unrealistic one sided expectations. Set the expectations appropriately when the survey is distributed." Adam Sweet, CEO, 2 Brothers Moving and Delivery

Review Yourself

The performance review process is central to employee growth and development, which is critical to the success of your organization. It gives the business owner or manager an opportunity to examine what is going right, or not as well, and helps both parties to set goals and expectations for the months ahead. It is a key component of employee satisfaction and of employee engagement. Yet, what about you, the small business owner? Who reviews you? You should have a review program just like everyone else.

It is possible to have a 360 review process, in which your staff is asked to review you, or perhaps you have a partner and you have agreed to review each other. Still, chances are you have neither. That means you will go another year without feedback on your own performance.

You may say the success of the business is your performance review, but this is not necessarily the full picture. You are a key contributor to your business success, but it is not an indicator of the impact your performance has on the overall potential for success. The way you run your business is your performance. The skills you use, the way you behave, the habits you keep, and the way you manage yourself are not always visible in the business outcome.

Everyone, including the business owner, can benefit from an examination of their performance. If you do not have others who will take responsibility, then why not do it yourself? A simple self-review can help you to identify areas of strengths and weakness and provide valuable information for goal setting for your future.

If you have 15 minutes and a willingness to develop and improve as a small business owner, find a quiet place where you can reflect uninterrupted and follow the instructions below.

You will rate yourself on each of the areas listed below using one of the following performance indicators. I recommend you write that word next to each statement.

(U)nsatisfactory – (M)arginal – (M)eets requirements –

(E)xceeds (R)equirements – (E)xceptional

___ Works "on" the business.

___ Works "in" the business.

___ Uses resources in an effective manner including peers, partners, and outsourcing.

___ Plans effectively.

___ Is accountable to plans.

___ Has refined leadership skills.

___ Is an effective role model.

___ Manages time.

___ Recruits effectively.

___ Employee management.

___ Generates revenue.

___ Prices competitively.

___ Expense management including having a budget and managing that budget.

___ Invests in the future with training and development for self and staff.

___ Sets clear boundaries for work and life.

Add up each category. How did you do? If you are like most small business owners, you will have rated yourself "Meets Requirements" in most areas with only a few "Exceptional" and a few "Marginal" or "Unsatisfactory."

Now what? Take this list and use it as a springboard for goal setting in the months and year ahead. Focus on your strengths. Build on them. Give some time and attention to eliminating the "unsatisfactory." Then, mark your calendar to check your progress in six months and again this time next year. And, by the way, give yourself a raise in the next raise cycle. You deserve it!

DO IT!

If you do not have a performance management system, create one. Set up all of your employees for performance reviews. Use the reviews to analyze the quality of your staff and make plans to take action to improve performance, upgrade personnel and hire for the gaps.

COACH'S CHALLENGE

Review yourself. Identify your strengths and build on them. Identify your weaknesses and create a plan to eliminate them or fill the gaps with others on your staff.

COACH'S ADVICE

Face performance issues directly. Do not let them negatively impact your business.

Processes, Systems, Operational Efficiencies

In every small business there are tasks such as bookkeeping, accounting, contract management, administrative support, workflows, policies, procedures, scheduling, inventory, and many more that must be performed in order for the business to continue safely, securely and efficiently. They are critical to overall performance in so many ways that they cannot be ignored. Strangely, these are also the areas a majority of my clients tell me they do not have well defined, under control, or in smooth working order. Nine out of 10 clients rate themselves "below average" in performance in one or more of these categories: administration, processes, systems, or operational efficiencies. If you are one of those business owners pay close attention — making progress here will do more to improve the performance of your business and the joy in your life as an owner than almost anything else you can do.

Let us start by admitting that most of us have a goal to create enough revenue to hire or outsource as many of these functions as possible. It is rare for a small business owner makes a choice to support themselves in all functions because they enjoy every task. They describe these responsibilities as "necessary evils" or worse, ignore or avoid them until they are surrounded by boxes of receipts and unfiled taxes, or worse yet, they are overwhelmed and thinking seriously about giving up on their decision to be a small business owner.

The good news is there is plenty you can do to make these functions easier to manage.

Be Organized

Systems, processes, and efficiency all start with the practice of organizing — organizing spaces or information. It is that simple. There is a massive amount of information out there on how to become more organized, but you do not have time to waste on learning and relearning the best system of the moment. You can gain just as much benefit from following the "lessons I learned as a teenager" version below.

Organizational Tips

- If you do not need it do not buy it.
- If you do not use it do not keep it.

- Touch it one time. Decide what to do with it. Do it.
- Read the directions the first time.
- Have the right tools for the project.
- Have a place for everything and put everything in its place.
- Don't put off until tomorrow what you should do right now.
- Break big stuff into small pieces.
- Record things that are important in the place you can find it.
- Anything hidden under your bed (or in your desk) is trash.

When you are disorganized you cannot find what you need when you need it. You lose time, money, and energy that you can never recover. Be organized. It matters. If you do not know how, hire someone to help you. There are many small businesses out there today who have a mission to help their clients be as organized as possible.

Create Systems

This will be a short section. See the real answer below in "Record processes and procedures."

You may ask, "What does create systems mean?" Quite simply a system is your processes and procedures written in a step by step format. Your "systems" are those things you do to perform the service or create the product that you offer. So, when I suggest you "create systems," what I really want you to do is to find the most productive and efficient way to create the product or service you want to offer and then make sure everyone who has any part in delivering that product or service uses the same system to get the same result.

Processes and Procedures

Now that you know how you do those things you do to get the results that you want, record them. Teach them. Train everyone on your team to follow or implement the system in the same way every time. What you will get is uniform results and efficiency. This will save you time, money, and create a high quality product. It will also become your insurance against any one person(s) having all of the intellectual property or being the only one who knows how to "do" something that is critical to your business success.

Like everything else in your small business, if taking the time to record processes and procedures becomes a task you may not have time for, I recommend you share the load. Delegate portions to everyone who participates in your system or, if you are the only participant, break it down in manageable pieces. Record the process or procedure as you perform it. Spread the creation of the documentation over a short period of time.

Once you have processes and procedures recorded, keep them updated. Mark your calendar to update them on a regular basis — quarterly or twice a year are the most common.

ADVICE FROM YOUR PEERS

When JR decided to hire his first employee he knew that finding the time to train them was going to be a challenge. He was willing to commit time for this important task, but he did not anticipate that he would have to do it twice in quick succession. When his first employee left suddenly after just a few months JR could hardly believe he was again faced with committing valuable time to train someone new. "Record the processes and procedures as you train a new employee, or, better yet, let them record it as they learn. Let them break it down into step-by-step actions and task them with keeping the training manual up-to-date," was JR's solution.

Manage Your Time

In my initial interview with new clients I ask them to list for me the top five challenges they are currently experiencing. Depending on the industry and business, they list a variety of issues, but universally over 90 percent of them identify "time management" as one of their top challenges. This leads me to conclude that if there is one thing most small business owners can agree on it is there never seems to be enough time to do all there is to do. A small business owner could have something to do every minute of every day. You are the only one who can decide how you will spend your 24 hours. The choices you make will result in your feelings of being accomplished and organized or overwhelmed and exhausted. Managing time means managing your priorities.

Low vs. High Value Tasks

When faced with a long list of things to do and given a short block of time to complete them, owners often look at the list and determine which tasks can be knocked out right away. It seems more productive to clear them away and then tackle the project which needs more energy, research or undivided attention. This is dangerous. It is easy to get involved in one small project after another and before you know it, you are adding the more important or valuable project that you delayed to your tomorrow's "to do" list over and over again. The result is a lot of low value tasks are completed and nothing of high importance has been accomplished. It also means your sense of urgency is heightened and stress level has risen.

The good news is there is a "fix" to this productivity challenge. All it takes is a simple change in behavior. You probably already have everything you need to manage your time. The basic tools are a calendar, paper, pencil, day planner, and/or computer. Now all you need to do is arrange your tasks in order of priority — not in ease of completion.

What should I work on first?

The simple answer is to spend your time on our highest value priorities. The dictionary describes a "priority" as the *state of having most importance or urgency* and "value" as *to rate something according to its perceived worth, importance, or usefulness*. When you put these together you have a formula for business time management success. Figure out what items have the most worth to whatever you are trying to accomplish, place them in order of priority and accomplish them in that order. Sound simple? It can be.

In an effort to refocus on areas of importance it is critical you have a full understanding of where you are spending your time. The best way to do this is to record your efforts and analyze them. Follow the tips below to assist you in being more time efficient.

Tips for Managing Your Time

1. Spend your time on tasks with the highest value. Ask yourself, "what value does this activity have?" If the priority is not high enough, say "no" or push it lower on the list.

2. Focus on "moving forward." You have a vision. Every step you take should move you closer to that vision. As you are trying to decide what to do with your time ask,

"Does this activity move me forward?" If you cannot answer an emphatic, "yes," then redirect your time.

3. <u>Plan your work and work your plan</u>. By now you should have a strategic action plan. Once you have that plan, review it regularly to make sure you are following your map to success. Spend time only on activities that help you move closer to the vision you have defined for your planning period.

4. <u>Get organized "your way."</u> Use what works for you. To determine what works best, you must examine your preferences. You must decide whether you prefer paper or technology. "Paper" people need to touch and feel their organizer. When forced to use mobile devices and electronic gadgets they get extremely frustrated. "Electronic" people will cringe at the mere suggestion that you print anything and are entirely comfortable storing all their information in an electronic system. The key is to use something that works for you.

5. <u>Learn to say "no."</u> As the old saying goes, "you can't please all the people all the time." The same goes for doing everything anyone wants you to do when they want you to do it. You know that only those things which you have identified as important will help you reach your goals. It is essential that you learn the art of saying "no" to those things that do not have the right value priority. Be honest but firm when you tell requestors you have other things taking priority at this time. You might then offer

an alternative delivery date or time if you believe your schedule will allow it.

6. Track time. If you are paid by the hour then "time is money." Make sure you are charging the right amount by tracking time with a time tracking program. You can find a wide selection on the internet ranging from "free" to "major investment." Pick one that is right for you and your needs.

7. Delegate and outsource. If you do not need to do the task yourself, delegate or outsource and give over the autonomy and authority needed for others to be successful.

Outsource

In small business the mantra should always be, "do what you do best, and outsource the rest." As you grow in size and revenue you have this choice. Start by asking:

- What do I want to do myself and what do I want to hire someone to do?

- Do I want an employee or should I hire a service or contractor?

- Who do I hire for first?

These questions seem simple enough, but small business owners seem to struggle with making the leap. Each time someone is hired to do something you could do, your spouse could do, or someone you already have on the payroll might squeeze in to their schedule, you will likely stop to consider how you will cover the additional expense and hesitate to engage a new employee until you are certain you can cover it. Do not make the mistake of waiting too late.

As challenging as it might seem, I would recommend you hire as soon as you need help. To be prepared for that I recommend you have a plan and a budget so you will know how the structure and expense of your business will change when you hire.

Start with the positions which are most important to your business and those that will allow you to focus on your highest and best use. As an example, a majority of my clients outsource bookkeeping as quickly as they can afford to. That typically translates to within the first three years. The function is important, it is one most business owners do not enjoy, and it is a relatively low investment.

If you are having trouble justifying the cost, most people need only to calculate what an hour of their time is worth. In the example of hiring a bookkeeper you will assume the value of your time is worth $50-75 dollars an hour or more. Bookkeeping is typically available at or below this price range (with higher prices charged by CPA firms that offer bookkeeping services at the higher end). You can hire someone else to do it for you and reclaim your time to find more clients, develop programs or services, network, etc. If your excuse is you "do it on your own time" such as weekends, you should reconsider this philosophy. What is an hour of personal time worth to you?

Here are a few functions that are easily outsourced:

- Bookkeeping, accounting, tax preparation
- Digital marketing and SEO (search engine optimization)
- Social media
- Advertising
- Human resources
- Recruiting
- Facilities management, repairs, and cleaning

ADVICE FROM YOUR PEERS

"Block time for you and for your business. It really has made my life fuller because I am not breathing, sleeping and digesting work." Chris Pero, Consultant, Pero Art and Frame

DO IT!

Evaluate how you spend your time. Where is it being wasted? Take action to make corrections.

COACH'S CHALLENGE

Hire as soon as you are ready. Have resources set aside to cover several months of the expense. Take full advantage of the additional resource(s). Justify the return on your investment at 60 and 90 days.

Facilities and Equipment

Needs for facilities and equipment vary widely for different business types, from a desk in your basement to multiple locations in multiple states. Most small business owners know what their needs are and meet those needs as soon as their budget allows.

Some struggle to make the commitment even when they believe the investment will contribute to business growth and opportunity. It is to this group that I share the following advice.

Facilities

For all of you readers who have already secured the perfect location with the right landlord at the best price and the right footprint to meet your needs for the next five or more years, congratulations! You have mastered a major component of the business success equation — the right location and facility. For the rest of you that know you could grow your business, attract new clients, have more dedicated work time, or be more productive, read on.

Lori had worked for a major national retailer for many years. She understood the power of having your "shop" in the right location. When she opened her own human resources consulting firm for small business she worked from home and met her clients at their location. That worked fine for the client appointments but Lori found she was easily distracted in her home office. If it was Monday and the laundry was piling up, she would stop to do a load. If it was Friday and the shopping needed to be done, she might scoot out for an hour or two to shop. What she was not getting was the full amount of available time dedicated to working "on" her business.

Like many others, Lori was a bit worried about adding fixed expenses so early in her business. Income was inconsistent and some months were already tight on operating capital. Still, after some discussion Lori decided to give it a try. She found a space she could afford, in a location she could be proud of, and signed a lease. She was not prepared for what happened next. Almost immediately she became more productive. She found more time to focus on marketing. She arranged for clients to meet her in her office, saving drive time and travel expense. Lori also found she had neighbors that were potential strategic partners and quickly made new professional friends. This was not all. Clients who had resisted her program suddenly saw Lori as a legitimate option for their needs. They were comfortable having Lori interview their potential employees and her contracts soared. In just six months Lori found her rent was far from a concern and in just two years she moved from that location to a higher grade building in a higher traffic professional community.

Are you like Lori, afraid you will be biting off more than you can afford? Here are a few things to consider and a few questions to ask.

- The increase in business is often significantly more than the cost of the facility. How many new clients or sales dollars will it take to afford the facility? Do you believe you can count on that type of gain?

- Having a dedicated facility is an outward display of your belief in the possibilities for your business and sends a message to your client community that you are here to stay.

- Having dedicated space changes the way you think about your business. My client Chris says it makes her feel she is finally "successful."

- Having a dedicated space puts you in touch with more potential clients. Your facility sign is advertising. How many potential new clients might see it every day?

- Having your own facility can offer you an opportunity to build partnerships and professional relationships with others that can promote your business. Be sure you select a location that will give you advantages and then make a plan to build relationships.

Having your own facility could offer an opportunity for passive income. Depending on the size of the facility and your usage, you could have room for a sublet. Plenty of business owners sublet enough space to pay their facility expenses.

As you move forward there are a few precautions to take. You should be looking for the right balance in satisfying your current and future needs with cost. Secure the space you need for only the period you think you will need it. If you are growing you may want a shorter lease to allow you to move. If you are at the size and level you want to be you may want a longer lease to lock in the best price. Keep in mind every landlord wants good tenants for as long as possible. Be sure you do not let a leasing agent pressure you into taking too much for too long.

You also have the option of purchasing your own location. If you choose this route, you are creating an asset for your business. To be sure it fits into your budget and is a good investment you will want to talk to both your real estate agent and your accountant.

DO IT!

Assess your situation and then decide if the time is right to get or upgrade your facility or facilities. If you find you have more space than you need or you are not spending the time in your space to justify the cost, let it go or sublet it.

COACH'S CHALLENGE

Find the right balance in facility needs. Getting more than you need steals your profit. Signing a lease for too many years can limit your opportunities.

Equipment

You need the right tools to do any job well. What you do not need is more than the job requires.

Today it is easy to get pulled in by the allure of ever-changing technology. Buy it today and then upgrade with new "bells and whistles" tomorrow. It seems we can never stay current.

It is important to remember you control these decisions. These types of capital expenditures can disturb your cash flow and your profit. Determine what you need and invest — but do not over invest. Be profitable so you can invest more later on the newest and best.

Keep the following in mind to make the best decisions for your needs:

- Do a full examination of your needs.
- Identify what is needed to deliver the product or service you offer.
- Make the investment you feel will get you the best return.
- Be clear about the amount of sales it will take to cover the investment and know that it is within your capacity.
- Avoid being pressured into buying more than you need for the next 12-36 months.
- Have a plan and a budget for upgrading equipment as it is needed.

DO IT!

Evaluate your current equipment needs. Make sure everything is in good working order and will support your vision. Identify any future purchases you will need to make and plan for them including setting up a reserve fund for any which are above your normal expense level.

Legal and Compliance

One of the strategies most often ignored or poorly developed by small business owners is legal and compliance. Shocking, right? If you are not an attorney you are probably not an expert on the legal codes and statutes which regulate your business in your city, county, state and country. Not being an expert is not an excuse. When you are a small business owner you must make it your business to learn the rules and then comply. The best way to do this is to hire an expert.

For help with this strategy I turned to just such an expert. Jim is a business attorney who specializes in keeping small business owners out of trouble. He makes it his business to keep his clients in full compliance with all governing regulations through education, audit, and situational action and advice. I asked Jim what he felt were the most common mistakes made by small business owners. He began by saying, "Most business owners do not know what they do not know." This can get even the most intelligent owner into trouble. He went on to list a few common mistakes and offer advice on how to handle each.

He says, "While owning a small business involves constant learning, it's important for owners to candidly assess their strengths and weaknesses and to seek professional advice when needed. An ounce of prevention (risk management advice and implementation) usually is worth at least a pound of cure (fines, civil penalties and lawyer fees).

Common Mistakes Small Business Owners Make

1. Wrong 'Entity' selection: Some business owners automatically assume they must incorporate to be in business. Some never bother to consider their options and operate as de facto sole proprietors or undocumented partnerships. Consult your business lawyer and your CPA before making a decision.

2. Missing or inadequate governing documents: While corporations are required by law to have written bylaws which set forth who runs the legal entity and how they do so, LLCs have fewer formal requirements. As a result, many LLCs, particularly those formed without professional assistance, have no written documents spelling out who is in charge and what happens in case of disagreements. Likewise, any business with two or more owners should always have a buy-sell agreement specifying how and when owners may sell or transfer their respective ownership interests.

3. Not using written contracts: Oral agreements may be enforceable, but not putting it in writing leaves open the possibility of a "he said/she said" dispute. Every business should have a written contract with the person or entity paying them for goods or services.

4. Employment issues: Hiring employees is a significant step for any business. It's also a frequent source of

legal problems. Employment laws are constantly changing, so it is highly advisable to get professional help with hiring and firing procedures, payroll withholdings, employee manuals, and written employment agreements. Businesses that rely solely on independent contractors instead of W-2 employees must take extra precautions to ensure that contractors are truly independent. If a contractor is determined to be a misclassified employee, the business can be exposed to fines, penalties and significant legal liabilities.

5. <u>Not protecting intellectual property</u>: Your business name, logo, and website content can have significant value. Likewise, if your business creates inventions, develops unique processes, or writes its own software or applications, these too are assets that should be safeguarded through patent, trademark, or copyright protections.

6. <u>Lack of succession planning</u>: Whether you are a sole proprietor or a large corporation, it's important to have a plan for retirement, death, or disability of an owner. Often that involves a buy-sell agreement between co-owners, but it may also include plans to transfer the business to a new generation of employees or family members, or selling to a competitor or investor. Likewise, any transfer of a business for economic value has potential tax consequences for buyers and owners. As the saying goes, failing to plan is planning to fail.

7. Not having the right professional advisors: Even the smallest sole proprietor needs trusted advisors. Establishing relationships with a competent, cost-effective business attorney as well as a CPA makes it easier for your business to stay out of trouble rather than having to get out of trouble. Also, getting your professional support team lined up ahead of time means you can address emergencies immediately.

Enough said. Jim's advice is the advice I would give you.

If you are just starting out, you may think you have nothing to lose by creating your own contracts or setting up your own entity through an online service. The right start is the best start. View legal support and services as a critical expenditure. Find an attorney who specializes in working with small businesses and make it a part of your budget to get the support you need to protect your business.

DO IT!

Be sure you find a business attorney and form a relationship. Look for one that specializes in small businesses and has some experience in your industry. Have an audit done on your business practices annually as a prevention and protection measure.

COACH'S ADVICE

Pay for the professional services you should not be doing yourself. Many small business owners try to do all of their legal work on their own or through an online resource. I know of many situations that could have been avoided with an hour's consultation with an attorney. This is not an area to be penny wise and thousands of dollars foolish.

Executive Development and Leadership Skills

Recently a client said to me, "I think I am a great small business owner but I am a lousy leader." I was shocked he viewed himself that way. I started thinking about how many small business owners may or may not be effective leaders. They know how to be brave and courageous. They are tenacious and dedicated. Taking risks is part of their charm. Still, how many know how to "lead?"

Before you add staff you may get away with using your charm, courage, or fearless attributes to push your business forward. Once you are not in the business alone you must use your leadership skills. If they are not adequate, stop and develop them.

Leadership is critical for a small business owner. The skills contributing to these characteristics will help you to build a high performance team and create a culture of acceptance, creativity and productivity.

Small business owners and small business leaders are not synonymous. A small business owner is a person who had an idea, resources and commitment to open their own business. A small business leader is someone who starts as a small business owner but has developed skills that also make them an effective leader. People listen when they give advice. Others follow their lead. Many are influenced to seek their opinion.

A small business leader is not just an owner. They inspire others to share their vision. They also inspire others to perform at or above their potential while contributing their skills, abilities, and talents to catapult the organization towards the vision.

There are several skills that set and owner and leader apart. Let's focus on seven that are critical. Some of them come naturally. All can be more fully developed with time and experience. The more developed these skills, the more accomplished the leader. The more accomplished the leader the more successful they often are.

Leadership Skills for Small Business Owners

1. Communicating. Communication is the key to understanding. It includes not only verbal and written abilities but active listening.

2. Delegating. Delegation is the art of sharing control. It sends a message of trust and promotes growth in those that have been delegated responsibilities.

3. Influencing. Influence is having the capacity to have an effect on the character, development, or behavior of someone or something. This is a powerful skill and can have either a negative or positive impact on the individual(s) being influenced. In this case, we are referring to "positive" influence.

4. Coaching. No matter how accomplished we are it is difficult for any of us to see our blind spots. Coaching is a skill that points out these flaws or blind spots in such a way the individual is inspired to make a positive change.

5. Motivating. Motivation takes a spark of desire, guides it and tends it to exceed expectations.

6. Creating a safe place. Everyone makes mistakes. Creating a place and relationship in which others feel safe takes skill.

7. Role modeling. Actions are worth more than all of the above skills together. When you are trusted and respected your behavior becomes the pattern to follow.

Yes, developing these skills will take time and energy. Is it worth it? You decide for yourself. As stated earlier, a small business headed by a leader is likely to have more staff loyalty, more satisfied employees, lower turnover and higher productivity. Leaders are also more likely to have more time to work "on" their business once they have engaged their staff through delegation. They are likely to be viewed as successful in their communities and be asked to participate in industry decision making and leadership positions in professional organizations. Lastly, they are likely to report more joy in their work life as business owners.

DO IT!

Identify the leadership skills you want and/or need to develop most. Find people (coaches, consultants), programs (workshops, classes) or resources (books, online learning, podcasts, etc.) that can help you. Make time for skill development. Practice. Ask for feedback.

COACH'S ADVICE

Fight the tendency to think you can behave any way you want just because you are the owner. Leaders are humble and constantly evolving.

Be Prepared for the Unexpected

In business as in life there are things we simply do not control. These are things that happen "to" us — often with no warning. The range of possibilities is immense. You might experience anything from a natural disaster (hurricane, tornado, flooding, snowstorm or heat wave) to a personal tragedy (death, loss, divorce or illness). For most of us these experiences force us to make a full stop to attend to the issue or recover from the event. Sometimes, because we want to, and sometimes because we have no other choice. In any case, an event out of your control is best dealt with through preparation. To be prepared you must first identify the possibilities.

Striking a balance between being prepared and creating unnecessary worry or concern is always important. Step back and try to see your situation from an outside perspective. Do your best not to give this exercise any emotion. Undue concern can cause panic and even paralyze your movements. You can spend so much time worrying about what might happen you do not take advantage of the opportunities ripe for plucking. This was the case with my client Jennifer S.

Jennifer owned a very successful custom furniture company. She was ready to take her business to the next level. Her vision included adding a showroom where she would sell her furniture pieces and home accessories to the public. A long-term competitor was ready to retire and approached Jennifer about purchasing his showroom. It was in the perfect location in a market where Jennifer's target client shopped. The price was right, and her competitor was willing to assist her in the transition. We discussed the opportunity in several meetings. There seemed to be no business reason not to pursue this opportunity. But Jennifer had a personal concern. She was an only child and her parents were aging. Both were in great health, took very good care of themselves, and had high marks on recent physical exams. However, there was a history of heart disease in Jennifer's mother's family. In fact, several family members had either died of heart failure or suffered from heart disease complications. Jennifer was convinced her mother would be next. She worried a health event would come any day and she would have to step away from her business to care for her mother or to assist her father should her mother pass away. This fear was very real for Jennifer and she ruminated over it daily. So much so she was afraid to take advantage of the showroom opportunity for fear she would not be available to ensure its success. After much discussion Jennifer agreed to come up with a plan to support her in the unlikely event her mother grew ill over the start-up period. Jennifer created a budget including the expenses of a support team for both her business and her family. She negotiated with the retiring owner to be available for up to two years for direct support up to 20 hours per week. She identified a part-time manager who would be willing to work more hours if needed. She engaged a contractor to develop a process and procedures manual and a cross-training plan for her staff and management team. Working with her parents' financial advisors she put a long-term care plan in place for in-home or facility assistance.

Once all of the plans were in place something happened. Jennifer's fears regarding her mother's health calmed down and she signed the contract to purchase the showroom. Today, that showroom is the highest grossing custom furniture retail store in the region.

Do not be afraid of what "might" be. Take the time to identify any event you believe has a 30 percent or greater probability and then develop a plan. Know what you will do, where you will find resources, and how you will operate or behave. Do your best to predict what the consequences or outcome might be, then prepare specifically for that outcome.

As the probability percentage rises (50 - 90 percent) make sure you plan is solid enough to meet the challenge.

ADVICE FROM YOUR PEERS

"Learn how to take strategic risks. Strategic in that you have a plan A and a plan B; risks in that your skin in the game forces a level of success you wouldn't have been capable of otherwise." Adam Sweet, Founder, 2 Brothers Moving & Delivery.

Disaster Recovery Plan

I lived and worked in Florida, a state that has an annual hurricane season, for over 40 years. Based on that experience, my advice for every business owner is to be prepared in the event of a disaster — natural or otherwise — such as flooding, fire, weather events that disrupt service, death, illness, disability, major human error or sabotage and acts of violence. This would be any event that would interrupt service, destroy records, or make it impossible for regular work and regular work hours to be performed. Know what you will do and how you will do it long before it happens. If you never use it, great. If you need it, you will be overjoyed you have a plan in place.

Make sure you have:

- A record back-up program — computer and hard files, client contact lists, employee contact lists

- A communication "tree" — who will call who and when.

- Alternative means of notification for clients and employees

- Alternative access to your money (branch banking in multiple locations will usually suffice)

Predictions and Preparedness Exercise

The world around us is never static. Change is constant. Much change is something outside our control. These are considered "threats" to you and/or your business. The likelihood of them happening is often low, and for this reason we often ignore them all together. The best way to address these is simply to be aware of them and be prepared.

Is there anything outside of your control for the term of your plan? This could be:

- Change in the economy.
- Change in your staff or organization structure.
- Personal changes or demands on your personal time (health, family, other responsibilities)
- Changes your competitors will be making.
- Regulations or policies that guide your business.
- Any changes in technology requiring you to change or your target to change
- Any clients' changes — expanding, contracting, selling, bringing in new decision makers
- Acts of nature — winter snow storms, hurricanes, tornadoes, etc.

Record your answers in the form below:

Event	Be prepared with:

DO IT!

Be prepared. Take the time to know what will happen in any event you can imagine.

COACH'S ADVICE

Be prepared, but do not give it too much energy. Let the plan take away the worry instead of contributing to it.

Exit Strategy and Succession Planning

You may think just because you plan to work for the foreseeable future you do not need an exit strategy. While knowing when or how you will exit your business may not be high on your list of priorities, it should certainly be on your radar. When you are within as many as 10 years out and as few as five, your exit should become a part of your planning process. Avoid waiting until one to two years before you plan to make a change. By that time your options become more limited.

As you begin to plan for an exit I recommend you find a sale intermediary, often referred to as a business broker. This individual can assist you in a valuation of your business and help you to position your business for a sale. If you do not know one, ask your peers and professional network for a recommendation. Once you have been introduced, confirm your business type is one they have experience with. Ask for references. Then fully utilize their services to help you understand what you can expect and how you should prepare for the outcome you want.

Be prepared for the unexpected. Your view of what your business is worth may be very different from the business broker's based on a number of important factors. The sooner you can address them the better your opportunity to adjust positively impact the outcome. Risks associated with a high concentration of revenue from a few key clients, or ownership of underutilized intellectual property could have an impact on value. Another such issue is the historic and projected growth rate of your business and how it compares to others in your industry. These are just a few of the factors. Connect with the professional and let them help you to maximize the sale of the company you have worked so hard to create.

To prepare personally contact your financial advisor. Make them aware of your plans and timing to be sure it is considered in your financial positioning.

If you do not plan to sell your business you have a variety of other options including continuing in the business in a different position or at a different level of involvement. You may just decide to offer fewer service hours to accomplish this change, but if this is not possible, you will need to replace yourself. You need a succession plan. Knowing who will step into key roles in your business will help you make difficult decisions. Having time to groom these individuals will help you make a smooth transition.

DO IT!

Spend time thinking about the future of your business. Make decisions on what you most want to happen and then start to take action. Talk to anyone you see as a part of your future plans. Find a business broker and contact them. Take their advice on when you should start to put your strategy into action.

COACH'S ADVICE

Do not assume the people you see in your future business want that role. Talk to them to confirm.

Love It!

Love It!

Focus on the Big Stuff

The late Stephen Covey, author of *First Things First* and *The 7 Habits of Highly Effective People,* described a prioritization system he called "Big Rocks First." It is still appropriate and powerful today. Search for the YouTube dramatization of Covey demonstrating his system in which the audience is asked to fit a few big rocks (which symbolize priorities), smaller rocks or pebbles, (which symbolize the less important tasks) and sand or smaller pebbles (which symbolizes distractions) into a bucket (which symbolizes our available time). They try lots of combinations — without success. Finally, Covey instructs them to start with the big rocks (priorities or highest value) followed by the smaller rocks, and then the sand. Voila! It all fits!

As a small business owner, your day (the bucket) may often feel like it is overrunning with rocks, pebbles, and sand — and sometimes water. There is always more to do than you have the time for. To fit it all in you must identify what is most important to you in both your business and personal life.

Once you know what is most important, block out protected time and assign that time to your priorities. Try not to give too much time or attention to the things that do not matter. Fit in items between priorities and "does not matter" as you can. This is the same premise as the "80-20 Rule."

The Pareto principle, or 80–20 Rule, is based upon the research of Vilfredo Pareto (1848–1923). The principle states that approximately 80 percent of results are derived from 20 percent of effort. Put another way, 80 percent of results are created by 20 percent of activities. Given this, it would seem that 80 percent of business activity does not directly contribute to success, while the remaining 20 percent makes a significant difference. The 20 percent is the "big stuff." This is what counts. When you accomplish the big stuff you will see success. When you are successful you will have more love for your business and your small business lifestyle.

Need I say it again? Let all the little stuff go!

LOVE IT!

Block your calendar and protect the time you blocked.

COACH'S CHALLENGE

Block time to work on your business. Block time to enjoy your life. Protect the time you blocked. Both are critical to your success and your joy.

Follow the Green Lights

Have you ever had a situation in life — personal or business — when you were not sure what to do next and the answer just showed up? It was almost as if a light came on or the path lit up. You may have felt the universe was answering your call for advice. If we act on the opportunity, we find our problem is solved or our options become clear. The path is there for us to take if we just look for the lights. I like to imagine them as green, symbolizing "go" and "grow."

Recently my client Jonas, a private tutor, had an opportunity to work on a special project with a political candidate. It was his lifelong dream to be involved in a high profile campaign but Jonas had a full calendar of students and knew when the campaign had concluded he wanted to return to his practice. What to do? He was at a crossroad and there did not seem to be a good answer. He felt he would need to say "no" to his dream and keep his practice alive or lose significant income in the process and have to rebuild his practice on his return.

One of the ideas that came out of our brainstorm was for Jonas to spread the word to teachers without full time positions to gauge if someone would commit to covering his clients for three months. Before he even put out the word, he got a call from a teacher about to retire who needed a few months to blend her job end date and social security eligibility dates. She was a perfect fit.

While there she helped him to evaluate his processes and update some of the material he was using. Everyone was a winner — but especially Jonas. He had a wonderful experience in the political campaign and returned to his practice energized and ready to recommit to his clients. He had no client loss.

The best news about green lights is you do not need to do anything to make them appear. They just do. Follow them. If it feels right, it probably is. Green lights are just another indication that you are doing exactly what you should be doing.

ADVICE FROM YOUR PEERS

"If you are struggling every day to make any amount of progress and are overrun with obstacles and roadblocks, take another look at why you own your own business. Owning your business should feel "right." You should know that you are doing exactly what you should be doing. Opportunities should just show up, and when they do take advantage of them." Dr. Andrew J, Internal Medicine

LOVE IT!

Raise your awareness. Take time to notice the "green lights." Respond to the little nudge to take advantage of an opportunity. You will know when you are ready to take action. Be ready.

Build Your Business on Your Terms

The most important concept in loving your lifestyle as a small business owner is to create the business you want. From very early on you will have to resist the influence of others trying to tell you how it should be done. You may have to be reminded that part of the allure of being a small business owner is to create the business on your terms. As long as you are meeting your own needs as a small business owner you can consider yourself successful.

Sarah owns a creative design company. She creates custom patterns for anything from designer throw pillows to fishing waders. She is also a wife and mother with special circumstances. She cares for her aging mother and, after years of hoping for a family, now has a two-year-old daughter. Sarah was once a work-a-holic who committed

60-70 hours of her week to her corporate responsibilities. Now she has built a business around her new life priorities and has very clear boundaries on her workday. She works on her business a maximum of 20 hours each week in order to have time to be with her daughter and support the needs of her mother. Just because her work time is limited does not mean she is not serious about her business. It just means it is limited to the parameters she has set.

As a small business owner you have the power to set boundaries on time, scope, target vision and more. You may have worked through those parameters before you opened your doors but, if you did not, you will want to take time to reflect on why you opened your business and how you want it to fit into your life. You might want to go back to "Know What You Want" in the "Plan It!" section of this book. Read it again and define what you want. Once you have decided on your parameters, stick to them with consistent behavior. Do not cave-in to the pressure to be bigger, broader or work longer.

Caution: do not set expectations that exceed your parameters. To want more than will fit into the restrictions you have imposed will leave you frustrated and lacking. Once you set your boundaries, be realistic about what your work time can yield. Do not set a goal for 30 billable hours if you block only 15 available. Be realistic in your goal setting and realize you can change the work parameters at any time.

ADVICE FROM YOUR PEERS

"Be the driver of your passion and you'll always get where you want to go. There are many things I lacked passion for initially in my business. I have learned to love those things that count most and the rest you just practice, practice, practice." Adam Sweet, Founder, 2 Brothers Moving and Delivery

LOVE IT!

You are the architect of your small business. Build it your way. Review what you have created. Is it what you wanted? If not, what needs to change?

COACH'S CHALLENGE

If you find your business is "more" or "less" than you intended it to be, vow to make changes to bring it back in line with your vision.

Be Mindful

It is important to be mindful every day in every way to get the most from your life. Your business life is no different. It is our tendency to find what works, and then repeat it over and over again. This is rooted in an attitude of "if it isn't broken don't fix it." Sometimes this is exactly what you should do. But you will not know if the "old" way is the "best" way if you do not stop to pay attention to the present. What are the current circumstances? How have things changed? How have I changed? What adjustments do I need to make in my business or in my life to accommodate the changes? These are questions you should ask every day.

Mindfulness is a state of active, open attention to the present. When you are mindful, you observe your situation and your thoughts and feelings from a distance — without judgement. The practice of mindfulness often involves meditation. If you enjoy meditation practice, then by all means continue, and be sure you bring your business into practice. If you have never tried mediation but would like to, I recommend it. It is one of the best ways to relieve anxiety, lower stress, and to be aware of how you fit into your world.

For those of you who do not want to practice mediation or struggle to find extra time, here are a few short mindfulness exercises you can incorporate into your work day.

1. Two-minute daily work launch. Instead of rushing from your home to your office or to your desk, flinging open the computer, rushing to check your cell phone for messages and your e-mail for emergencies with only seconds to spare before the first client arrival, or opening the

shop doors, start your day with a full two minute start-up routine. Leave your electronics in the "off" position. Sit down at your desk or counter. Look around you. Notice the smell, the light, the cleanliness of your space. Pay attention to the energy in the room. Smile. Take a deep breath. Say out loud or under your breath, "Today will be my best day ever in business."

2. Take a breather. Between clients, over lunch, or whenever you have a break in your day, stop to just breathe. Close your eyes if you like. Breathe in and out slowly and completely. Pay attention to what one breath feels like. Notice how your lungs feel and the sensations in your nostrils. Lower your shoulders. Relax your stomach. Let your toes spread out in your shoes (or better yet take them off).

3. Prepare for difficult conversations. Many small business owners avoid conflict with clients, employees or partners. If you are one of those, or even if you are not, you can improve the outcome of any tough conversation by being prepared. Take a few minutes to review the situation from your point of view and from their point of view. Ask yourself, "What are they trying to tell me?" Identify what you want the outcome to be and why. Then ask yourself how you want them to see you in this interaction. Breathe deeply. See an outcome that is good for both of you in your mind's eye. See it resolved. Be prepared to listen more than you talk.

4. Effective meetings. Don't just save mindfulness, share the practice. Start meetings with a mindfulness exercise. Ask each member to take a moment and identify to themselves what they came to accomplish. Ask each member to leave any distractions they have outside the room reminding them they can pick them up at the door on the way out. You might point out the smell of coffee or lunch. Ask everyone to enjoy that for a few moments. Always ask them to turn off the electronics! Avoid disturbances and distractions.

5. Close your day with a mindfulness exercise. Leave a few minutes at the end of every day to put things away. Tidy up your space. Dust the furniture and water the plants. Now, pause for a moment to think about what you have accomplished today. Be sure your phone is off or put away and you can have this minute to yourself uninterrupted. If you cannot count on privacy, consider doing this exercise in your car before you leave the parking lot. Be mindful to leave any anxiety, ill feelings, or special challenges in your office. They can be picked up in your morning routine on your next office day. Exit to life.

ADVICE FROM YOUR PEERS

The secret to my success, especially early on, was to be clear on what I was building, what it meant to me and to be committed to doing whatever I needed to do to get there. Small business is rewarding and full of challenges with a steep learning curve. By being clear on my mission and seeing the small victories...I was able to weather the challenges and difficulties more easily." Sandra E. Stryker, Founder, Life's Work Physical Therapy

LOVE IT!

Create a mindfulness practice. Block the time on your calendar. Protect the time you blocked for this purpose only.

COACH'S CHALLENGE

Commit to this practice for 72 days. That is what it will take for mindfulness to become a new habit.

Set Boundaries

Whether you are just getting started or have owned your business for a while, having the success you want and still having time to enjoy the fruits of your labor can be a challenge. You are the only person that can set boundaries for the way you work and the way you live. If you do not have boundaries, your business may steal the joy right out of your life.

A boundary is the point or line beyond which something should not, cannot, or may not proceed. In the same way a good fence makes good neighbors, clear boundaries make for healthy relationships in the work place and between work and home. Ultimately, they become the building blocks for the way you live your life as a small business owner and a component of your business success formula. Set and reset boundaries as your life requires.

Diane has a very aggressive plan to get from where she is today to a nationally recognized name brand in just a few years. I have no doubt that she can reach her vision. I also have no doubt that boundaries are a challenge for Diane as she rockets towards her success.

A 15-hour work day is not unusual for Diane. She and her partner Jill have, from the beginning, had an understanding that the early years would require sacrifice. They have always agreed they would do whatever it takes to reach their vision as quickly as possible. This sounded doable in the excitement of starting their exercise products company. As the years have ticked by and they are only half way to their vision they have begun to question whether the sacrifice is too much. Life has changed and now it may be time to adjust. Two years ago they adopted a baby and both want to be involved parents. Jill's mother is aging, and she finds she needs increasingly more time to care for her. The demands of life and their life priorities are now different. It is time to adjust the boundaries.

Work vs. All Other Areas of Life

When I talk about boundaries with small business owners they come back with questions. They want to know, "If small business ownership is a "lifestyle" why are boundaries between work and life important? Are boundaries even possible in the small business lifestyle?" My answer, is "Yes, boundaries are necessary to maintain balance and yes, they are possible."

Anything to excess is out of balance. Balancing the duties of work and the responsibilities of other areas of life give you the opportunity to enjoy and grow in a multitude of ways. It keeps life and work exciting. It gives you time to rest from one responsibility while undertaking another. It also takes away the excuses of ignoring one's responsibility to focus on something different.

The next question I get is, "What are the right boundaries?" Business owners want to know what percentage of their time should be spent working on or in their business versus with their family or attending to their own personal needs. This question is much harder to answer. Boundaries are different for different people. The biggest challenge is that most small business owners push the limits of their boundaries no matter what they try. Almost without fail, work wins more often than any other area of life. The fact that work wins out is not necessarily a problem for the business owner — but it may create a problem in other areas that are important to them, like family, friends, self-care, etc.

ADVICE FROM YOUR PEERS

"When I first started my business, I took my phone with me everywhere. I answered every phone call. I never truly had time off. I was so afraid I would lose a client by not being available every minute. Would I really have lost that client? Absolutely not! Everyone takes a vacation, or should. Now I leave a message that informs callers when I will be back and when they can expect to hear from me. It works every time. I have never lost a single client as a result of scheduled time off." Chris Pero, Consultant, Pero Design, Art, & Frame

With Your Spouse or Partner

In the early 1990s I was transitioning from my "old" career to my new role as a coach and consultant. While I was working through the education part of this transition I found I was not as busy as I wanted to be. My husband owned a mortgage company and was shorthanded. I had a brilliant idea. I could work for him, keep his costs down, and fill those empty hours in my week. This turned out to be a bad idea for a variety of reasons. First of all, I did not view this as a "real job." After all, I was just filling in and I was not getting paid. That meant I worked when I wanted to and not when he needed me to. Second, I did not show him the right amount of respect. He was my husband, not my boss. Third, it was just temporary. I did not take the time to know what I really needed to be a productive employee. My work was not the quality he would have hired. All in all, I was a terrible employee and he was a frustrated boss.

I can count on one hand the number of real arguments we have had since we were married. You know the kind. They are the ones where you huff off and do not speak for several hours. They are the ones where there is yelling and name calling and you sometimes say things you regret. Two of those five arguments happened in those few months we worked together. There was only one solution: I fired myself! (See — even now I imagine I had more authority than I did.) If I had only known then what I know now about what it takes to work together while maintaining a loving relationship with your spouse I am sure I would have never printed the business card.

If you work in your business with a partner or spouse you may find yourself in a situation where there is a lack of clarity about where work ends and your relationship begins. The balance you are striving for is not as difficult as it may sound, but it does take commitment, clear understanding and expectations in the following:

- Specific business hours — work time versus relationship time

- Roles and responsibilities — who plays what role; who has final authority
- Personal responsibilities versus work responsibilities
- Communication when the system is breaking down — how and when
- Respect — always respect.
- Knowing who will help if you are stuck in conflict — who do you trust to sort out the differences

It is certainly possible to have a healthy work relationship while maintaining a healthy and loving couple relationship. I work with people who do all the time. It takes practice, an open mind, a willingness to work through the challenges, and the realization it will not always be perfect. Most importantly, you both agree no matter what, your personal relationship is the most important.

With Employees

If only I had 100 dollars for every time a small business client has asked me how to [terminate, separate, return to a less intimate] relationship with an employee I could afford that villa in Italy that is on my "before I die" list.

It always seems like a good idea to build a close relationship with your employees — but how close is too close? What happens if you need to reprimand or even terminate that employee? Maintaining a friendly but professional relationship is the key to retaining all your options in making the best decisions for your business now and in the future.

Knowing where the "lines are drawn" helps all parties understand what is expected and provides a sort of "playbook" on how to gain high marks on work performance and leadership within your organization. It is also helpful to put systems into place from the start, avoid misunderstanding and send a message of fair treatment to all employees.

Having healthy boundaries with employees reduces conflict in your work day and is important to a joyful work life.

LOVE IT!

Talk to people who are important to you about setting boundaries. Listen to what they need from you and tell them what you need from them. Then decide how you will set your boundaries. Once you agree to them, keep the agreement. Check in often on how it is working. Give others permission to approach you with concerns.

COACH'S ADVICE

Do not think you are different from all other business owners. Do not think you do not need boundaries to manage your life. You are not — and you do.

Be Committed to Wellness

For most small business owners there is no business without the owner. This means a priority for every small business owner should be to take extra special care of the driver of the business — the business owner. That sounds simple but is surprisingly one of the most difficult commitments for many business owners to make. I have stories too numerous to tell on this subject about owners who have sacrificed sleep and relaxation time, have over worried, over imbibed, and under nourished themselves, among other things. They all end the same way. There is a long period of time when the health of the business owner slowly slips and then one day something happens that jolts them back to reality. It is usually an illness, accident or exhaustion. Work is forced into the background along with reduced income or a decline in business success while the owner is forced to pay attention to recovering. In almost every case, the situation could have been avoided altogether if only the business owner had attended to the basic needs of wellness in a steady and consistent way. This requires setting boundaries on work time to allow for wellness time.

The message is this: treat yourself like the important asset you are. Take very good care of it. Block time for exercise, meals, vacation, physical check-ups, and socializing. The payoff is higher than you might think.

ADVICE FROM YOUR PEERS

"Having a successful business does not mean you are not allowed to have a "life." Take time off. Take care of yourself. Prioritize your health. You will be a better owner and boss. You will be your best self for your clients. That is what they pay you for." Mike Newman, Massage Therapist

LOVE IT!

You cannot enjoy your business if you are not well. Prioritize wellness and the time it takes to achieve it.

COACH'S ADVICE

Do not wait until you are successful to prioritize your needs.

Conserve Your Energy

We all know them — those people that drain your energy. You can almost feel it seeping from your body when they are around. These are people who feed on the good nature of others and are almost never satiated. Their negative attitude, uncooperative nature, and resistance to any idea that is not their own is almost always a symptom of something is out of alignment in their life. It could be low self-esteem, resentment, anger, or fear of almost anything. The cause does not matter. You cannot "fix" them. All you can do is try to understand them and avoid exposure by not engaging in relationships with them as clients or employees, and certainly not as partners. Think of it this way. Each of us gets only so much energy every day. If we are to accomplish all we want to accomplish and enjoy the lifestyle we have chosen we have to conserve energy for the right activities.

Here are a few scenarios you might encounter and my recommendations on how to deal with them to maximize joy in your work and life.

Avoid Clients who Drain Your Energy

<u>The vampire client</u>: I first heard this term from my strategic partner, Lori. I could not have described them better. These are the clients who always want more than they pay for. They want to ask just one more question, get just fifteen minutes of "free" advice, one last revision, or one more serving. They will drain your resources, your

time and your energy. These clients are hard to spot. They look like all the others. It is the behavior that is different. They take more than they pay for. They always want something for free. They count on your generosity and your desire to avoid conflict.

Solution: Be assertive. Be clear about what you offer and for what price. Develop messages that protect you from "giving it away." For example, if you have a client that overstays their appointment or the time allotted you might give them a warning. ("Our time is almost up. We have just ten more minutes. What would you like most to do before our time ends.") Or make them an offer. ("I have a few more minutes to offer you if you would like to extend our time.") Then charge them if they stay. You can also apologize but be firm. ("I'm sorry, if you want that additional piece it will be another $xx.")

<u>The unmotivated client</u>: This is a client who does not want to be a client. They are not motivated to participate and are only in the relationship because someone else has convinced them to buy it or be there. This client often does not make their own appointment nor do their own research. They communicate their needs through someone else; usually someone who has tried to help them but cannot. Someone else makes their arrangements or appointments for them. They are also those who do not want to pay until they have everything they came for and

yet they never get their needs met so you may find yourself chasing the money.

Solution: Set policies that protect you from this group. I have a policy that I do not work with anyone who does not make their own appointment. You might also have payment policies or pay-up-front arrangements if you find this is a group who wants the service but does not pay or pay on time. Be sure they sign agreements that spell out the role of all parties.

<u>The unrealistic client</u>: This client wants more than you can give them. They have an unrealistic and maybe even a fantastic expectation of what is possible. They typically play along for a while and then become disgruntled once they realize their expectations will not be met. Often they blame you as the provider and want their money back or refuse to pay the final installment.

Solution: Offense is the best defense with this client. Be very clear about what is possible. Ask for feedback often and restate what is possible. Have them acknowledge agreements with initials or signatures. If you can determine that they have unrealistic expectations before the work begins or purchase is made, consider not engaging.

Avoid Employees that Drain Your Energy

Your employees are a reflection of your company mission and vision. Clients measure their experience by the treatment they experience from all of your staff members

— good and bad. They expect you to have chosen the very best talent to deliver what you promise.

If this is not enough reason to hire the best and avoid the rest, here are some more reasons not to hire the right people: these are the same employees that are difficult to manage, represent your highest turnover, lower the morale of other staff members, create conflict, and reduce both productivity and profitability. These employees drain your time, your bank account and your energy. Be on the lookout for employees that are:

- Disrespectful
- Rule breakers
- Gossips
- Negative attitudes
- Attention getters!
- Know it alls
- Irresponsible
- Blame anyone but "me" types.
- Loud, conversation dominating, annoying.

Any of those mentioned above should be identified and swiftly dealt with. Do your best to identify this behavior prior to hiring. Know what questions to ask and interview them multiple times to learn as much as possible about their behavior. Consider having them do "on the job" interviews or work in a temporary capacity to test their workday demeanor.

If they slipped past the interview process, do not try to change them. These behaviors are often deeply rooted and difficult to modify. Follow your performance management process and do not be afraid to terminate them if the behavior persists.

Avoid Partners that Drain Your Energy

Partnering with one or more people in business ownership can be rewarding. Working in tandem for a common vision and mission can be exhilarating and energizing. Sharing ideas, responsibilities, and success should be a wonderful experience.

It can also be challenging if you are not a good match. It might start out with great potential, but you will quickly find working with people who are not your best match is a draining experience. Facing each day can become drudgery. You will begin to dread the interaction that will most often result in conflict.

There is good news! You can avoid partnering with those who are not a good match for you. Spend the time it takes to vet each other thoroughly before you enter into permanent arrangements. You might try working on a project together or sharing research responsibilities for an idea you have. Along the way, be honest about the assessment and ask for input from other stockholders.

The solution is to partner with your best match and only your best match. Find someone with whom you:

Share a vision: They want what you want and when you want it.

Share a mission: They have the same or similar motivation to own a business.

Compliment strengths and style: You fill the gaps for each other. Each of you has a role to play and together you are stronger and more effective.

Keep agreements: They do what they say they will do when they say they will do it.

Committed to success: They are willing to do their part to get the outcome you both want.

Are respectful, humble, good communicators and loyal.

Anyone that falls outside these guidelines will drain your energy. If you are thinking about a partnership do not be hasty in the development stages. Take your time. Court each other. Get to know each other. Learn to trust and respect each other. Then, become partners.

ADVICE FROM YOUR PEERS

"I wish I had learned earlier that you do not have to work with every client or keep any employee that does not see the job you gave them as an opportunity. I could have saved myself countless hours of pain and suffering." Shawn G., Owner and Photographer, Perfect View Studio

LOVE IT!

Examine all your relationships. Do they bring you joy? Do you look forward to spending time in their company? Do you benefit from knowing and working with them? If not, make changes.

COACH'S CHALLENGE

Terminate relationships that drain your energy — personal, professional, or employee —that are not healthy no matter how difficult it might be to make the change. You can never see how enjoyable your life as a business owner can be as long as you have these relationships in your work day — and life.

Build a Community for Support

Many small business owners tell me they often feel isolated. Solo owners or those without senior level peers often describe being drained from the responsibly of making all the decisions and shouldering all of the risk. They can be confused about whether the decisions they make are the best for them, their industry, their marketplace, or their clients. My first and best advice is always, build a community of resources that will serve you well.

Not just anyone will do. It takes careful selection and relationship building to get the right group of members. They fall into several categories, each with their own purpose and all of them very important.

Professional Resources

Your resource community should be comprised of individuals or groups to fill your gaps in knowledge, experience, and expertise to build and operate a successful business. These might include a financial advisor, marketing expert (digital and more traditional), a human resources expert, graphic designer, branding expert, digital marketing expert, and a business broker to name a few. Talk to other business owners about their professional resources and gather ideas on what other resources to include in this group.

If you are new to a market or client type, find someone that has worked in that area or with that group for a longer period of time. If you are new to a profession, find a mentor. Seek resources who have education or knowledge in areas that will make you a stronger, better business owner.

Do your homework. Be sure the resources you invite to your community share your values. Make sure they have a stellar reputation. Check their credentials. Get references.

Check the internet to see what others have had to say about working with them.

Take your time. One of the biggest mistakes business owners make in building community is to try to build it too quickly. Take your time. Let the relationships unfold. Be slow to commit to anything long term. Be sure your resources earn your business and your loyalty while you earn theirs.

Build for the long term. This is the type of relationship that should grow with you. Find resources that will be in business for the long term. Let them know you want a long term relationship and are looking for others who want the same.

Peer Groups

Peer groups can be invaluable as you grow and change. Members play a similar role as an advisory council, or board of directors. They want to learn your business and are willing to contribute to your success by offering feedback, advice, sharing experiences and resources, and playing "devil's advocate." You can start a peer group of your own, but it is not necessary. Today they are available in almost every city. In-person meetings are the most powerful, but you can also find a variety of options by phone or videoconference if you live and work in a more remote region.

Find a group that works for your schedule. Peer groups meet regularly, usually monthly, from between a few hours to an entire day. Be sure the group you choose can fit into your schedule. You will need to make a commitment to be a part of this type of group. Missed meetings and not fulfilling your commitments in between is frowned upon and will ultimately cost you the seat if you do not participate fully.

Find a group to fit your budget. Peer groups typically charge a fee. The amount ranges from less than $100.00 to well over $1,000.00 per month. With research you should be able to find a price and membership package that matches your budget. Do not overpay for the same opportunity. There are a number of franchise programs that charge higher fees than a group formed by a professional organization or a local business consultant, and they do not offer any more for the money. If you are concerned about the expense, perform a return on investment (ROI) analysis on membership. How many new clients would you expect to get by being a member of a group like this? Subtract the cost of membership plus your time and you will have a rough return on your investment. Some of the value may be in your development. Be sure to account for this. You might also think about how many new clients or how much more revenue you would need to generate to make it worthwhile. Can you visualize how this group could help you reach that goal?

To be sure it is a good fit, start with a visit. Every group should allow you to visit the group once or twice before you decide to become a permanent member. During your visit pay close attention to how the group and members make you "feel." This group should inspire you. At the conclusion of the meeting, you should walk away with new ideas and energy to explore them. You should feel the members understand you and your business and are willing to contribute to your success. You should want to get to know the members of this group and feel you can learn from them.

Once you have found one to meet your needs, I recommend you try to meet individually with some of the group members to gauge their success as a member and to decide how you might work together to both be more successful.

There is always strength in numbers. Find a group that suits you well and be a committed participant. The contribution to your success can be more than you imagine.

Trusted Advisors Team

Every business owner has a need for advice. Sometimes it is just nice to have and other times it is imperative to the safety and security of the organization. What is important is to know when to turn to professionals for help to keep you and your business out of trouble and to keep stress in check. Here are the few professionals I believe are critical for every small business as a trusted advisor.

An Accounting Professional

The planning and budgeting you completed in the Plan It! section are the beginning of good accounting practices. There is another element that is more than just nice to have — an accounting professional as a trusted advisor.

As a small business owner, you may have decided to wear all of the financial management hats. You may keep your own books and prepare your own taxes. This may be fine for the early years of your business. But as soon as possible, engage an accounting professional who you can rely on as a partner in your business. Make it a part of your plan to find and develop a relationship with an individual or a firm to help you manage your business by the numbers.

Find an accountant before you need one. Even before you engage them fully in the practice of managing your financial picture add an accounting professional to your trusted advisor team. An accountant should be one of your first partners. Meet to understand how they like to work with their clients and describe your business goals. This initial meeting should be free. If it is not, keep looking.

Find the best fit. Not all accounting professionals are the same. Some specialize in working with individuals or larger businesses. Take your time finding an accountant who is a good fit for you and your business. Look for an accountant who works with small businesses. You might also ask how many clients they have in your industry or business type. The more they know about how you do business the more valuable their advice will be.

Look for a chief financial officer. You will probably not have a dedicated staff member to act as your CFO. This means you can benefit from finding an accountant who is willing to play the part. They should be willing to discuss your financial strategy and help you to balance your budget. They should be willing to educate you and give you advice when needed.

Be certain they fit your budget. Like most professionals, accountants are available for a wide range of fees. Larger firms typically charge more. Pay attention to when they charge and for what. As a small business owner who views an accountant as a member of your advisory team you will want to have access to them at a cost you can afford. Some accountants charge for each minute they spend with you or for you. This means they will charge for every e-mail you send them, every short telephone call, and all of your strategy meetings. Talk to your accounting professional candidates about how they will charge you. If possible, find one who has a flat fee for tax and accounting services that fits your budget.

CPA vs. accountant: CPA's (Certified Public Accountants) are accountants who have passed a licensing examination. That means all CPA's are accountants, but not all accountants are CPA's. Which is best for you and your business? Many small businesses use the services of an accountant, and there are many competent accountants serving small business. Most of the time and for most circumstances an accountant can meet your needs, but there are specific circumstances in which using the services of a CPA has advantages. The best reason to engage a CPA for your business is that a CPA is eligible to represent you before the IRS, while an accountant is not. Should you be audited, you will need that representation. Another reason some may choose a CPA versus an accountant is that CPAs are required to remain current on tax codes and laws and fulfill continuing education mandates and accountants are not.

An Insurance Professional

Many small business owners only think about insurance at renewal time, when they have a claim, or need to fulfill requests for coverage confirmation. Insurance is not just a "nice to have" it is a "must have." The need to have the right coverage should not be taken lightly. The minimum coverage may meet the needs of your landlord, license, or mortgagor but it may not be enough to protect you against a variety of circumstances you do not control. It can sometimes be the difference between a thriving business and "out of business."

The goal of having an insurance professional as a member of your trusted advisor team should be to help you to select the right combination of personal and business coverage, deductibles, limits, premiums, and self-insured risk to give you protection and peace of mind.

Once you find this advisor, let them help you create coverage that is best for you now and in the future. Have a plan that spans more than just a single year. Update it annually or more often as your business changes. Ask about coverages that help you protect yourself, your family and your business. You might discuss professional liability, auto coverage, long term care insurance for owners and key employees, key contributor life insurance, disability, umbrella coverage and anything specific to your business needs.

There are a number of factors to consider when finding the right insurance professional to add to your advisor team. Some of them are listed below. The most important factors are not. Factors critical to a successful relationship are that the insurance professional shares your values and is committed to giving you and your business the attention it deserves.

This is a time when you do not want to be a small fish in a big pond. Be sure your business matters to them. You also do not want to be a number on a computer screen time zones away. Look for someone local you can meet with face-to-face and get to know. The best resource starts with a strong "relationship."

<u>Broker vs. agent</u>: Is the best relationship an insurance agent or an insurance broker? The answer is either will

do if they bring with them the right knowledge and experience, understanding of your needs now and in the future, and have the willingness to partner with you and your business for your success. Both agents and brokers are insurance professionals and either could be a valuable member of your team.

You can find the right professional for your advisor team in either camp but you will want to understand the difference before you begin the search. "Captive" insurance agents are employed by and work on behalf of an insurance company. They can only offer services from the company that they are appointed with and they are compensated directly by those companies. These captive agents may be reluctant to tell you if there is a coverage gap in their policy that the company doesn't fill.

Brokers do not typically work for a single insurance company. They represent a number of different companies and often build their business on finding the best price rather than providing the most thorough coverage. Brokers can charge a brokerage fee as long as it is disclosed.

Look for experience and company rating: In your selection process focus on the experience, knowledge, reputation and references of the insurance professionals you are considering. Every insurance professional has a unique set of skills, abilities, experience and accreditations. Find one that will offer you references on how they have served others. Take the time to check those references. Be sure you are working with someone who suits you and your business best and has a track record of consistency, fairness, responsiveness, reliability and excellent customer service.

It is often helpful the insurance professional has experience working with small business and in your industry, or at the very least your market place. Their learning curve on your needs can be shortened and they can be more effective in less time.

Not all insurance companies are the same. Look for financial strength and the ability of the company to meet its ongoing financial obligations — for instance, paying your claim if the need ever arises. It is easy to check the rating of the company or companies that offer you coverage. For an overview of the rating process and ratings on most companies you can turn to A.M. Best Company, a global credit rating agency that provides an independent third-party evaluation with regard to life, homeowners and other insurance products. Find them online at www.ambest.com.

Notice I did not mention anything about premiums and prices. All you need to know is that insurance is a highly regulated industry. Premiums must be approved by the Insurance Commissioner in each state. Ask your advisor candidates to explain how rates are developed and how they might differ. Keep in mind insurance professionals are human and sometimes they too get busy and just sell the least expensive plan they can. This is the easiest, least time consuming sale and often what the client thinks they desire — but it's important to find someone willing to explain their recommendations rather than simply signing you up for the cheapest policy.

ADVICE FROM YOUR PEERS

"The right insurance professional should be willing to advise you so you can make an informed decision. They should help coach you on appropriate coverage based on your risk tolerance." Drew Johnson, ChFC, CMA, Agent, COUNTRY Financial

A Business Attorney

As my professional friend and business attorney Jim says, "The most important role I can play for my small business clients is to keep them out of trouble." Jim emphasizes there is tremendous cost and risk for a small business if a dispute turns into arbitration or a lawsuit. In addition to the court costs and attorney fees there is loss of work time and possible fines and settlements. At the very least there is the cost of the distraction.

No one likes to think they will ever have a need of a business attorney for more than just business entity creation or contract reviews. If you never need legal assistance, great, but do not wait until the need arises to try to locate and form a relationship with a business attorney. This is a resource you want on your advisory team from the very beginning. If they know you and your business it will simplify the process, lower your level of stress, and increase your level of trust.

Often an initial consultation is free, but do not let a small fee deter you, it is more than worth the relationship. Shop around for someone who specializes in working with small business and is priced for your budget. These specialists understand your needs. You will find them in smaller firms or operating as a solo practitioner. Do not let their practice size or style concern you. What you are interested in is their track record and experience. Ask for references and check them. Check their state bar association record.

Understand how they like to maintain relationships when you do not have any active issues. You may even find a small business attorney who has a special "small business retainer program." These can be a good match for your needs.

Often I have clients ask about online "do it yourself" legal services. I cannot recommend these services; neither can I deny they may sometimes be adequate. It all depends on the issue and the need. If you want to be safe, find the right business attorney and let them handle your needs. This is not an area to look for a "cheap" alternative.

A Business Coach

You knew this was coming — everyone needs a coach! You may have raw talent and experience. You may have a track record of success. As a small business owner, you almost certainly have a willingness to take risk and bear responsibility, but why go it alone? Add a business coach to your trusted advisor team. At the very least a coach should be of zero cost to you by helping you create enough additional revenue to cover their fees. The right coach will help you do a lot more than that. With their guidance and encouragement, you can push through your comfort zone and reach a higher level of success. Skilled coaches help you see roadblocks and obstacles that keep you from reaching your full potential and offer you resources to fill needs and promote your growth.

Just as with your other trusted advisor team members, not all coaches are equal. Find one who understands your industry, has experience with your issues and challenges, and can give you references to support their track record.

Always work with a coach you feel "gets you." You should expect to feel comfortable with a coach in the first 1-3 meetings. After that, if you still struggle to 'connect' they may not be the coach for you.

Do not be afraid to try more than one coach. You will learn something from every coach you work with. Six months is the minimum time frame to see results. I recommend you give the relationship a chance, but do not stay too long. Gain the advantage from multiple experiences.

ADVICE FROM YOUR PEERS

"I thought having a business coach was a luxury. It almost felt arrogant and extravagant. It's not. Frankly, it's the most effective way to build a business and not lose your mind in the process. My reasons for hiring my business coach, Sherry Jordan, may sound like trite business-speak, but hear me out. A good business coach, like Sherry helps me prioritize. She helps me articulate my dream and keeps me on track. She's objective about my business. She's not emotional and yet still is a cheerleader. She speaks the truth. She challenges, listens and distills. She sees the big picture and helps create a process so I don't have to reinvent the wheel. She keeps me accountable." Tracy Bagli Hooper, Founder, The Confidence Project

LOVE IT!

Identify open spots on your resource team. Record the action to locate, contact, or meet with potential members. Record an action to ask professional contacts or other small business owners for referrals. If you already have these partners, consider an action to set up a meeting to discuss your plans for this year and beyond. Review with them your vision and budget for the plan period. Ask for advice.

COACH'S ADVICE

Do not go it alone. But remember, the company you keep can make you stronger or drag you down.

Keep Inspiring Company

In her book, *It Takes a Village: And Other Lessons Children Teach Us,* former First Lady Hillary Rodham Clinton presents her vision for the children of America. She focuses on the impact other people outside the family have, for better or worse, on a child's well-being, and advocates a society which meets all of a child's needs. I have a similar vision for small business owners.

Small business owners are impacted, for better or worse, by the people they surround themselves with. Their needs are met by friends, family, other business owners, business resources, professional groups, institutions, clients and others. Each of you has a choice on who you allow to be in your "village." Choose well. Choose people who have high standards for themselves and everyone they share their time with. Choose people who see the possibilities in their life, their business and in yours. Choose people with positive "can do" attitudes.

Choose people who will inspire and support you. If you do not know anyone like this, start your search.

You can find them surrounded by other inspiring professionals. Find one and you will find many. All small business owners need to be surrounded by others successful small business owners. Start there! Then identify people or types of people you feel can inspire some change in you or spark movement on projects you are working on. For example, if you want to improve your self-confidence, identify people who are confident and spend time with them. If you want to write a book, find people who have published one and get to know them. You will find they are happy to share their experience and even tips to save you time and money.

ADVICE FROM YOUR PEERS

"If you do not have any friends who are self-employed, find some. It is a lifestyle that has to be experienced to be understood. Having friends who can relate and/or inspire you are part of the formula for success. You cannot have too many sources for emotional support, or inspiration."

Tara Davisson, Founder, Jenkins Davisson, LLC

LOVE IT!

Who are the five to 10 people you spend most of your time with? Do they inspire you? Are they like-minded? If you cannot say you have a full complement of inspiring personal and professional friends make it a point to search for them and develop relationships.

COACH'S ADVICE

If you find you are surrounded by people who do not inspire you it may be time to change the company you keep.

Do What You Do Best—Always!

When given the opportunity we will all gravitate towards the "thing" we enjoy the most. Why? Because this is where we find the most joy and where we feel most accomplished and confident. It is also where we know we make the most profound contribution. So, why not do what we do best all the time? For most small business owners this can sound like an impossible dream.

Small business owners, especially those in the early years of start-up, find they are doing something they do not enjoy doing as much as thirty percent of the time. It is the cost of owning it all.

Often, to own your own business you accept responsibility for areas that do not interest you or plain and simple, bore you. That is what accounting was for me. For you it might be inventory, ordering your own supplies, or cleaning the office bathrooms. With the right business growth plan this is not a scenario that lasts very long.

As soon as possible, you, the business owner, should be taking advantage of your choices to do what you do best and delegate or outsource the rest.

There are some very good reasons why small business owners should stick to doing what they do best. The first and most important is because it brings the most joy. That is part of 'loving' your business. The more you enjoy what you are doing the more worthwhile living the small business lifestyle will be. The more you can do what you truly enjoy the more likely you are to enjoy owning your business.

The second reason is because it is your highest and best use. This thing you do best is often the service, ability, or talent that inspired you to open your business in the first place. It may be the business.

Any time you are doing anything but what you do best you are not nudging the business forward towards more sales, more clients, more revenue, and more profit. If you focus on what you do best you will reach your business goals more quickly. The more quickly you meet your goals it is more likely you can afford to do only what you enjoy most.

If you need more reasons to focus on your strengths than those listed in the paragraphs above you can include: you'll feel the most confident; you'll feel the least resistance; you'll make the fewest mistakes; and your tasks are accomplished more quickly.

If you are not in a place where you can delegate or outsource, make sure you are working towards those goals. Identify what you will outsource or delegate first. Update your budget to include the costs of hiring or outsourcing. Know what it will take to get you to this place and get there as quickly as possible.

Delegate

There are several reasons why delegating is critical to small business owners. 1) As already stated, it allows you to do what you do best; 2) it allows you to reclaim time for executive level responsibilities such as planning, strategy, leadership, decision making and organizational development; 3) it helps you to build a stronger team through engagement; and 4) it improves efficiency. Owners get caught in the feeling that delegating is relinquishing control. Often there is a struggle with identifying which responsibilities can be carried out by others, delegating those responsibilities and then getting out of the way so that others can complete their assignments. All of this is just part of perfecting the art of delegating. Mastering this skill takes practice. The sooner you get started the sooner you will be comfortable identifying who you can delegate what to.

<u>Identify the tasks</u>: Start by taking time to identify all the tasks you complete in a given period of time (e.g. day, week, month). Now, examine which of these tasks really

need your involvement. Could any be delegated to someone else?

Identify who you will delegate to: Now, decide who you will delegate them to. Who is capable? Who can learn them if they are not yet ready? Who is available? Who has asked for more responsibility or opportunity?

Be clear on your directions and expectations: Do not just hand these tasks off and hope they are completed to your satisfaction. Be clear on how you want them to be carried out, when, what you expect the results to be, and how you want to receive feedback on the results, etc. There is a fine line between setting clear expectations and micromanagement. One is critical to the success of delegation. The other is sure to contribute to failure.

Check-in on the results: You should check in on the results, but be careful not to hover or over manage. It is reasonable to expect reports on progress or feedback but you must ask for that and then be clear on how you want to see that information. Ask them to tweak the information until you can see a full picture from the reports.

ADVICE FROM YOUR PEERS

"Now that I outsource bookkeeping, tax preparation, social media, search engine optimization, and human resource support I cannot believe how long it took me to make these moves. I was a slow learner. I worried about the expense. I wish I had fit those expenses into my budget earlier. I more than pay for them with time I spend building new partnerships and developing new business." Diane J., Owner, The Bird House

LOVE IT!

Identify what role(s) you most like to play in your business and clear the way to focus on that role or roles. If need be, outsource, delegate or eliminate. If your budget does not allow for that now, make a plan to move towards this state of being. Prioritize the changes. Update your budget to include the costs.

COACH'S CHALLENGE

Practice delegating. Start small if need be, but practice. Make a commitment to allow others to complete the tasks, projects, or functions without your micromanagement. This is the only way to see what they are truly capable of.

Invest in Yourself

In the previous section it was stated you should always do what you do best. This is true. Not only should you do what you do best, but you should build on what you are already good at. Invest in yourself. Decide what you want to do better and learn or practice until you master the new skill(s).

Build on Your Strengths

In work and in life, you are your best asset. We are always looking for ways to improve our chances to succeed, to get the job done, to make more money, to be more of what we want to be or have more of what we want to have. Often we feel we have little, if any, control over what we receive — when in fact we have more control than we realize. The choices we make and the actions we take make all the difference in the outcome.

It all starts with an awareness of our strengths, abilities, talents and attitudes. As a small business owner, most often there is no one to help you identify your strengths and encourage you to build on them. In the "Do It" section of the book you evaluated yourself as a leader/owner. What did you learn? What do you do best? While you can always strive for a bit of improvement in your areas of weakness you may find you get better results if you focus on building on your strengths. At the very least you will enjoy this development process more.

Training and Education

Wallis, Duchess of Windsor is famous for having said, "You can never be too rich or too thin." She might be right, but I would add to that, "too educated or too knowledgeable." For you see, another famous British figure and philosopher, Francis Bacon, said it best: "Knowledge is power." When what you know contributes to your power to succeed why not learn as much as possible?

In our annual planning sessions all of my clients set goals for training and education. Some do it because they are required to maintain licenses or contracts, but even if they are not, it is an area that I emphasize as being important to ongoing success. You may think you know it all or that you know enough to have a successful business. I would argue you are already losing a grip on the future of your business if you believe that to be true.

Just think about how much the world has changed since you were a child, since you graduated from high school, college, maybe even since you started your business. Change is constant. With change comes the need for you to adjust, to learn and upgrade and stay current. Identify what you need and what you want to learn, and make time to do so.

Development

Abraham Maslow's quote, "What a man can be, he must be," forms the basis of his theory that all humans have need of self-actualization. Self-actualization refers to a person's full potential and the drive and desire to reach that full potential. You might think of it as a desire to accomplish everything you can or to become the most you can be. For example, one person may have the strong desire to become the leading authority on a medical procedure and another may strive to become an ideal parent.

For each, their self-actualization equals a sense of accomplishment.

Maslow suggested that to reach your fully actualized self you must pass through several stages of development, master those and then move on. Let's apply Maslow's theory to your business self. I think we can all agree every small business owner has potential that can be developed and to reach that potential we must first attempt and master certain other skills.

What does your view of a self-actualized business owner look like? Are you working on the skills and experiences you will need to reach your full potential?

ADVICE FROM YOUR PEERS

"Small business is perfect for those who are lifelong learners. Be open to change as you learn and prepare your teams for change. It keeps work life exciting, challenging, and provides opportunity to grow yourself, your team and your organization." Sandra E. Stryker, Founder, Life's Work Physical Therapy

LOVE IT!

Identify your strengths. Then identify how you can build on them. What classes might you take or experiences do you need to further develop? Record actions you plan to take.

COACH'S CHALLENGE

Accept that you will never know it all. Commit to learning something new every day. Encourage others on your team to learn. Be a good role model.

Take Time to Reflect and Refresh

Growing up with vibrant and precocious siblings, the activity in our house was always on high and the noise level was often at a fever pitch. My mother, a fun-loving and patient woman, would generally ignore us until she would hit her limit. It was at that moment we would hear her shout, "I can't hear myself think!" This meant we all needed to lower the volume and, depending on mama's tone, we may need to vacate the premises. Mama needed to regroup, reorganize, plan, and rejuvenate for the next round of managing the children, the household, and her own very busy life.

Time to think, reflect, and regroup is important for everyone. We all need quiet time to find our center, challenge ourselves, and adjust our course of action. As a small business owner who works with other small business owners I frequently find this time is undervalued. Often it is the first thing to go when the schedule starts to bulge. But, in fact, it should be the last thing to go. Why are we so willing to give up something so important?

The owner is so focused on what they are losing or giving up they do not see what they are gaining. When any small business owner schedules "regroup" time or even "think" time it generally means taking time away from the business. If you are also a provider of the service or support, it is also time away from revenue generation, administration, or one of the other dozens of roles that you play in the day-to-day operation. For most, time away feels like time that has to be recovered.

Let me remind you that time to think and recover are also your responsibility. It is part of the time you dedicate to working "on" your business. It is your way of being the best you can be. Have you ever tried to take a test on no sleep or run a race after skipping a few meals? You might start out ok but you lose steam fast. It is hard to sustain your energy and make it to the conclusion or finish line. Trying to run a business with no time to restore your energy will have the same impact. The first symptoms will include grouchy behavior, resentment or anger. Relationships at work and home will start to suffer. As you continue to ignore the need you may find you get sick more often or depression will creep in. If the need continues to be ignored you may find a variety of things will happen but at the very least you will change the way you feel about your business. You may decide this is not the lifestyle you would have chosen, and you do not want it anymore.

If you are still not convinced taking time away is important here are a few more ways to justify this time to work "on" your business by taking care of yourself:

1. Think time results in clear direction. You are more likely to get where you are going faster if you have clear directions. Without it, you can go in the wrong direction and must make corrections that cost you time and money.

2. Think time helps you clarify what you want. Knowing what you want will help you focus your resources. It reduces trial and error. It improves your profitability and your efficiency.

3. Think time allows you to gain a clear vision. Having a clear vision will help you retain employees and clients. People want to know where you are going and if they should go with you. If you are clear on your vision then you can craft messages that will allow them to make choices about loyalty.

4. Time to think means time to restore your energy. Being at your best all the time is difficult for small business owners. Research tells us you are your most productive following a break. Although vacations or extended time away is something you should make time for, just a little time away from your regular routine is valuable. Being our best means we give our best to get our best.

5. Making time will save you time. Yes — taking time away to think about where you are going and how you are going to get there or what you want will actually help you

get it. Some say you will save as much as four times the amount you spend on planning. Just one day spent thinking and planning can save you four days in execution.

Even though it may feel like a loss of productivity, without refreshing and thinking time you are running at a rate of diminishing return. Diminishing return means you will get less for the same effort than if you were fully prepared. Translated, this means there are no rewards for working past the amount of time you can be effective. Accept this and put time on your calendar to refresh and renew.

Reflection Time vs Vacation

There are two kinds of reflection time. One is scheduled regularly, often weekly, and is time you will spend reflecting on needs, accomplishments, opportunities and planning. You might also use this time on personal development or research. It is time away from your regular routine spent working "on" your business. I challenge my clients to block out one half to one full day a week for this purpose.

The other type of time away is vacation time. Before I begin a relationship with new clients we spend time setting goals and identifying challenges. Over and over exhausted business owners report they want more time to spend with family and enjoying life and then confess they have not had a "real" vacation (more than a few days) in years. Taking a vacation goes on the top of the goal list for those owners. Most are surprised when they successfully take a vacation and return to find they are more productive and enjoy their business more.

How much is enough?

As I mentioned above, regular reflective time can be satisfied with one-half to one day a week. Vacation time is a different matter. The answer is, take whatever it takes for you to rest, relax, recover, and return to your best self. This amount is going to be different for different people. The tendency is to take too little time rather than too much. When I poll my new clients, the majority tell me they have not had a two week vacation in years, if ever. Most have not had more than a weekend in the past twelve months. This is not enough.

If you look around at mandated vacation schedules set by corporate giants you can deduce that the more responsible the position the more undisturbed time one needs to refresh. I come from the banking business, and many executives in that industry are required to take two weeks consecutively. There is a message in this policy. For me it says that you cannot get the full effect of time away unless you have sufficient days to recover. I can assure you that an awful lot of research has gone into the development of that policy.

How do you make the time?

Just make the time. Put it on the calendar. Make it a priority. Develop a plan well in advance if you need coverage or back-up.

If you need to justify this time to refresh here are a few facts:

- You are most productive following rest.
- You are your company's best asset. Rest is an important part of protecting that asset.
- Prioritizing self-care is part of role modeling which is a leadership behavior.
- The number one reason most owners give for starting their own business is to have flexibility with the way they spend their time. If you do not take advantage of your control over your own schedule you are not meeting one of the goals you set for owning your business.

ADVICE FROM YOUR PEERS

"When Sherry suggested that I block out a full day on my calendar I was skeptical. I could not imagine how taking time for myself could possibly help me catch up with all the work I had to do. As it turns out, she was so right! I look forward to Thursdays and I protect them. No one sees me on Thursday, not even my closest friends." Jordan C., Landscape Designer

LOVE IT!

Put time on your calendar to reflect, plan, and develop. I recommend one day per week. Protect that time. Put time on your calendar for vacations. Plan them in advance.

COACH'S CHALLENGE

Prioritize reflection and vacation time. You are worth it! If you must, think of it as an experiment then examine the benefits. Repeat.

Trust Your Inner Voice

We all have one. It can be described as a semi-constant internal monologue we have with ourselves or as "thinking in words." More commonly you might recognize it as the nagging feeling that you have forgotten something or the mental tug to drive down a certain aisle in the parking garage to find an empty space. It is also the one that shouts inside your head when you say "yes" and instantly wish you had said "no," or when you agree to engage a client you know is not a good fit and then regret your decision the moment they are out of your presence. We all have this trusted companion with our best interest in mind. This "little voice" wants us to grow to our full potential. This inner voice will keep us out of danger and help us to avoid pain, but most of us do not trust it nearly enough.

When you own your own business, you must find a way to trust your inner voice more. Sometimes this inner voice is the only advice you will get. This inner voice will save you time, money, embarrassment and much more. It knows you better than you know yourself and is in touch with what you really need — not just what you say you want. I am going to put myself on the line here by saying, “I have never, ever, received bad advice from my inner voice— not once.” Think about it. Have you?

My client Ann tells marvelous stories about how her inner voice is the source of her success. She calls the voice Harry (after her dad). Harry is Ann’s “partner” in a self-publishing company. She has real conversations with Harry about who to work with, and what to do when and how. When Ann does not listen to Harry’s advice, she pays the price. Those projects tend to take longer, be more difficult, and yield lower returns. When she does listen, projects slide easily through the process and the product sales exceed expectations. As it turns out, Harry is the best part of Ann. He guides her to the right clients and projects. He challenges her to “play” bigger, to take risks and push the limits. Because no business is ever perfect, this same inner voice helps her to restore confidence and brush off disappointment when challenges arise.

Listening to your inner voice does not come naturally for most of us. It can frequently seem like chatter you wish you could turn off. It might be too faint or overshadowed by another little internal companion, the inner critic (picture the character on your shoulder with the horns and pitchfork). The critic showers us with self-doubt. It whispers to us that we are not capable, smart enough, strong enough, expert enough, offer something unique enough or good enough. The little critic has its place. It helps us to balance our thinking. In the end, your kinder, gentler inner voice (the one with the halo) should be your guide.

I am still working on the name of my inner voice but I can attest to the importance of abiding by its counsel. Many of the most important decisions in my life and in my business have been based on a hunch, a feeling, or my intuition — all of which are nothing more than a whisper from this inner voice. Can you hear yours? If you cannot it may be because you block the message or you question the intent. Let me assure you your authentic inner voice has your best interest in mind — always! Trust your inner voice. Have courage and follow it.

ADVICE FROM YOUR PEERS

"Plain and simple find your inner voice and trust it. Together you will find success." Ann Bulllard, Founder, HBC Publishing

LOVE IT!

If you are not in touch with your inner voice, work on gaining awareness. If you are, listen to what it has to say and resolve to learn to trust its counsel.

COACH'S CHALLENGE

Take a chance. Follow the advice of your inner voice just once and see what happens.

Live the Vision

Millions of small business owners are out there waiting. They are waiting to wake up one morning and know they have reached their goals. Then they will start to live the life they have earned. Looking for signs in their bank account, in the news, or in their community, they are sure when they reach "success" it will be announced. Then and only then can they really begin to reap the benefits of all they have accomplished. Then and only then will they feel like they have "made it."

Sound the horns — you have already made it. Being a small business owner is not for the faint of heart. It is not easy to trust your ideas or instincts. It is not easy to accept that you and you alone will be responsible for your success, your livelihood and often for the care and comfort of others such as your spouse, your children or your parents. You are already a success! You can, and should, start to live your vision of success today. Be the person you expect to be when you [fill in the blanks]. Be that person now! I know this may not sound easy. It does take practice. But it's worth it. After all, having a life you love was one of your primary reasons for owning your business.

Create a Mental Image

Walt Disney is famous for having said, "If you can dream it, you can do it." Translated it means you first must believe "it" is possible. The same is true in small business success. You, and only you, can create your future. It all starts with a clear image of what you expect your business to be and who you expect to become.

Who do you want to be? How will you look, behave, and think when you reach your fully actualized goals as a business owner? Can you see the picture? If not, spend some time with it. Etch those details clearly in your mind and start to see yourself that way. If you meditate, incorporate those images into your practice. Make a list. Create a dream board. Do something that will be visible to help you to become crystal clear on the image.

If you're struggling with this, you might look at other successful small business owners. Find a few you admire and examine the reasons you admire them. What characteristics do they have you want to develop? What about skill? You might even look at the material things they have acquired or the recognition they have achieved. Borrow them until you create your own image.

Be the Image

Once you have a clear picture of who you will be, begin to live up to that image. Act the part. Dress the part. Put on the image just like you would a suit of clothes and wear them every day. Start to ask yourself, "How would the future me handle this situation?" and then act. Practice being the future you until you become that person.

Outline a plan to develop the skills you want to develop. Get help and advice in any area you feel you are not equipped to master.

LOVE IT!

Take the time to be clear on your image. A project like a dream board is often helpful. Find images in magazines or on the internet that represent different aspects of your image. Paste them on poster board or copy them to your computer screen. They should be visible every day. Once you have the image, put yourself in the picture.

COACH'S CHALLENGE

Give away or throw away anything that does not support your new image. I started by cleaning out my closet. You might do the same. Wear only clothes that are worn by the image in your vision.

Be an Optimist

"If you don't like what's happening in your life change your mind." – His Holiness the Dalai Lama

"If you don't like what's happening in your business, change your attitude." – Sherry Jordan, Coach

Success begins with an attitude. Yes, you have an impact on your overall success by the way you think and what you believe. Your beliefs can be the difference between having it all or nothing at all.

As a child my sweet mother, often mentioned in this book, gave me great snippets of wisdom. One I am most fond of and often repeat is, "Honey, the only thing you really have control over is your attitude." What my mother was trying to tell me was I could choose to be optimistic or pessimistic and my choice would have an influence on the outcome of my situation. I offer you the same advice.

As a business owner it is very important for you to have the right attitude — one of success and optimism. You must believe you can succeed, win and have it all.

Optimism costs nothing. It is not a line item on your budget. It is yours to control. If you are the slightest bit pessimistic you are probably already saying, "But, I am just made this way. I was born a pessimist. My glass is always half empty and that has kept me safe for years." Even if you want to change, you may not think you can.

Good news! Personality researchers have discovered that we can change some traits or qualities once thought to be scripted at a very young age. They have identified one of these traits as optimism.

Pessimists are skeptical of everything. They are certain that if there is a potential bad result, it will happen to them. They think positive outcomes are for someone else and, when good things do happen, they tend to overlook them or believe they are accidental.

Optimists seem to believe they are destined to suffer less, recover quicker, and have the outcome that, even if it is less than optimal, is necessary to propel them on to extreme happiness. So, what difference does it make? In scientific studies, optimistic people are found to be healthier, rated higher in employer surveys, feel less helpless and even have stronger relationships — including marriages. They are better liked, and considered to be more fun. Shouldn't we all want that? If you answer "yes" to this question, and you are a pessimist, how do you morph into an optimist? The simple answer is practice. Here are few practical practice tips:

Surround yourself with other optimists: One of the fastest ways to change your attitude is to borrow one. Find people who have a positive attitude and emulate it.

Don't just think, act: Be aware optimism is not just relentless cheer or "positive thinking." It is more about what you do and the actions you take.

Be persistent: When at first you don't succeed, try, try again! Optimists do not give up. They learn from mistakes and keep going. They find another way and try it.

Pay attention and keep a record: When good things happen to you, acknowledge them. A great way to do this is to keep a note on your calendar. You will be surprised how many "good" things happen in a week.

Bad news in small doses: No one says you should live "uninformed," but you also do not need to read every news source, or see every report. I recommend you pick a news resource that gives you the full extent of the news important to your work, family and community and leave the rest. Constant review of the same news is reinforcement! This includes blogs and rumor sessions around the water cooler. It might also include social pages and videos.

Argue with yourself: Ask yourself, "Why not?" If you are someone who normally thinks everything is a long shot, argue, "Why?" Learn to question why you think the way you do. Looking at situations rationally often helps to justify a positive outcome.

Expose yourself to humor: It has been said you can only have one emotion at a time. Choose humor — then sadness and pessimistic thoughts have no place to live.

Old habits die hard. The question you should ask is, "Will it be worth it?" How might your life and business change if you can think about it more positively? Only you can answer these questions, but remember your attitude is a choice.

ADVICE FROM YOUR PEERS

"There is never a good time to start a business and never enough time to build a business. Life will get in the way. The have to's the should do's, the honey do's will all happen. So will the unexpected. Life is not linear. Build your business anyway. If you don't, somebody else will take your dream. It is your dream, your idea, your business plan, your impact to make, your financial future. Get going. And, by the way, enjoy! That's part of the point, right?" Tracy Bagli Hooper, Founder, The Confidence Project

LOVE IT!

Are you a pessimist or an optimist? If you are an optimist, great! Carry on. If you are a pessimist vow to make changes and practice optimism.

Spread Good Will

As new business owners are getting started they almost always hit a point where everything stops. After months or even years of networking, selling, building, and promoting, growth and flow stalls. The phone does not ring. The projects dry up. No one walks through the door. You begin to wonder if the success you were experiencing was a fluke or ruse. You might even fear you have made a terrible mistake and question your reasons for opening your own business. Over the years I have worked with hundreds of clients who have had this experience and my advice is always the same: give something away to get it rolling again. Yes, give it away!

What you give away is completely up to you. I give free sessions to someone who is opening a new business or a workshop to a charity I am fond of. Many of my clients give away a product or a service to someone who has been loyal, or in response to a kind gesture. Why does this work? Giving ignites feelings of well-being and good will. Those feelings lead to confidence. Confidence attracts [insert a long list of good things].

This does not mean you should "go broke" to feel good. Make wise and meaningful choices about what you give away. Put pro bono and donation costs in your budget.

Spreading goodwill can also be sharing advice or experiences. Anything you do to help someone else succeed, save time, save money, feel more confident, or restore their hope is a check mark in the "done good" column. You should reap real benefits, tangible benefits, from goodwill gestures. Expect them. Enjoy them. Commit to doing more of them.

ADVICE FROM YOUR PEERS

"Giving something away is magic. It acts like a restart button. I would never have believed it but when I reported in my accountability group that I was having the worst month ever in my business someone said, "Give something away. It always works for me." I tried it and it works. I am not going to question it in the future. Just do it."

Lauren Prescott, Owner, Sundown Spa

LOVE IT!

If you are "stuck," give something away. Be sure it is meaningful but not prohibitive to your success.

COACH'S CHALLENGE

Do one good deed every day.

Celebrate Everything!

Both children and adults enjoyed the journey of J.K. Rowling's character Harry Potter from poor misunderstood boy to a storybook hero. I was one of them.

One of my favorite scenes takes place in the first book when Harry has his eleventh birthday. On the day of the event, ignored or forgotten by his family, Harry decides to celebrate alone. He draws a birthday cake in the dust on the floor, blows out pretend candles, and has his own little birthday celebration.

Just like Harry, you need not wait for validation to celebrate milestones or accomplishments. It is nice to share, but do not wait for someone to recognize you have met your goals, achieved success, or received awards. Plan your own celebration, big or small, and spread the joy you are feeling in knowing you crossed the finish line. You worked hard. You deserve it — and sometimes you are the only one who will know.

Call your peers and share the good news. Invite them to a lunch to share the moment. Choose a special restaurant or a special dish or dessert.

Share your story in your peer group or accountability group. Remember in doing so you set a great example for the other members to do the same.

Send yourself some flowers or buy a new plant for your office.

Buy a reminder gift such as a plaque or artwork for your business.

Take a photograph and display it for everyone to see.

If you have employees, share "wins" in a staff meeting. Acknowledge others who contributed. Treat them to lunch. Fly balloons. Hang banners. Turn on the music. Give yourselves a round of applause.

Do not hesitate to include everyone you care about. Anyone important to you will want to share your milestones. This is not bragging. Think of it as humbly giving them the gift of being proud to know you and all you have created. Make it special and enjoy yourself. Indulge in the glow of the hour and warm embrace of receiving praise. Be a receiver.

No matter how or what you decide — celebrate.

ADVICE FROM YOUR PEERS

"The number one characteristic that has led to my current success is humility. As a business owner you're expected to know it all and do it all, but the truth is you can't. Believe me I've tried. Even though I have an MBA and come from a family of entrepreneurs my biggest success has come from accepting I don't know it all and asking for help. Whether it's been from my business coach, mentor or peer groups, some of the best ideas that have led to profit or other business success have not been my ideas. Instead of faltering the many times I should have, with their help, I've been able to turn turbulence into terrific opportunity." Nick Footer, Founder, In2itive Search, LLC

LOVE IT!

Mark your calendar to review your accomplishments every month. Share them. A staff meeting is a great place to share them. If you do not have a staff or staff meeting share them with your coach or peer group. When you reach milestones share them publicly on Facebook, your newsletter, throw a party, or whatever feels right.

COACH'S CHALLENGE

Be humble when you are asking for help but bold when you are celebrating.

A Gracious, Well-Planned Exit

Over the years I have had dozens of small business owners tell me that they plan to work as long as they are on the right side of the dirt. Some even tell me this was one of their motivations for starting their own business — they could not be forced into retirement. It may be your plan to work long after a typical retirement age but do not use this as an excuse not to plan for retirement. Part of loving the business you own is the knowledge that it is providing for you and anyone you are responsible for today or in the future. Think of a gracious and well planned exit as having an escape route in case of fire. You may never need it, but you want to know it is there.

Sell it or keep it?

When your days of business ownership come to an end you have choices to make. Will you keep it and change the role you play — or sell it. Maximizing either option takes planning. Selling your business may seem simple but there is much to consider. Not every business has the value you might think it has. You are often the most valuable asset and without you the business may be worth far less than it is with you performing the services or guiding others who do.

Have a Succession Plan

Succession planning begins long before you have any thoughts of exiting your business. From the very beginning, or very soon thereafter, you will want to begin to develop plans for your future. Part of those plans should be who will take over if, or when, you are not there. Surround yourself with people who have potential or who are already as good or better than you are in whatever role you play. Engage them in plans for the future and understand how their career goals might overlap or intertwine with the future needs of your business. Carefully, and without promise, help those people to understand how they might be a part of the future of your business. Set goals for experiences they should have and education or development they might need. Be sure to let them drive the process. You never want to force anyone into a position they do not want — including your children.

If you have children who work in the business do not assume they will want to take over. It is not always the case they have an interest in a leadership or executive role. They have to be suited for the role and ready. If they are interested, and well suited, then help them to get ready. Start early and set long term goals to groom them for the role you have agreed upon. Transition parts of the role to them as early as possible and support them as they grow into those roles.

If your children do not want to succeed you, do not force them. Let them know you are looking for leaders for the organization's future and work a steady plan to find those leaders, hire them, train them, and turn over responsibility to them.

Save for Retirement

Many small business owners have all of their assets tied up in their company. They do not save for retirement but rather have a plan to take what they need from the business when the time is right. This plan is often flawed. Start by knowing what you need and then understanding what your business can provide.

A large part of planning for retirement is being clear on what it will take to live in the manner you have chosen and funding that with something other than Social Security. Develop a budget on your own or with the help of your financial advisor or financial planner. Once you know what is needed, your ongoing operating budget should include a designated percentage of income or funding for retirement. How you use these funds should be a discussion you have with your financial planner or advisor. They will want to look at the whole picture and then give you advice on how to be ready at different ages.

My plan includes an exit at 62, 65, 67, 68, and 70 years old. I will rely on contributions from a variety of savings and investment areas to continue the comfortable lifestyle I have earned. You deserve the same. Having it and never using it is so much more comforting than needing it and not having it. Create peace of mind. Steadily grow a fund for retirement.

Be Open to Change

Recently I have had the opportunity to work with a number of very successful business owners that are ready to begin handing over leadership in their business. All of them are over 65 but not yet ready to retire. They want to continue working in the business in a meaningful role for an undetermined number of years.

Each of them came with similar questions, "How do I know it is time? How do I transition to a new role and still feel like a contributor? How do I give up control?"

There is not an easy solution to the challenges this transition can create, but it can be simplified. You begin by identifying what role(s) you will be leaving behind, who is the best fit to fill the role(s), and a target date to fill them. Now you create a plan to shift the organization structure and execute on it.

You will also decide what role you will play after the changes have taken place. This may be a role you will play temporarily or for as long as you feel you are willing or able. Examine that role carefully. Outline what your responsibility will be. Decide how many hours a week, month, or year you want to work. Do you want to be in an ancillary role such as Chairman of the Board, or in an advisory role only with no set office hours? Will you be involved in business activities or decision making only on an as needed basis?

Whatever you decide, the most difficult part will be relinquishing control. Since you will most likely have been the primary decision maker in your business it will not be easy to hand over responsibility to someone else. Be aware it may be a challenge. Communicating to others you recognize it may be a challenge. Be prepared to practice the change realizing it may take time and help from a business coach, consultant or other professional.

ADVICE FROM YOUR PEERS

"Address your exit early. Include everyone that you think might be involved. If you have children that you think might want to succeed you, do not wait until it is time to make the transfer. They might surprise you by saying they are not interested. Making this change is hard enough without extra challenges or surprises." Will J., retired retail store founder

LOVE IT!

How long do you plan to own your business? If you do not know now, start to think about the options. Have a plan for each one. If you believe others may be involved in the transition, start to have conversations with them about your plans. Get their feedback. Understand their interests. Get legal advice if needed. Contact a business broker for a valuation and advice if you are within 10 years of making the change.

COACH'S CHALLENGE

Do not be afraid to ask questions about your exit early. Like everything else in small business ownership, a successful exit requires planning and careful execution.

Love "Her" Like You Mean It

In all my years of working with small business owners I have known only three, after much reflection and discussion, determined being a small business owner was not for them. These fine people returned to the work force of corporate America and are still there. Even for the other more than 99 percent there have been days when they wondered why they chose small business ownership. Stomping or crying, and sometimes cursing, they declared they were throwing in the towel. But after a bit of rest, reflection, and a thorough inventory of their reasons for staying or going, they always returned to the business they created. They loved "her." She was a thing of their creation — how could they leave her. Yes, content small business owners not only love but are "in love" with their businesses. They are kind and understanding when things do not go well. They are strong when the business needs them to be. When "she's" confused the owner finds answers. Owning a small business becomes a part of who we are. While we always have a choice to walk away it is not in our DNA to give up easily.

If you are to be happy in the small business ownership lifestyle you must accept your business is now a responsibility and be willing to embrace it for better or for worse. When all is going well and the sun is shining bright, celebrate. When you are feeling overwhelmed, ask for help. When you are stuck, dig deep and find a new spark or a new product or a new group of people to inspire you. When the days look dark, persevere because the sun will come out again and you will find you are right where you should be — living and loving the small business lifestyle.

ADVICE FROM YOUR PEERS

"Take it from me you can be more successful if you love what you do (have a passion), surround yourself with good folks, balance work and play, get away so you can have perspective, and appreciate and enjoy all parts of your life!" Karen Selig, Co-Founder, Psychological Services of St. Augustine, Inc.

LOVE IT!

Rate your love affair with your business on a scale of one to 10 every day for a month. If the average is five or greater, keep working on it. If it is four or less, consider your options.

COACH'S CHALLENGE

Small business ownership is not an easy way of life but it should be rewarding. If you are not finding rewards examine the "why." If you determine you are expecting too much, give yourself some time or reduce some of the demands on yourself. If you determine your "place" is somewhere other than small business ownership, ask for help and make a change.

COACH'S ADVICE

It is a privilege to serve the world in your special way and with your special gifts. If you have a gift to share, share it wherever it is best for you and the world.

RESOURCES

There are endless resources available for small business owners and more available every day including *Lead Like You Own It, 10 Essential Leadership Skills for Small Business Owners* my next book.

I have listed a few others that I recommend to clients or that clients have recommended to me. You will find something for almost every subject and every schedule. Consider using audio versions that you can listen to between home and work or moving between clients or jobs . . . great time management trick!

This is not a complete list as the information available grows daily. Explore! You will find what resonates with you.

Book References

1. *Crucial Conversations by Patterson, Grenny, McMillan, Switzler*

2. *The 7 Habits of Highly Effective People* by Stephen R. Covey
3. *First Things First* by Stephen R. Covey
4. *Guerilla Marketing for Small Business* by Jay Conrad Levinson
5. *Finance for Non-Finance Managers and Small Business Owners* by Lawrence W. Tuller
6. *Profit First* by Mike Michalowicz
7. *The Ultimate Guide to Electronic Marketing for Small Business* by Tom Antion
8. *Hire With Your Head* by Lou Adler
9. *The One Minute Manager* by Kenneth Blanchard
10. *The New Rules of Marketing and PR* by David Meerman Scott
11. *The 25 Most Common Sales Mistakes and How to Avoid Them* by Stephan Schiffman
12. *80/20 Sales and Marketing* by Perry Marshall
13. *The E-Myth* by Michael E. Gerber

Podcasts

1. Small Business Big Marketing – Timbo Reid
2. Entrepreneur on Fire – John Lee Dumas
3. The Smart Passive Income Podcast – Pat Flynn
4. The Ziglar Show – Zig Ziglar
5. Build Your Tribe – Charlene Johnson

Online Resources

Allbusiness.com

Browse this site for forms and agreements that might be helpful for you and your business. They also offer podcasts and videos on a variety of business topics. www.allbusiness.com

Austin Family Business Program

The Family Business Program, College of Business, Oregon State University, prepares family businesses to balance the well-being of the business, the family, and the individuals as they address business challenges and maintain a health family life. www.familybusinessonline.org

Bizstats.com

This site offers a variety of useful financial ratios, business statistics, and benchmarks you might use in planning, analysis and forecasting. www.bizstats.com

Entreprenuer.com

This resource is provided by Entrepreneur magazine. Here you will find articles, books, and valuable thought pieces. This is a great site to follow. www.entreprenuer.com

Census Bureau

The Census Bureau serves as the leading source of quality data about U.S. population and economy. www.census.gov

U.S. Copyright Office

101 Independence Avenue SE Washington, DC 20559-6000. 202-707-3000. www.copyright.gov

Harvard Business Review

Harvard Business Publishing (HBP) is a not-for-profit, wholly owned subsidiary of Harvard University, reporting into Harvard Business School. The mission is to improve the practice of management in a changing world. While not specifically a resource for small business the resources and information are valuable for all business owners. Subscribe to e-mail newsletters such as "Management Tip of the Day." https://hbr.org

Internal Revenue Service

The IRS helps small businesses and self-employed through its tax center. www.irs.gov/businesses/small

Minority Business Development Agency (MBDA)

As a part of the U.S. Department of Commerce, this agency was created to foster growth of minority-owned business in the United States. For more information: 888-324-1551 or www.mbda.gov

Occupational Safety and Health Administration

To learn more about federal health and safety standards employers must provide for employee protection. www.osha.gove/dcsp/smallbusiness/index.html

Small Business Administration (SBA)

The SBA provides a wealth of information and resources to help small business owners navigate any stage of business growth and development.

www.sba.gov/smallbusinessplanner/index.html

Service Corps of Retired Executives (SCORE)

SCORE offers free advice, education, and resources to small business owners. The services are particularly helpful for start-ups. www.score.org

Womenbiz.gov

There are many women-owned business resources. Search for them in your area. This one is the gateway site for women-owned businesses selling to the federal government.

www.womenbiz.gov

Acknowledgements

THIS BOOK IS THE culmination of a lifelong dream. From my earliest memories, I have wanted to be an author. It has also been a labor of love. I have labored and others have loved me in spite of it. I am grateful to my family, friends, colleagues and the wonderful group of small business owners I have been privileged to work with for their support and permission to share their stories.

I offer special thanks to those few whom without any one of them this book would have never been completed.

First, I want to thank my husband Dennis, who loves me unconditionally and believes in me when I do not believe in myself. He is the one who encourages me when the delete button is in overdrive or the trash can is overflowing. He is the one who has sacrificed weekends, nights and holidays so that I could write, revise, research, or just prepare for publication. He is the one who reminded me that this was a process and work worth completing when I was ready to throw in the towel. He never failed to tell me that, no matter what happens, I will always be the world's best coach to him. Thank you Dennis for your boundless love and energy, for countless hours of "porch time" listening, and for being the best partner a girl could ever ask for.

Thank you to my mother Gwen Bullard, long departed and constantly missed, for teaching me patience and setting the example that a woman determined can do anything. She was, and still is, the voice on my shoulder that gently reminds me that I am loved and accepted just as I am. I wish you were here for the launch party, Mom.

Thank you to my Dad, Felix Bullard, now also departed who knew about this project and was so proud of me for following through on a lifelong dream. He reminded me that so many let their dreams go unfulfilled because of "not so real" responsibility, and then regret that they have done so when it is too late. I did it, Daddy! Even if no one reads it, I have met my goal. I know you are smiling down at me even now.

To my kids and the spouses that love them, Andrew and Rosie, and Todd and Courtney, thank you for your constant love and acceptance. Your pride in my accomplishment means so much to me.

Heartfelt gratitude goes to my great friends Susan King, Monica Fuqua, Holly Rittenhouse, Diane Keane, Betsy Cavanna, Lori Rush, Sharon Lamb, Tammy Williams, Jill

Goldsmith, Sandy Stryker, and to my friend recently lost, Linda Baker, who listened and supported (and listened and supported) during the many years it took me to get from conceptualization to publication.

Thank you to Beth Boulden, who shared so many great tips for this first time author, without whose help in formatting and resources, in everything from programs to book cover, I could not have completed this project on time or on budget.

Finally, thank you to Anish VonAhlefeld and Nick Footer for helping me to get the word out and giving me a digital voice. I appreciate all you did to make this book happen.

Also By

Plan It! Do It! Love It!

Plan It! Do It! Love It! Workbook

Lead Like You Own It!: 10 Essential Leadership Skills for Small Business Leaders

www.ingramcontent.com/pod-product-compliance
Lightning Source LLC
Chambersburg PA
CBHW071532200326
41519CB00021BB/6456

* 9 7 8 0 6 9 2 4 7 8 6 1 5 *